WAS

WAS

A pastime from time past

RICHARD DREW PUBLISHING
GLASGOW

First published 1975 by Thames and Hudson, London

This edition first published 1990 by
Richard Drew Publishing Ltd
6 Clairmont Gardens
Glasgow G3 7LW, Scotland

© David Daiches 1975

The publisher acknowledges the financial
assistance of the Scottish Arts Council in the
publication of this book.

British Library Cataloguing in Publication Data

Daiches, David 1912-
    Was: a pastime from time past — 2nd ed.
    1. Edinburgh. Jews. Social life, history.
    Biographies
    I. Title
    941.34004924

ISBN 0-86267-286-4

Printed and bound in Great Britain by
Cox & Wyman Ltd, Reading

Contents

PART ONE

Poets

WAS IT TENNYSON who said that if you gave him a word, any word, he would find a rhyme for it? The word Tennyson itself rhymes very nicely. Benison, for example, and venison.

> O Tennyson, Tennyson
> Give me your benison . . .

Can you imagine old Alfred with his black beard hanging over you with benediction? Blessing is a better word, though. 'God make you as Ephraim and Manasseh', my father would say separately to my brother and myself (in Hebrew, of course: *Yesimcha elohim ke-ephraim vechimenassah*) on Friday evenings, after coming home from *shul* (synagogue) for the inauguration of the sabbath; he would place his hands on his son's head as he said it, with a kind of loving perfunctoriness. For years I never knew what it was he said. More formal, and more eloquent, was when he gave the old priestly blessing, first in Hebrew and then in English, at the end of his address to a boy celebrating his *Barmitzvah*:

> May the Lord bless you and keep you;
> May the Lord turn the light of his countenance on
> you and be gracious unto you;
> May the Lord turn his face towards you
> And grant you peace.

It sounds better in Hebrew, which is the original language of blessing. You had to make a separate *b'rocho*, a blessing to God, for everything – for bread and fruit and wine and for recovering from an illness. And you said 'Bless you' to someone who sneezed.

A somewhat demented Highland minister once wrote a long letter to my father in which he tried to demonstrate that Gaelic was really a transmogrified form of Hebrew and the original Scots were the Lost Ten Tribes. Later, when I studied Gaelic, I looked for resemblances, but they were not significant. Gaelic is good on blessings too, though.

Alasdair Mac Mhaighstir Alasdair has the Highlanders say to Bonnie Prince Charlie when he was about to leave Scotland for ever after the unsuccessful Jacobite rising of 1745–46,

> *Gum pill thus' a ris air n'ais oirnn,*
> *Beannachd leat le neart ar graidh.*

> Till you return again to us
> Blessings on you, with all our love.

Yes, Gaelic is good on blessings. Even 'goodbye' is a blessing: *beannachd leat*, a blessing on you. Then there is *beannachd Dhia leat*, may the blessing of God be on you. (We have forgotten that goodbye is God be with you, but the Gaels haven't.) The Gaels are less good on peace: *sith* is less used and less evocative than *shalom*, which is at the same time an ideal, a blessing and a greeting.

These comparisons and contrasts between Gaels and Hebrews fascinate me as they fascinated James Joyce; but mine is not the Leopold Bloom complex, I have no mystical view of the Jew as the symbol of modern alienated man, wishing to be part of the society in which he lives but always remaining slightly other. No, it is simply the Scottish-Jewish combination in my own experience. Take old Tennyson again, and this time consider venison rather than benison. Scott's stag at eve had drunk its fill where danced the moon on Monan's rill, and it would have become venison had it been caught. Venison was a Highland meat, as it was an ancient Israelite one. Now therefore take, I pray thee, thy weapons and thy bow, and go out to the field and take me venison, said old Isaac to his son Esau.

> I do not think that Alfred Tennyson
> Shared old Isaac's love of venison,
> I do not think that ever he saw
> Deer with the eyes of Scott or Esau:
> He saw himself as poet *and* seer,
> Yet stags (alas) he saw like Landseer.

The Monarch of the Glen. I knew an English girl once who in childhood saw a painting of the Trossachs with stags in the foreground, and thought ever afterwards that a trossach was a species of deer. But *I* read 'The Lady of the Lake' at school and had to memorize large chunks of it, which I still recite with the greatest pleasure. Scott invented the Trossachs with this poem. My father bought a little tartan-bound edition of 'The Lady of the Lake' on his first visit to the Trossachs some time in the 1920s, and I used it at school.

There is a pleasant inn there now called the Covenanters, at Aberfoyle, and it has tartan all over the place: what the Covenanters, who hated the Highlanders to a man, have to do with tartan or the Trossachs I can't think; but the inn has a nice bar and pleasant rooms. Crossing the bar (to quote Tennyson again) you move to pleasant window seats where you can be private and at the same time be part of the general company.

> Twilight and evening bell,
> And after that the dark!

T. S. Eliot was more direct: 'Hurry up please, it's time' sounds through a section of *The Waste Land*. Who reads Tennyson now?

> Any one
> For Tennis-on?

Yet his broody nostalgia and sense of isolation speak for us very well.

We were born nostalgic, scenes of childhood reminding us, even when we participated in them, of something else, something other, something before – perhaps some symbolic or Platonic scene of domestic happiness, fireside communion. True poetry, said Keats, should strike us as almost a remembrance. Why do we feel so often: almost I have been here before? Almost. It's not *déjà vu* (though there is that too) so much as a fleeting sense that this experience stands for something else. Waking up on an Edinburgh morning after a spell of cold winter weather to find rain, and a warm south-west wind blowing, the whole world mildly wetly windy, smelling it as you open the front door and leave for school, blown almost off your feet as you cross the Meadows, you accept the change as portentous. It speaks of something you have always always known. But what? You simply surrender to the undefined awareness. You? One? I? Virginia Woolf used to modulate (in Mrs Dalloway for instance) from she to one to I in presenting her characters' reveries, simultaneously distancing the reporter and universalizing the experience. I remember. You remember. One remembers. The English use of you, like the French *on*, indicates a certain mateyness, a desire to identify the person you (there we go again) are addressing with oneself (yourself?) and with universal experience. And notice that now I have thrown in a we, which can be similarly used. We are such stuff as dreams are made on. You are such stuff... One is such stuff... I am such stuff . . . A gentleman who kept, I think, a small jeweller's or watchmaker's shop once regaled us at the Edinburgh Jewish Literary Society with speeches from *Hamlet*. He declaimed:

Me father. Methinks me sees me father.

He was carried away, borne into a universal first person accusative singular.

That society met on Sunday evenings at Foresters' Hall, which belonged to the Ancient Order of Foresters; but they were a benevolent society and no Robin Hoods. No venison there. But rows of chairs and a platform with a table and two chairs, and a visiting speaker on 'The Ethics of Spinoza' or 'Manasseh ben Israel and the Return of the Jews to England under Cromwell' or reminiscences by a High Court Judge. My father always gave the inaugural address, generally on some ethico-religious topic. His initial Ladies and Gentlemen, so beautifully articulated and soaring up into a lovely cadence on Gentle, his black frock-coat (not cut-away, not swallow-tail, as an artist posthumously imagined him once, but square, like Gladstone's), his black bow-tie, his trim little beard, and eloquence, eloquence. Methinks me sees. Then question time. 'Excuse me pleess, doctor' (they always called my father doctor), 'dat Moses Mendelssohn you talked about, is dat de same Mendelssohn dat lives above his shop in South Clerk Street? No? Not de same? Tenk you doctor, tenk you.'

'Isn't etticks vot matters,' another asks, 'etticks, not observance?' (A good question, and asked every year for I suppose some twenty years.) The difference between Greek and Jewish etticks (ethics)? An attack on Attick etticks?

> It's most problematic
> If Jewish or Attic
> Provides the best ettick.
> Is peripatetic
> The way you suppose is
> More useful than Moses?
> Work it out on your own?
> Or two tablets of stone?

My father believed in the two tablets of stone: revelation is the only guarantee and the ultimate sanction of moral laws. Prescription therefore for a sick world: take two tablets.

But tablet in Edinburgh was also something quite different, a kind of sweet, akin to the Sassenach fudge but harder, available in a variety of flavours and colours, pink, white, brown, but the brown was chocolate or toffee flavoured, not ginger, like the pale brown sticks of Edinburgh rock. Sassenach rock is hard and mint flavoured and always pink outside: as a child I knew nothing of it, nothing, knowing instead that strangely textured Edinburgh rock made by Alexander Ferguson, sold in tartan boxes with pictures of Edinburgh Castle on top, and the white mint flavour was good but the pale brown ginger was quite simply the best. You got a box (there goes that you again) on special occasions; it was not ordinarily bought or consumed. Wind round the persons, like numbers changing on a station departure board or on a bus at its terminus: I, you, one – he.

He. He is so obsessed with ways of making the stick of rock last longer that he hardly tastes it. He licks gently, bites off a tiny piece and lets it dissolve slowly in his mouth, wraps the base round with paper to prevent it dissolving in his hot hand. But it will go, it will go. He knows that however he contrives it, there will come a time when it is not there. This bitter knowledge – the paradigm of human finiteness – is already deeply entrenched in him. He sees week-ends approaching, Friday golden-coloured, the last period at school, then home for two free days. Friday night, its blessing, its candles, its festive tablecloth, is but the gate to two whole school-free days. Saturday, the sabbath, the walk to shul across the Meadows, the service, the return, the leisurely midday dinner, the sung psalm before the grace after meals (When the Lord turned the captivity of Zion, but in Hebrew, and a melancholy tune), the sleepy afternoon over a book, then the secular Saturday night with still a whole un-used Sunday holding off Monday morning and school again: then Sunday itself, loaded with homework for the morrow, for the school always set heavy homework for the week-ends, tainted with the shadow of Monday, so hardly to be enjoyed because of the taint, and Sunday night with the prospect of a cold early rise out of a warm bed to confront an icy room and bare linoleum. It came, it came, and, oddly enough, when it came it was all right, it was there, he was in it, and dread anticipation vanished in experience. The pause be-tween anticipation and being in it haunted him. When he played golf (on Braids no. 2 course, schoolboys twopence per round) he was obsessed with anxiety as to whether his drive would be a good one, and so drove unthinkingly, wildly, to be quickly in a position in which knowledge replaced anxious anticipation. It was the same with bathing in the sea. It was cold to the ankles, what would it be like when he was right in, what, what? He wanted to know, but most of all to have known. So he plunged in wildly, head under the water, to terminate the terrible wondering and replace it by certainty. Exams were like that too. The day before the exam he would say to himself, tomorrow by this time I shall know whether I did well. And the day before the results were due he would say, tomorrow by this time I shall know my mark, know whether I've come first, and tomorrow is there, waiting for me to enter it, there is nothing I can do to hasten it or stop it; in the end I shall have known. Was ever child so conscious of the future perfect tense? He looked to the future to show him what he was going to do, to make it into what he had done. It was not that he disbelieved in free will (though he did not think explicitly in such terms), but he knew that whatever he chose to do, and did, would inexorably become something about which he no longer had any choice at all, something past. He wrote a poem when he was eleven, called 'To Time'. He addressed Time rhetorically, asking it if it would never stop. But he knew that it was a rhetorical question, and that it wouldn't.

It was years before that – he must have been five, or just six, for it was in the last year of the First World War – that he asked a man the time on the way home from school, and the man answered, 'Time the war was over'. He thought of the war then as a long, dark tunnel within which the two sides continuously fought at close quarters one endless perpetual battle with furious movement and noise.

Tennyson was an evening poet – the long day wanes: the slow moon climbs – and Judaism was an evening religion. But there was no Tennysonian elegy in the evening welcome of the Princess Sabbath, the Bride Sabbath: Come my beloved to welcome the Bride, the sabbath eve hymn began: all was triumph and a shutting away of week-day cares. Why Tennyson, then? Because Tennyson was the first poet he was aware of; because his sense of rhythm was somehow bound up with the rhythms of the sabbath eve service; because his mother used to recite to him, the first poem not a nursery rhyme he thinks he ever heard, Tennyson's 'Brook':

> I come from haunts of coot and hern,
>   I make a sudden sally,
> And sparkle out among the fern,
>   To bicker down a valley.

Coot and hern? Haunts of? Mysteries, mysteries, enchanting mysteries. Sudden Sally? He had heard of Sally in our Alley somewhere, but this Sudden Sally was something different. He knew the brook went on and on; that, his mother made clear, was the point of the poem. And it played – played games, played music, two kinds of played:

> I chatter over stony ways,
> In little sharps and trebles, . . .

He knew about sharps and trebles. He could read music, and play simple pieces on the piano. So he could see how funny and clever it was to have the brook chattering in little sharps and trebles. But most of all the brook spoke for itself. Its noise was like speaking: that was funny and clever too. A brook of course was a burn, and how well he knew the Braid Burn that ran behind Blackford Hill almost into Mayfield Road. They walked there often, and in places the burn really did chatter, but he looked in vain, often and often, for fish.

> And here and there a lusty trout,
> And here and there a grayling.

He didn't quite believe in grayling, surely a literary fish, but trout were real, and he longed to see one, to catch one. He would trail a string with a hook at the end in the water as he walked, hoping that somehow a real fish would get itself caught, that he would pull up the string and find it. Why this desperate desire to catch fish, that ran right through his childhood? On holiday on the Fife coast he would watch the fishing-boats set out and come back, but there it was not the fishing so much as the actual movement of the boats on the water that captured him. A boat going up and down in a swell was splendid to watch, and even driftwood riding the waves as they came in to break on the beach gave real joy. At home in his bath he would make little boats out of bits of wood and match-boxes and the whole point was to ruffle the water so that they went up and down. Legs made a good harbour, where the boats could shelter from the stormy water outside. The thought of rafts was very pleasing: how wonderful if it would rain so much that you could sail down the street on an upturned dining-room table. He heard or read somewhere about floods, and was envious. Noah's flood, however, he never really took seriously. It achieved God's purpose, doubtless, but it was too contrived, and the tedious specifications of the ark did not sound like a real boat. Gopher wood, forsooth! And all those cubits. Still, gopher wood wasn't as bad as shittim wood, which was also in the Bible. That was downright embarrassing.

Fish could be caught in rock pools by the sea, but fish in burns were much more elusive. At Leven, where they went one summer when he was nine, there was the Scoonie Burn, but nary a fish could he ever find there, for all his patient waiting with line and hook and worm. Bob Merry, who was the funny man among the sea-side entertainers who performed in a little box-stage on the shore, once hilariously mis-sung the opening line of a song as

> While sailing down the Scoonie Burn.

The Scoonie Burn was pretty tiny, and this got a loud laugh from the children standing appreciatively outside the enclosure (to go inside the enclosure you had to pay, and sat on folding chairs). At intervals one of the entertainers would come round with a collecting box, chanting Anyone desirous? The children wished him well, but had no money to give him. The entertainers wore navy-blue blazers with brass buttons, white trousers, and naval caps. The girls wore white dresses. One of the men would introduce the next item, taking off his cap and staring inside it before he announced what it was to be: it took the children a long time to realize that he had the pro-gramme pasted inside. There was a serious baritone who sang 'Lochnagar', Ian Maclean who sang Harry Lauder-like songs, the splendid Bob Merry; there were three ladies, one young and pretty – but what did she sing? She twice turned a somersault on the stage and revealed paradisial white panties. The other lady was older, a contralto – perhaps it was she who sang 'Lochnagar', and the bari-tone sang 'The March of the Cameron Men'? Wee Betty was at the piano, and would start the performance with a thumped out medley of song-tunes, ending with the group's signature tune which heralded their opening chorus. When the afternoon performance was over, the rock pools called.

He admired Bob Merry, but considered he himself could do as well. He wrote new words to Bob Merry's tunes and sometimes in-vented tunes and words together. He wrote a song satirizing wide plus-fours, which had become fashionable, and linking the satire to the housing shortage. The singer appealed to the wearer of a pair of these capacious garments to rent him space inside. The last four lines ran

> Have you rooms to let in your baggy breeks,
>   Please do not say no,
> For we've been thrown out of our old home
>   And we've nowhere else to go.

The tune had a rather pleasing lilt. That, as Joyce might say, was when he was jung and not easily Freudened.

His music-hall gifts, if one may call them that, were applied with great gusto to the humours of Edinburgh Jewish life, and especially to the language of the immigrant members of his father's congregation. There was a baker named Plantsy whose name provoked some splendid rhymes (and some poetic licence, for the first verse introduced Mr Plantsy's auntsy, who had a supererogatory s, and Mr Plantsy's pantsies, which in those days were inevitably undergarments and not trousers), and Mr Asher Solstone, whose parked car slid into what he called 'de barrication' at Peebles Hydro, on which the resourceful Mr Solstone did not panic but, in his own words, 'sent at vonce for de insoorance', or in the words of the song with which our hero entertained his family

> And though his brains they were but poor 'uns,
> He sent at vonce for de insoorance.

A car was a relative rarity in those days, at least for him, and when Dr Matheson came to visit our hero's mother in his Ford, the children were allowed to sit in it, and sometimes the doctor would take them a ride for half a mile or so before letting them out so that they could walk home. Once or twice he took them to his garage behind George Square where he kept guinea-pigs. If you hold them up by the tail, their eyes fall out, he told them, and they believed him, and then learned it was a joke, for guinea-pigs had no tails. Dr Matheson wore a bowler hat and large leather driving gloves, and when he came to the house he would deposit his hat upside-down on the silver tray which stood on the hall table, then lightly cast his gloves into it. He laughed like a pantomime demon, actually exclaiming Ho Ho Ho, and our hero could hear the Hos rolling down the stairs from his mother's bedroom or out of his father's study. Ho ho ho Dr Matheson, you are safe from comic rhymes, for even Tennyson could have found no rhyme for your name.

Between George Square, where Dr Matheson lived, and the short street where his own family's house kept respectable but far from opulent terraced company with others, lay the Meadows, his playground, wide expanses of green bounded by railing, crossed by paths, chief of which was the Middle Meadow Walk with the jawbone of a whale near its entry. The jawbone of a whale? Yes, it criss-crossed in an arch; you walked underneath; it was from a real whale, yet it was hard to image those unfleshed curves as ever having chomped and chewed. Neither fish, flesh nor fowl they were now, curiously cleansed and devitalized, witness to impersonal anatomical knowledge. The jawbone of a whale is as big as THAT, some city official must have thought, and proposed setting one up there as a perpetual lesson to the citizens on the wonders of nature. The Meadows were a loch once, the Burgh Loch, though he knew none of this at the time, partially drained in the seventeenth century, wholly drained in the eighteenth by Mr Thomas Hope of Rankeillor, president of The Honourable Society of Improvers in the Knowledge of Agriculture in Scotland. He knew Rankeillor Street, running between Clerk Street and St Leonards, and for that matter not far from Hope Park Terrace, also called after Mr Hope of Rankeillor. He didn't know, either, that Rankeillor was the name of Mr Hope's Fifeshire estate, and that those so much looked forward to, so lingered on, so re-created in the mind after the event holidays on the Fife coast were linked, nominally linked one might say, with those shabby-genteel Edinburgh streets where so many of his father's congregation lived, far from rich but managing a determined domestic comfort: Buccleuch Street, Rankeillor Street, Richmond Street, Crosscauseway, St Leonard's Street, between George Square and the King's Park where Arthur's Seat raised its couchant lion shape over the city; old stone-built flats, Edinburgh's first New Town before the more splendid, more internationally enlightened New Town to the north. And here now were the aforesaid Mr Plantsy the baker, and Mr Kleinberg another baker, and Mr Brown the butcher with his rabbinical beard, and Mr Lurie another butcher, and the Jewish family who lived in the house familiarly known simply as Drei-und-dreissig – 33 Buccleuch Street. Drei-und-dreissig, which is Yiddish although (as he discovered later) also German, symbolized for him Jewish Edinburgh, the mingling of the traditions of the old grey city with those of newcomers from Eastern Europe, who came fleeing persecution and outrage to lead humble lives in humble occupations in Scotland's capital and to pick up a Scots-Yiddish language that disappeared within a generation unrecorded, a lost feast for linguists.

My father purchased the eastmost house on the south side of the Meadows; and there the next twenty-two or twenty-three years of my life were passed. We had about eight acres of ground, partly in lease and partly our own; and nearly the whole country to the south of us, though all private property, was almost quite open. There were very few fences south of the Meadows. The lands of Grange, Canaan, Blackford, Braid, Mortonhall, and many other now enclosed properties, were all, except in immediate connection with the mansion houses, unenclosed; and we roamed at pleasure till we reached the Pentlands, or the deserts of Peeblesshire. A delightful region for wild and active boys.

That was Lord Cockburn, reminiscing in the 1820s about his childhood in the eighteenth century. There were no estates now at the eastern end of the Meadows, and the open country to the south was now built into streets – quiet, genteel, well-to-do streets for the most part, Dick Place, Lauder Road, Grange Loan, leafy and desirable localities, perpetuating the names of ambitious and successful Lord Provosts of Edinburgh. Grange House went from the Dicks to the Lauders, and in the Register of Entails for 1757 we find Mrs Isabel Dick of Grange, and Sir Andrew Lauder of Fountainhall, entailing the lands and estate of Grange. They were cousins. He was the fifth baronet of the old and honourable line of Lauder, and she was the only child and heiress of William Dick of Grange, whose arms, argent a fesse wavy, azure, between three mullets gules, were thenceforward quartered with the rampant griffin of the Lauders. Red mullet, *triglie alla Livornese* (it was years before our hero discovered that joy), three moreover, enclosing a fesse wavy, a coat of arms to the Dicks, gefillte fish on a blue plate to the Goldstones who now lived where once Lauder rode.

> The acres were broader
> In the days of Lauder
> But it was harder
> For Lauder's larder
> To furnish fish
> On an azure dish
> Than for Mrs Goldstone to provide gefillte fish on
>   an ancestral blue ashet.

Ashet? Certainly; this Scots word from the French tripped lightly on Mrs G's lips. 'Ess, mein kind, ess. Plenty more on the ashet.' It was not gules exactly, brown rather, for these islands produced a wholly British version of the fabulous gefillte fish, originally on the Continent boiled and chopped before being re-inserted in the fish's skin but now, in Britain only, boiled or fried, the friedliest being the best, fried Friday fish, sabbath welcoming chopped fried fish pancakes, pan-fried fishcakes, to be eaten cold with pickled beetroot or horse radish soaked red in beetroot-juice, Jews' juice gules, downwards to darkness via red gullet. Shalom. Green peas be with you. Every sabbath welcomer a Gastronomer Royal. Once in royal David's city they sang at school in Class B, and he knew this was a hymn (a hymn and not a her, he explained to his little schoolmates with childish laughter, because it ended with Amen and not with Awomen) and not kosher, but it had a nice tune and anyway wasn't he himself of royal descent, come down step by step from Dovid Ha-melech? That was proved in his grandfather's book. That book knew nothing of Dicks or Lauders nor of the Edinburgh gentry who once paced the Meadows where now the grandson played. There has never been in my time, wrote Lord Cockburn, any single place in or near Edinburgh, which has so distinctly been the resort at once of our philosophy and our fashion. Under these trees walked, and talked, and meditated, all our literary and scientific, and many of our legal worthies. There were different Edinburgh walkers now. Some, elderly and bowed, walked stooped with their hands behind their backs, meditating ages of outrage. Mr Goldstone (or if it was not him it was another) once complained to the rabbi that when he made a suggestion he got noding but abusement, and our hero composed a song:

> Up and down the busy street
> Mr Goldstone walks,
> Moving slowly with his feet
> While with his hands he talks.
> He pauses as he goes along
> To spit a little spit,
> And then he sings a little song:
> These are the words of it:

> (CHORUS)

> Verever I am, verever I be,
> Everybody laughs at me,
> Dey laughs at me for deir amusement;
> Votever I do, votever I say,
> It's oi-oi-oi and it's oi-oi-vai,
> For I get noding but abusement.

The tune – without which the words fell very flat – was suggested to him by a song in *That's a Good Girl*, the first musical comedy he ever went to see; it had Jack Buchanan and Elsie Randolph. And just as, years before when he first heard Bob Merry, he was convinced he could do at least as well, he walked home across the Meadows certain that he could compose both words and music of better, brighter, wittier songs. He would compose whole acts in his head as he walked to school with the catchiest tunes and the most scintillating rhymes, and he could see the accomplished gestures of the singers nudging the audience into rapture. Heard melodies are sweet but those unheard are sweeter: he knew at once that Keats was right. Years later he met an American music student who had changed his name from Katz to Keats: from Tympan Alley Katz to unheard melodies, perhaps, he thought (or hoped). Meanwhile, inside the tramcars, he read almost daily: Keatings kills bugs, flies, moths, beetles, . . . An old established exterminator.

> Perhaps while Keatings killed the bugs
> The bugs were killing Keats.

Bugs were various, and the kind you chased around the tree gave the smart schoolboy a chance to utter the dread words bugger and bloody in affected innocence. How daring to recite AT HIGH SPEED

> I chased the bug around the tree,
> I'll get his blood, 'e knows I will.

You could also ask an innocent chum to say the word Puck while pulling the corners of his mouth apart with his fingers. This produced a dread word whose meaning nobody knew, but it was dread. Much dreader than simple mockery of institutions:

> Salvation Army free from sin
> Went to Heaven in a corned-beef tin.
> The tin was greasy,
> They slipped out easy.

That, he knew, was not very witty and not very grammatical; but he enjoyed saying greasy with a long-drawn-out vowel and a very zeddy s.

In the Meadows these verses were ventilated in freedom and conscious daring. The young descendant of King David, or at least of generation upon generation of rabbis who had inhabited ancient Palestine, France, the Rhineland, Holland, Russia and God (literally) knew how many other countries before washing up in Scotland, trod those acres where once – let the historian tell what once. Where the Meadows now lie there lay for ages a loch coeval with that at Duddingstone [ah, he knew Duddingstone Loch well enough, and caught sticklebacks there, bringing them home in jars], some three-quarters of a mile long from Lochrin, and where the old house of Drumdryan stands on the west, to the road that led to the convent of Sienna [that gave its name to Sciennes Road, his Sciennes Road, round the corner from his own street, and his father conducted Hebrew classes in the evening at Sciennes School – what would Our

Lady of Sienna have said?] on the east, and about a quarter of a mile in breadth – a sheet of water wherein, in remote times, the Caledonian bull, the stag, and the elk that roamed in the great oak forest of Drumsheugh were wont to quench their thirst, and where, amid the deposit of marl at its bottom, their bones have been found from time to time during trenching and draining operations. The skull and horns of one gigantic stag (*Corvus elephas*), that must have found a grave amidst its waters, were dug up below the root of an ancient tree in one of the Meadow Parks in 1781, and are now in the Antiquarian Museum. The corvus elephas had drunk his fill where danced the moon in the great oak forest of Drumsheugh (great oak forest? genteel Drumsheugh Gardens in the West End of the New Town?). One stag that was never venison, whose flesh received no human benison, unsung by Scott, unrhymed by Tennyson.

2

How HEROIC is the heroic couplet? Pope's pride and passion.

> Nor will Life's stream for Observation stay
> It hurries all too fast to mark their way:
> In vain sedate reflections we would make,
> When half our knowledge we must snatch, not take.

No clash of arms there (though it takes some determination if not courage to say aloud quickly 'must snatch not take': you were aware of this I hope, Pope?). But when Marmion egged his army on, that was heroic, that was how our hero rendered the saga of Judas Maccabeus, Scoto-semitic heroism, brassy and blatant. But life's stream would not for observation stay, it hurried all too fast, Maccabeus and Iscariot, Pope and Pope – not only the poet and the pontiff, but two aspects of the pontiff himself, the history-book facts, Gregory the Great, Innocent III, Pius IX a kindly man of less than average intelligence (according to Falarope Major *apud* Huxley), figures in European history, in exam questions, but Gregory the Great wrote to the Bishop of Palermo that in the same way as the Jews should not have licence to practise in their synagogues anything more than is allowed them by the law, so they should not suffer any disability in that which is conceded to them, which wasn't bad really, but Innocent III was the real villain of mediaeval clerical anti-semitism and the Fourth Lateran Council was no exam question for Jews and Pius IX allowed the forced baptism of children and refused to do anything about the terrible case of Edgardo Mortara, the six-year-old Jewish boy kidnapped by papal police and forcibly baptized. Oh there were popes and bishops with copes and mitres who stood in his mind with inquisition fires, ghetto walls and cruelty cruelty: in vain sedate reflections he would make when facing these figures now in a Scottish history class-room now in Jewish memory. It was easier to surrender at one time to this feeling and at another time to that, moving the face round to different lights, changing the self almost, but what became of the whole man then? He knew about syntheses, cultural adjustment and reconciliation, and the well-balanced mind and body; *mens sana in corpore sano* his father, who quoted Latin and even Greek as readily as Hebrew, would say, a humanist ideal, and he knew too that he must learn everything everything about history and culture from the Greeks and the Romans right up to Rupert Brooke's Grantchester with its knowing use of the optative in the Greek quotation so relished by Mr Paulin the Greek master. And during prayers at school he sat outside with the Catholic boys, jointly excluded, outsiders all, common foes of the innocent hymns warbled by massed boys on the other side of the door, learned by heart in spite of everything. Hallelujah he knew of course – fancy them knowing that Hebrew expression, had been his first thought – and it flowed through the door as the chorus of a puzzling hymn about all the saints who from their labours rest. Saints were not his cup of tea; patriarchs, yes; good men of old, great men of old; gentle scholars like Hillel, heroes like Judas Maccabeus, father-figures and leaders and setters of examples. But saints, with dishes round their heads? Saint Joan somehow was different, and could be admired because there it really was a case of the right against the wrong (the wrong-doers included the English, but that was all right, for Scotland was on France's side in the Hundred Years' War). So he sat on the hard bench in the ante-room of the school hall with the Catholic boys and the train boys (who arrived too late for the beginning of prayers) and learned the hymns in spite of himself. In some there was no offence at all, and when his piano teacher wanted him to learn the special kind of chord playing that accompanies hymns his father got hold of a collection of hymns suitable for Jewish singing which included some of those that came through the door on school mornings. Metrical psalms and paraphrases were another matter: they were learned by heart in scripture lessons, which it was all right to attend if they weren't doing the New Testament, and in memorizing these he learned quickly about the temptations of inversion in strait-jacketing words to rhyme and metre:

> In pastures green. He leadeth me
> The quiet waters by.

Buy my quiet waters, buy, buy! It was ludicrous but somehow charming, and the tune was ravishing. But he could not dwell long in those boxed-in quarters. Farewell, pastures green. Quiet waters, 'bye.

In the *machzor* or prayerbook for New Year's Day there were some mediaeval hymns, *piyyutim*, of great intricacy, full of complex biblical allusiveness, and a note to the English translation of the book (done in Austria) explained that these particular hymns were not translated: these poems, it read, are unapt for translation by which they would receive a curled appearance. But the metrical psalms in English were not curled but excessively straightened. The first Scottish Psalter of 1564, printed at Edinburgh by Robert Lekprevik, aroused the wrath in the next century of Thomas Fuller, who said the versifiers had drunk more of Jordan than of Helicon and sometimes they made the Maker of the tongue speak little better than barbarism, and have in many verses such poor rhime that two hammers on a smith's anvil would have made better music. Flat and homely, said another critic. *Lech lecha*, said God to Abram, Get thee out of thy country, and from thy kindred, and from thy father's house, unto a land that I will show thee. *Lech lecha*, Lekprevik, the psalms you printed are not for the elect.

> I wil my wayes with wisedome guide,
> Till thou may state erect:
> And walke vprightlie in myne house,
> As one of thine elect.

But the worst metrical version of the psalms ever known in Scotland was that of her king James VI. The sycophantic Francis Hamilton may have written on that king's death

> Wee waile not IAMES, who learn'dly did rehearse,
> King Davids Psalmes in his owne royall verse,

but King James was not King David, and no worse verse did ever bard rehearse:

> That mortal man most happy is and blest
> Who in the wickeds counsals doth not walk
> Nor yit in sinners wayis doth stay & rest
> Nor sittis in seatis of skornfull men in talk
>   But contrair fixis his delicht
>   Into Jehouas law
>   And on his Law both day and nicht
>   To think is neuer slaw.

At school, however, the version they had to learn by heart began:

> That man hath perfect blessedness
>   who walketh not astray
> In counsel of ungodly men

nor stands in sinner's way,
Nor sitteth in the scorner's chair:
But placeth his delight
Upon God's law, and meditates
on his law day and night.

No popish polish, admitted, but singable at least. Ernest Hartley Coleridge, editing the *disjecta membra* of his uncle the great STC, had him liken a Pope to A. Pope. The Pope may be compared to an old lark, who, though he leaves off soaring and singing in the height, yet has his spurs grow longer and sharper the older he grows. But why on earth – or in heaven – should Coleridge have likened any Pope to a soaring songbird? He didn't. STC's manuscript reads: 'Pope like an old Lark who tho' he leaves off soaring & singing in the height, yet has his Spurs grow longer & sharper, the older he grows.' Pious nephew, misunderstanding, supplied the definite article; uncle was talking about the poet not the pontiff. Pontiff, oddly enough, rhymes with *yomtov*, colloquially pronounced yontiff, originally Hebrew for good day, that is holy day, and then Yiddish word for such a day: Good yontiff, they say to each other emerging from shul. The story that a wandering Jew, given an audience by the Pope on Passover, greeted him with 'Good yontiff, pontiff' is probably apocryphal, but apocryphally probable. The Apocrypha, however, has always been accepted by Roman Catholics, as distinct from Jews and Protestants, as genuine biblical books so the story may well be true to the Pope though to the Jews foolishness. A strange thing, though, that the Pope and the whole Roman Catholic way of doing things had in some moods, in some senses, a warmer connection with his friendly Jewish feasts and fasts; the waving of palm branches on the Feast of Tabernacles, the white-robed chanting on Yom Kippur, the pattering of prayers in an ancient foreign language at speed, seemed more congenial to Rome than to Geneva. Yet the committed Old Testamentness of Scottish Presbyterians, his schoolfellows' respect for Jews as the People of the Book, their recognition of him as a relative, as it were, of the people they had to learn about in scripture, all came down on the other side. He learned early how sympathies changed with moods: Edinburgh Castle was as Scott saw it, guarding mine own romantic town, or it looked down on the Graham Street Synagogue and on the house in Kerr Street where the *shamos* or beadle sold passover wine without a licence, marked Frying Oil. So too he preferred Catholics to Protestants or Protestants to Catholics according to whether he was thinking of a congenial ritual or of the hooded figures of the inquisition. One thing, he used to say, that Judaism and Roman Catholicism had in common was the religious value they accorded to high-speed praying. The pious Jew knew mile-long prayers by heart and went through them in mutterings of supersonic speed: it was often a point of pride in shul to finish one of the long silent (or quasi-silent) prayers before your neighbour. Our hero himself was no slouch, and made it a point of pride to move at speed yet without skipping so much as a syllable. It exercised the tongue marvellously, and this was to come in handy when he told those Scottish music-hall jokes which had to be presented in a rich Scots at a breathless rate. He was good at that, and attributed it to his earlier piety. Burns talked about three-mile prayers an' hauf-mile graces as a phenomenon of Scottish Presbyterianism, but the Hebrew grace after meals took up six pages in the Authorized Daily Prayer-book and was gone through by heart in a mixture of muttering, recitation, chanting and singing. Before meals there was a brief blessing for bread. The canny Jews saved their real thanks until after they had made sure that they had eaten. The blessing, by the way, like all Jewish blessings, was to God for having provided the food or whatever it was, never on the article provided. This and us bless, the short Christian grace he was often to hear, always struck him as odd, asking a blessing on things and on ourselves. Bless this house and so on. All Jewish blessings over objects or on particular occasions began with the formula, Blessed art thou O Lord our God. He was the one to be blessed. True, people are blessed in the Bible: blessed shalt thou be in the city, and blessed shalt thou be in the field: but the man who walketh not astray in the first psalm is not *baruch*, blessed, but *ashrei*, which perhaps means something more like happy. *Baruch* was rendered *benedictus*; Baruch Spinoza became Benedict Spinoza, but what did the word really mean, he wondered, and how can man bless God? The priestly blessing invoked God's blessing on man, paternal blessing asked God to make one good and happy, but man's blessing of God? He wondered if God needed it. More and more he combined worried questioning on such matters with cheerful performance of ritual and observance of taboos. He was offered a tin of baked beans with pork on a youth hostel walking tour at Kinlochewe, by Mr Cameron the grocer. Not eat pork? Quite right, few people up here do, but these tins contain VERY LITTLE PORK. But the size of the bits was irrelevant, as in the case of the servant-girl who pleaded that her illegitimate baby was a very little one. The idea rather than the fact of eating any animal upset him, and he preferred not to think about what really happened. As for the Jewish method of killing animals for food, his father always maintained it was painless and humane, but if it was not cruel to the animals it was certainly cruel to the slaughterer.

Pope saw no problem here:

> Know, Nature's children all divide her care;
> The fur that warms a monarch warm'd a bear.

Rachmonos for the bear, pity for the poor animal. *Rachmonos*, a Yiddish word from the Hebrew meaning pity or mercy, was invoked once on a poor horse which bore the well-nourished body of an Edinburgh Jewish lady whose husband had made good and who now wanted to follow the ways of the gentry. *Rachmonos fur de pferd*, pity for the horse, said Levinson the *chazan* (cantor) when he heard of the lady's activities. Archaeologists discovered King Solomon's ample stables, but since his time, or since the author of Job described the war-horse pawing in the valley and rejoicing in his strength and saying Ha ha among the trumpets, the Jews have not been a horsey people. Perhaps they went in more for mules, being a mulish and stiff-necked people, reproved by their own prophets for obstinacy. At any rate, that early Zionist Joseph Trumpeldor formed a Zion Mule Corps of 650 Jewish volunteers in 1915 (the volunteers were Jewish men; the mules were conscripted and were probably not Jewish). The Zion Mule Corps served at Gallipoli. 'These men have done extremely well,' wrote General Ian Hamilton to Vladimir Jabotinsky on 17 November 1915, 'working their mules calmly under heavy shell and rifle fire, and thus showing a more difficult type of bravery than the men in the front line who had the excitement of combat to keep them going.' Cannon to right of them, cannon to left of them volleyed and thundered, and they worked their mules calmly, denied the more obvious glory of a cavalry charge. As a child he came across in his reading the word Calvary, which he always read as Cavalry, though exactly where he found the word is difficult to say: not in any Jewish source, certainly. But he knew that Jesus was said to have been crucified there, and thought perhaps the Roman Cavalry had a hand in it. He did not of course find the word in the 23rd chapter of Luke, for Jews did not read the New Testament, nor did he know then that Calvary rendered the Greek *kranion*, skull, *golgotha*, Aramaic *gulgulta*, Hebrew *gulgolet*. The whole business of the crucifixion was pretty ghoulish, appropriate to a region of skulls, a horrible event, he agreed, but that Christians should therefore worship the cross was something he found completely puzzling. He would not conceivably, however, have mocked his schoolfellows' religion and was astonished when they mocked it themselves, singing:

> At the cross, at the cross,
> Where we played at pitch and toss,
> Till the bobby came and chased us all away:
> He ran after Fatty,
> Who tripped on a tattie,
> And now we are happy all the day.

Jesus of course was always an embarrassment to Jews. He was one of our boys, the thought ran, who was elevated into a God and presented as our enemy by those who so elevated him. Was Jesus then a Jewish prophet, unorthodox perhaps (but they all were), who was posthumously made anti-Jewish by malicious gentiles? He was shy of ventilating such points in discussion at home. When you are grown-up you can study the New Testament and understand what happened, his mother told him, explaining why he was withdrawn from school scripture lessons when the New Testament was studied. You had to know an awful lot to be able to read the New Testament without getting the wrong idea, evidently. Jews never said Christ, and they rarely mentioned Jesus either; when they did it was with a certain embarrassment, as though not knowing where to place him. He was sometimes referred to with ambiguous familiarity, as Yoshke, diminutive of Joshua, and once, only once, he heard his father repeat

> Yoshke
> Took a droshke
> And went to Mosky [Moscow]

but when he expressed interest in the intriguing rhyme his father looked confused and changed the subject.

There were cabs, if not droshkes, in Edinburgh then; two or three waited in a stand at the top of Marchmont Road, and there was a horse-trough at the bottom of the road, into which he used sometimes to peer, fascinated by what he thought were tiny fish swimming about but which must have been larvae. Once, when an aunt and cousin from London were visiting, he rode with them in an open cab round King's Park, and recorded the feat in a snapshot taken with the family's newly acquired no. 2 Brownie. But taxis were now commoner, always a machine of joy, suggesting the annual ride to the station before going off for a holiday by the sea or the luxurious journey to the King's Theatre for the Christmas pantomime. The theatre was a rare treat, but the pantomime was never missed. He remembered all the songs for years, especially those let down on a screen for the audience to join in singing:

> A big fat fly flew by,
> By Flo the fat fly flew . . .

His mother's name was Flora, called Flo by her sisters, and this gave a special flavour to the song. Filled with fear and dismay, Flo flew home and strange to say – she was startled in her flat by another fly. The singer demanded to know

> If the fly that flew by fat Flo's flat
> Was the fly that flew by Flo.

They saw a dramatized version of *Little Women* at the Lyceum Theatre, and it was so soon after the First World War that they felt it proper to make the sympathetic Mr Behr, whom Jo married, into a Frenchman. He wore a little dark pointed beard and said zis and zat. It spoiled the illusion really, because he knew that in fact Mr Behr was not French but German. He saw a dramatized version of Scott's *Rob Roy* at the King's Theatre when he was eleven, and he was ravished when between two acts Di Vernon came in front of the curtain and sang 'O whistle and I'll come to ye my lad'. He saw no incongruity in having the action interspersed with songs, and when Bailie Nicol Jarvie sang

> Some say the deil's deid, the deil's deid, the deil's deid,
> Some say the deil's deid, and buried in Kirkaldy.
> Others say he'll rise again, he'll rise again, he'll rise again,
> Others say he'll rise again and dance the Hieland Laddie,

he was carried away with the humour of it. The evil Rashleigh had his face painted a corrupt green. Rob Roy himself had a red beard, and when caught and bound by the English redcoats it was splendid to see him burst his bonds with a flip of his arms and dash into the loch to swim to freedom. And when he sang 'Macgregor's Gathering', with those haunting words about the clan that is nameless by day (it was many years before he discovered why the clan was nameless), our hero felt a frisson go down his spine that was intensely agreeable. This was his first view of the Highlands, a stage set at the King's Theatre, with painted mountains and lochs and waterfalls, and one set with a full moon, reflected on the water. Later when he went to the Highlands he saw that it was all quite accurate. My heart's in the Highlands, my heart is not here . . . He was astonished when his father took down from his bookshelves the collected Hebrew poems of Tchernichovsky and read to him a Hebrew version of Burns's poem, in his Ashkenazi Hebrew pronunciation with strong stresses on the marked syllables:

Binós-horim líbi, libósi lo póh,
Binós-horim líbi aléi tseidható . . .

How could Tchernichovsky know about Burns, he thought? What was Tchernichovsky's heart doing a-chasing the deer? The book was on the dining-room table, resting on the red cloth that permanently covered it, and his father leant over it, reciting Hebrew Burns in his strongly rhythmic sing-song. It was in fact in this Hebrew version that he first heard that poem. (Years later he translated some of Judah Halevy's Hebrew poems into modern Scots, returning the compliment as it were.) Actually, deer came easily into Hebrew. The Hebrew word *tsvi* meant a stag, and was commonly used as a male proper name, as was *aryeh*, lion. His great grandfather had been called Aryeh Zvi, Lion Hart, and his brother was called Lionel after him. Lion Hart: Jews preferred the word hart to the word stag as a rendering of *tsvi*, because it was more easily adaptable to a proper name in European languages. When he heard at school and in Robin Hood books about Richard Coeur de Lion he felt a flash of recognition: there were Lion Hearts in his ancestry too. Wooden hearts were another matter: when he first read about Hearts of Oak he was puzzled. Heart of oak are our ships, all right. But heart of oak are our men? Who would want men with wooden hearts? Would that make them stronger and braver?

> I have withstood what other men
> Could never have withstood:
> My strength is as the strength of ten
> Because my heart is wood.

Hearts could be overdone in literature. In a school collection of verse he found that very unWhitmanesque poem of Walt Whitman's, 'O Captain My Captain', and one year it was set as the poem to be recited by contestants in the annual school elocution competition. But how on earth could one recite 'O heart, heart, heart, O the bleeding drops of red'? It was too much, really too much, and he did not enter the competition that year. Hearts with lions were all right though, and many years later it gave him a singular satisfaction to recognize that the Hebrew word *lev*, heart, was more or less identical with the Russian word *lev*, lion. They called Lev Tolstoy Leo Tolstoy, Lion Tolstoy. But of course he was really Lion Heart Tolstoy, Aryeh Zvi like his own great-grandfather, who for that matter had been born in Russia. Aryeh Zvi Tolstoy? A Tolstory.

Lion-hearted Richard, whose picture in armour with the crusader's cross in front was in his Robin Hood book, was not really a sympathetic character, although of course highly preferable to his disgusting brother John. Though Richard appeared at the end as a kind of *deus ex machina* to save Robin and his men, his crusading absence was not admired by our hero. The crusaders were great slaughterers of Jews in their path, and they perpetrated the most awful cruelties on Jewish communities both en route and when they got to Palestine. *The Talisman* was one of the earliest Scott novels he read, and he responded to Scott's portrayal of the subtle and civilized Moslems as compared with the mutually feuding hulking crusading Christians. He did not at first know what a talisman was, but he knew that a talis was a prayer-shawl, seen weekly in use in Sabbath morning services, and his first thought or perhaps merely idle fancy when he saw the title on a shelf in the dining-room book-case was that this was a book about a talis-man, a Jew renowned for stamina in praying. This was not so improbable, after all, for he had read a child's version of *Ivanhoe* and knew about Isaac of York and Rebecca. Scott might well have created a talis-man. But it did not take him long to learn that the odd Hebrew and Yiddish word that crept into ordinary conversation at home aroused bewildered stares of incomprehension at school. Perhaps, after all, Scott hadn't known what a talis was. In Latin of course it means such, of such a kind, used with qualis to mean as. He thought of a joke in the Latin class once – qualis talis? what kind of a prayer-shawl? – but there was no one else in the classroom, not the master even, who would have understood it, so he had simply to smile quietly to himself. There were in fact different kinds of prayer-shawls, of taleisim, the great big woollen ones with black stripes and enormous fringes worn by the old Yiddish-speaking members of his father's congregation, and the much smaller silk ones with blue stripes and neat little fringes worn nattily, like a delicate scarf, by younger members. He discovered a reference to Taliesin, the Welsh poet, and he wondered about the name. His father once talked at dinner about the *lex talionis* and its relation to the biblical eye for an eye, and some wag present as a guest said that if the hunted fox turned and bit the huntsmen it would be a case of Lex

Tally-Ho-nis. He remembered that for years, as he did a sentence he once idly read in a paper-bound volume called *Jerrold's Jest Book*: Mr Foote, on being asked by his hostess if he would venture on an apple, replied that he would be glad to do so were he not afraid of falling off. He added the mental footnote that Mr Foote was pulling his hostess's leg. There was a line, and one line only, of an abusive comic rhyme he heard somewhere

> Skinnymalinky long-legs, wi' umberella feet

that he relished for its expressiveness. There were girls like that on the streets of Edinburgh, shabbily clad, thin-legged, with old boots too big for them swelling out below; he would encounter them playing in the Meadows or in the adjoining thoroughfares, keelies they were really, but harmless, unlike their brothers, who could be friendly one moment and very nasty the next. If you played in the Meadows and on the streets, as he did, there was always the problem of keelies. He learned a great deal from them, strange dregs of facts, rumours of astonishing practices, glimpses of other ways of life. The genteel Jew confronting the very un-genteel gentiles. He realized now that class differences were in a way more important than religious differences (though he would never have used such terms). Gentility was common to his own family and to the families of most of his schoolmates. When he went to tea with the son of the minister at Duddingstone the scene by the Presbyterian fireside in the manse was no different in feeling and atmosphere from the scene at his own fireside, and though he had to watch out for the possibility of meat-paste among the sandwiches this was not important. But you couldn't go to tea with a keelie. Keelies didn't have tea, anyway, at least not his kind of tea: their tea was their main meal and probably included such inadmissible sustenance as ham-and-eggs. Ham, like pork, was the archetypal forbidden food, and ham-and-eggs (oddly, a phrase he heard much more often than bacon-and-eggs) was a symbolic meal, representing conspicuous non-kosher consumption. An uncle – his mother's only brother, a somewhat irreverent man – had taught him a song which he understood later was a parody of a hymn:

> There is a boarding-house
> Far far away
> Where they have ham and eggs
> Three times a day
> O how the boarders yell
> When they hear the dinner bell . . .

That is all of it he ever remembered. It stayed in his mind, that boarding house, where the thrice daily consumption of forbidden food proclaimed a flaunting of gentile-ness that had its own fascination.

There was a fascination, too, though of a different kind, in the thought of wicked drinkers in pubs. Drunk men were not an uncommon sight in the streets of Edinburgh in the period immediately after the First World War, and he would watch them staggering about with an awed curiosity. Once in the Meadows he saw a man actually consuming something out of a bottle and when he paused to stare the man cursed and then started to chase him. He fled in terror and on reaching home told with pride how he was chased by a furious drunkard who hurled whisky bottles at him. Later he was not sure about the hurled (a more splendid word in this context than thrown) bottles, but it seemed dramatically right. Beer and whisky were the drunkard's drinks, he knew, and he had not the slightest idea then what the difference was between them. Once in the school holidays he and his brother decided to follow Mr Grieve the plumber, who lived down the street, and see where he landed up. They were amazed and deeply excited to find, after quietly shadowing him across the Meadows, that he ended up in a pub in Nicolson Street. And this was in the middle of the day. Wine of course was quite another matter. It was poured ritually on sabbaths and festivals and sipped in honour of the holy day. *Kiddush*, sanctification, over wine, was such a central part of Jewish observance that he could hardly imagine life without it. Not that they drank more than a few sips, except on the Seder night, the Passover service, when four cups were compulsory. They had very small gilt cups precariously balanced on narrow bases, so that they frequently fell over, spilling their contents. This came to be part of the Seder routine. The wine they used was red and sweet, Palestine wine, Palwin or Bozwin or sometimes, more rarely, a kosher wine that perhaps did not come from Palestine called simply Levinson's No. 2. He and his brother had many a secret jest about Levinson's No. 2 and speculated lewdly about the process by which it was made.

Passover rather than New Year was the great signal of time. Each year in spring it came round and produced the same sense of excitement. He always knew what to expect: the removal of all secular groceries which could in any way be considered leaven or had had contact with leaven (he was never absolutely certain what leaven was, except that unleavened bread, matzo, was flat and crisp), the ritual destruction of its last traces, the replacement on shelves and in cupboards of ordinary dishes and ordinary food by dishes and food reserved only for this particular festival. And, before this, spring cleaning, with all the adventure of familiar furniture moved out, familiar rooms turned upside down and put temporarily out of bounds. Then the climax, the Seder, the ritual meal of freedom, with the traditional questions asked and answered and the long but constantly varied commentary in Hebrew and Aramaic woven through the evening, which ended in song that had by now moved from the religious and the celebratory to the inconsequential, like the ditty about the single kid that father bought for two *zuzim*. Every year the same song, the same kid, the same two *zuzim*, the same family jokes about the rate of exchange for *zuzim* or the character of Pharaoh. Where was Moses when the light went out? Not in the dark, like the Egyptians, for when the plague of darkness was brought down over the land of Egypt there was a thick darkness in all the land three days, but all the children of Israel had light in their dwellings. Still, he didn't really like the idea of the ten plagues, and shuddered at the slaying of the first-born. I know of no way, said Edmund Burke, of drawing up an indictment against a whole nation.

Edinburgh was not unsympathetic to these biblical reminiscences. At the foot of Morningside, recorded a nineteenth-century historian, the Powburn takes the singular name of the Jordan as it flows through a farm named Egypt and other scriptural names abound close by, such as Hebron Bank, Canaan Lodge, and Canaan Lane. Canaan Lane he knew well, and had often wondered at the name. But he did not know that in the secluded house of Milbank, westward of Canaan Lane, there occurred on the 26th of September, 1820, a marriage which made some noise at that time – that of Alexander Ivanovitch, Sultan Katte Ghery Krim Gery, to Anne, fourth daughter of James Neilson, Esq., of Millbank, as announced in the Edinburgh papers for that year. This personage, explained a writer in *Notes and Queries* in 1855, was the Sultan of Crimea, and had fled from his own country in consequence of his religion, and was being educated in Edinburgh at the expense of the Emperor Alexander of Russia, with a view to his returning as a Christian missionary, and his wife was hardly ever known by any other appellation than that of Sultana. According to Mr Spencer, he had not succeeded in 1836 in making a single convert. A likely story! The Sultan of the Crimea at school in Edinburgh, with his education paid for by the Tsar of Russia! But no more improbable than Egypt Farm and

Canaan Lane: it was Edinburgh reaching out towards his own background, which also included both Canaan and Russia. As for the testimony of the unknown Mr Spencer, he would have believed that, for he knew all about the futility of attempts to convert people. The Church of Scotland had its mission to the Jews and each year they reported on their activities to the General Assembly and each year his father wrote to *The Scotsman* to protest at the hypocrisies and dishonesties involved. No one in fact was ever converted in Scotland, though the egregious Sir Leon Levison, a one-time Jew of odd Levantine background who had turned Christian in foreign parts and tried to organize conversionist activities in Edinburgh, liked to make vain claims, for they gave him status. No passover knight he; he had already passed over to the majority religion where life was easier; but the douce citizens of Edinburgh regarded him warily. What will Sir Leon say? asked a master at school in heavily sneering accents when his son had been caught out in some offence of commission or omission. So he uttered no paean of praise to Sir Leon, whose name had probably originally been aryeh, lion; but now he was a lion whose pray remained elusive. The conversionists went abroad and tempted starving Jews with free soup; each one who came was chalked up as a conversion, and the same person coming several times appeared in the figures as several conversions. The Edinburgh rabbi did not like this a bit, and exposed the facts in the reports.

> Eve's tempter thus the Rabbins have exprest,
> A Cherub's face, a reptile all the rest.

This rabbin did not go so far as to stigmatize the tempter as a reptile, nor would he grant him a cherub's face, which in any case was unlikely, but he thought the behaviour satanic. It was his only quarrel with the Church of Scotland, where he found many admirers, and actually wrote a Hebrew grammar as co-author with an Edinburgh Presbyterian divine. The Scottish ministers regarded him as a sort of Jewish Pope, and though this was far from the truth ecclesiastically it had a certain poetic truth, for poetry to him ran naturally in rhymed couplets and once his son found in a pocket of the rabbi's only dress suit, which he had worn before he had married, a copy of a poem he had written to be recited at his elder brother's wedding, witty and polished, in its own way Popish. As God had said to Moses I am that I am so poetry spoke to our hero's father saying Iamb that Iamb. There were other metrical feet, of course, and My Heart's in the Highlands was dactylic in both Hebrew and English, but to him the great iamb was king of them all. The rabbi enjoyed the formal scansion of poetry, and used to sit down with his son and demonstrate the way the different metrical feet were built up of longs and shorts. Know then thyself, presume not God to scan, wrote Pope, but the rabbi scanned both God and Pope.

3

WORDSWORTH, in the course of a 200-word verse sentence whose structure yields only to repeated re-examination, refers to the power of literature on the developing mind,

> From Homer the great Thunderer, from the voice
> That roars along the bed of Jewish song,
> And that more varied and elaborate,
> Those trumpet-tones of harmony that shake
> Our shores in England, – from those loftiest notes
> Down to the low and wren-like warblings, made
> For cottagers and spinners at the wheel, . . .

The rabbi, who had enjoyed a classical as well as a rabbinical education, and could quote by heart passages from the Odyssey in Greek as well as biblical and talmudic texts in Hebrew, communicated to his son the compatibility of the great Thunderer and the voice of Jewish song. In sheer emulation of his father he memorized the opening of the Odyssey and rolled the Greek hexameters on his tongue, while on Sunday mornings he attended the rabbi's lectures on Isaiah which required the memorizing of long passages of Hebrew prophetic eloquence on the part of the young auditors. So it was *nachamu, nachamu ami* as well as *andra moi ennepe mousa*, and the two kinds of poetry cohabited in his mind without dissension. As for those trumpet-tones of harmony that shake our shores in England – and Scotland – he heard them equally in Scott's heroic poetry and in the more rhetorical passages of Shakespeare. In school he had to memorize large tracts of 'The Lady of the Lake' and several speeches from *Julius Caesar*, his first Shakespeare play. The former was not all heroics. Beside

> Speed, Malise speed! the dun deer's hide
> On fleeter foot was never tied.
> Speed, Malise speed! such cause of haste
> Thine active sinews never braced,

there was

> He is gone on the mountain,
>   He is lost to the forest,
> Like a summer-dried fountain,
>   When our need was the sorest.

Forest rhyming with sorest? Just a bit tinny, perhaps? He liked it, yet felt slightly uneasy. But there was no uneasiness at all, only uninhibited relish, at

> Wherefore rejoice? What conquest brings he home?

and the rest of Marullus' outburst against the commoners: he would recite it to himself with histrionic passion, loving the scornful repetitions of And do you now put on your best attire? And do you now cull out a holiday? and the concluding admonition:

> Run to your houses, fall upon your knees,
> Pray to the gods to intermit the plague
> That needs must light on this ingratitude.

As for the different movements of Antony's funeral speech, they enthralled him entirely, in spite of his moral preference for Brutus. Yet Wordsworth had it wrong. Homer was not for him the great Thunderer; he knew the Odyssey better than the Iliad, and it was the moving human detail not any great thundering that captured him. So they came to the wheat-bearing plain, and afterwards pressed on towards their journey's end, for so well did their swift horses carry them on. And the sun went down and all the ways grew dark: *duseto t' heelios skioonto te pasai aguiai.* As for Jewish song, it was no bed along which a voice roared. The plangency of the prophetic voice was what struck him most. *Purah darachti levadi* . . . I have trodden the wine-press alone, and of the peoples there was no man with me. He had no idea what this was about, but it seemed to him strange and shuddery. Jewish song? On Saturday nights, when the sabbath had departed leaving the beginning of a secular week, his father would sing in a desperately sad melody a song about the return of Elijah the prophet to redeem his people. *Eliyahu ha-navi, eliyahu ha-tishbi, eliyahu he-giladi* . . . Elijah the prophet, Elijah the Tishbite, Elijah the Gileadite, may he come speedily with Messiah the son of David. Sad too was the tune to which they sang the 126th psalm before post-prandial grace on sabbaths and festivals. They that sow in tears shall reap in joy. Though he goes on his way weeping, bearing the store of seed, he shall come back with joy, bearing his sheaves. The contrast was striking, and though it sounded a note of hope, of misfortune reversed into happiness, it was the picture of the sad man going forth weeping with his seeds that stuck in his mind: *haloch yelech uvachoh* . . . No roaring voice this, but a plangent record of suffering and of long-deferred hope. Chanukah, the feast of lights, was the festival that came about Christmas time and commemorated the restoration of the Temple after the victorious campaign of Judas Maccabeus against the paganizing forces of Antiochus Epiphanes. The Chanukah hymn, sung each evening of the eight-day festival after the candles had been lit, was a hymn of triumph. Yet in his father's massive prayer book, published in Jerusalem with a voluminous commentary, there was an extra verse to that hymn, which once, accidentally as it were, his father sang, after he himself had thought that the hymn was finished. The verse appealed to God to stretch out his holy arm and finally bring about the long-delayed salvation of the Jewish people. Punish the doers of evil for shedding the blood of thy servants, for salvation has been long delayed to us and there is no end to the days of our suffering . . . The verse, he learned, had been inserted at a time of pogroms in Russia, and was a desperate cry for an end to persecution and suffering. His father told him that it did not appear in most prayer books because the Russian Government had forbidden it, as reflecting on the Tsar's justice, and the majority of Jewish prayer books emanated from one part or another of the Russian Empire. But though he only heard it once, it echoed in his memory, and he looked it up and found it in the Jerusalem prayer book. *Ki archa lanu hayeshuah, ve-ein ketz li-mei haraah*: for long delayed has our salvation been and there is no end to the days of woe . . . Standing on the hearth-rug before a roaring fire, looking at the row of coloured candles, the dining-room table behind him set with a festive tea, he absorbed middle-class comforts of Edinburgh of the 1920s and could afford to enjoy the elegiac feeling that came with his sense of Jewish history.

But he could move easily from those loftiest notes down to the low and wren-like warblings of street and pantomime and seaside entertainers. The lyrical address to the chanukah lights, which appeared in the December 1926 edition of *The Family Entertainer*, a magazine edited and entirely written by himself, hand-written with one carbon copy, went side by side with varieties of comic verse, imitations of Lewis Carroll and Edward Lear and of music-hall jests and the songs of Scotch comics. He produced in another edition of his magazine a comic parody of the complete service for the seder, the haggadah, which he read aloud to an appreciative family after the passover meal. The rabbi looked indulgently on that parody of divine things which argued a familiarity with and a taking for granted of those things on the part of the parodist. In any case, there is not the division between sacred and secular in the Jewish religion that other religions seem to find necessary: the pious Jew regards himself as being constantly in the presence of God and feels free to include God in the most light-hearted of activities. It was early pointed out to him that the Hebrew language had no word for religion, and that Judaism was not a religion like other religions, not a creed, but a way of living.

The lofty and the low constantly rubbed shoulders in his mind and in his activities. He read 'The Ancient Mariner' at school and promptly proceeded to circulate among his schoolfellows 'The Rime of the Ancient Scavenger' which told, in Coleridgean rhythms, the touching story of an erstwhile chef at the Royal Hotel who spoiled the soup at a high formal dinner party and was cursed and driven to wandering and scavenging. And Stephen Leacock's stories inspired him to write a tale entitled *Muffled in Matzo-meal, or The Mystery of the Meshuggah Maggid* (mad preacher), which pressed into comic service virtually every feature of Edinburgh Jewish life and language that he could assemble. He made the most of that language. It was said that an Edinburgh Jewish watchmaker once emerged from his shop to accost a man who had been long peering at his shop window with these words: 'If you vant to buy a vatch, buy a vatch; if you don't vant to buy a vatch, take your nose out of my vindow.' In our hero's version he said: 'If it is your intention to purchase one of our time-pieces, kindly do so, but if, on the other hand, you have no such end in view, kindly remove your proboscis from my fenestration.' He found hilarious the notion of Mr Kaplan speaking such a sentence. A schoolmaster had once puzzled him with the sentence: 'Time flies you cannot they are too quick for you.' He naturally thought it was something to do with time flying, and couldn't make it out until the master explained that the sentence was designed to illustrate the importance of punctuation and the mysteries of inversion. Time flies you cannot: they are too quick for you. You can't time flies. But who would want to time flies anyway? Bob Merry once sang a song about flying:

> I'm an airman, I'm an airman,
> And I fly fly fly fly fly.
> Up in the sky

> Ever so high.
> Sparrows cannot catch me
> No matter how they try . . .

This was quite daft, like another song of Bob's, 'Right in the Middle of the Red Blue Sea' (nobody there but myself and me), and not at all clever. Then why did he like such songs? Why one moment could he recite with joy, I bring fresh showers for the thirsting flowers, right down to the triumphant concluding line of the poem, and the next meditate an absurd parody of it or think of some idle street-rhyme, some silly vulgarity confided to him by a keelie in the Meadows? Moods changed so quickly, language changed kaleido-scopically, rhyme and rhythm contributed their own kind of vitality to the day. Idly, as he walked to school, he would compose parodies of popular songs, like this one, to the tune of 'Happy Days and Lonely Nights':

> If you have a funny face
> Hide it in a lonely place
> Or always wear a mask.
> If you have a lengthy nose
> Use it as a garden hose
> Or as a vacuum flask.
> And if your legs are bandy
> You'll cut them off I'm sure
> For they will come in handy
> For giving to the poor . . .

The tune was that of a romantic slow fox-trot; he soon forgot the original words but the melody remained in his head. But his head also rang with the music of the Spenserian stanza and he started a long, meditative, broody poem in that stanza, enjoying the slow spreading out of the last line, happy in finding lingering words to fit. What'll I do when you are far away . . . ? a slow moaning song went. He changed it:

> What'll I do
> When the coo
> Begins to moo?
> When the coo
> Starts to moo
> What'll I do?

The thing to do when the coo starts to moo is of course to shoo the coo, which is what he did in the second verse. Beside the moan of doves in immemorial elms he put the moos of coos complaining to the Muse. The best use of the oos rhyme he once heard unexpectedly on the wireless. They were broadcasting something from Glasgow University students' rag week, and a voice recited in a strong Glasgow accent:

> Let Londoners gae silly
> Aboot their Piccadilly,
> And Americans may brag aboot their Wall Street.
> But if you want to booze
> The place that you should choose
> Is the bonny purlieus
> O' Sauchiehall Street.

Low and wren-like warblings indeed, made if not for cottagers then for slum-dwellers.

He was surprised to find that so often he sat down to write a Tennysonian elegiac poem, his favourite childhood and adolescent mode, and found his mood and intention changing as he wrote, so that a piece of nonsense verse or a parody emerged at the end. He first heard Gilbert and Sullivan at an end-of-term concert at school, when a fat master with a fine voice rendered songs from *The Gondoliers* and *The Mikado*. He discovered the Bab Ballads soon after that, and again he was stimulated to emulation. He was struck by the way in which two-syllable rhymes came out as comic, even, to his ear, when no humour was intended. He read 'Simon Lee the Old Huntsman' at school and thought he saw at once what was wrong with

> His master's dead, and no one now
> Dwells in the halls of Ivor;
> Men, dogs, and horses all are dead;
> He is the sole survivor.

His English master thought that the real blemish on the poem were the lines about Simon's poor old ankles swelling, and encouraged the boys to laugh at this Wordsworthian lapse, but he thought the rhyming of Ivor with survivor was more serious, for it showed that Wordsworth's ear could not tell him when a rhyme was funny. But why should it be funny? He tried experimenting with two-syllable and then with three-syllable rhymes, and found that the more the syllables the funnier the rhymes. He once began a poem

> Be patient all while I recount how once in far Nairobi a
> Black man was bitten by a dog and died of hydrophobia.

His greatest triumph there was to find a rhyme for business. The victim was a pedestrian, and went on foot about his business, without a car, i.e. tin-lizzy-less. A tin lizzy was a Ford car and by expansion any mass-produced car. Dr Matheson's car was a Ford, an open tourer, and in the summer the leather on the seats got pleasantly warm. One July day he was given a ride in the back seat; he was wearing a new school blazer and new grey shorts and the warmth of the seat and the bright newness of his clothes combined in his mind to symbolize festivity, celebration, summer gaiety. He felt handsome, and there came into his head the rhyme he had first heard in the last year of the war:

> When I was young I used to be
> The bonniest lad that you could see.
> The Prince of Wales he wanted me
> To go and join the army.

Not that he had military ambitions, but he would have liked to play in the pipe band of a kilted regiment. At 11 o'clock on 11 November the whole school would assemble in the playground, in front of the war memorial; the uniformed O.T.C. cadets would march past, led by the pipe band who first played a march then stopped in front of the memorial and played 'The Flowers of the Forest'. One of the several versions of this lament for Flodden was in his school poetry book. It began

> I've heard them lilting, at the ewe milking,
>   Lasses a-lilting, before dawn of day;
> But now they are moaning, on ilka green loaning:
>   The Flowers of the Forest are a' wede away.

The first line, he was told, was traditional, and dated from immediately after the fatal battle, and so was the fourth line, which was the refrain and also the title of the traditional air to which the song was set. He had to learn the whole poem by heart, and felt fiercely for the fate of the proud Scots routed by the guileful English as he recited

> Dule and wae for the order sent our lads to the Border;
>   The English, for ance, by guile won the day;
> The Flowers of the Forest, that foucht aye the foremost,
>   The prime o' our land, are cauld in the clay.

(But why was the two-syllable rhyme of order and Border not comic, like Ivor and survivor? For it certainly wasn't.) Jane Elliot wrote it, third daughter of Sir Gilbert Elliot of Minto. She was born in Minto House, in Teviotdale (not the Minto House in Chambers Street, almost opposite the Museum, which he knew, but that Minto House was the town residence of her family) in 1727, and she died in 1805 at Mount Teviot, then in the occupation of her brother, Admiral Elliot. She lived and died unmarried, greatly devoted to her father. She possessed a sensible face, a slender, well-shaped figure. In manner grave and reserved to strangers. In her conversation she made no attempts at wit, and, though possessed of imagination, she never allowed it to entice her from the strictest rules of veracity. She had high aristocratic notions, which she took no pains to conceal. Turning over Scott's *Minstrelsy of the Scottish Border* he discovered another version, written by the late Mrs Cockburn, daughter of Rutherford of Fairnalie, in Selkirkshire, and relict of Mr Cockburn of Ormiston. Her active benevolence, keeping pace with her genius, rendered her equally an object of love and admiration. But what a disappointment her poem was, after Jane Elliot's! It began

> I've seen the smiling of Fortune beguiling,
> I've tasted her favours, and felt her decay;
> Sweet is her blessing, and kind her caressing,
> But soon it is fled – it is fled far away.

Smiling and beguiling, blessing and caressing – not exactly comic, but highly suspect. You taste fortune's favours but feel her decay: he sought in vain for the logic of this sensory distinction. He was aware of the terrible temptation to parody rising up in him.

> I warn you be wary of eggs from the dairy,
> I've tasted their flavours and smelt their decay . . .

But he went no further. It was a kind of sacrilege. Flodden Field, that infinitely sad battle where Scotland's king fell and the land grew permanently darker, was too real for jesting. When news of the defeat reached Edinburgh the citizens hastily built a massive wall to prevent the victorious English from penetrating their city. This defence had many gates and towers, crenellated and furnished with embrasures and loopholes, and was of vast strength and height, with a terrepleine of earth in some parts, especially to the south. Descending from the Castle in a south-westerly direction, it crossed the Portsburgh at the foot of the Grassmarket, where there was a barrier called the West Port; and ascending the steep Vennel – where much of it still remains – to Lauriston, it turned due eastward to the corner of Teviot

Row, from whence it ran acutely northward to the Bristo Port. He used sometimes to go through the Vennel on his way to the Graham Street synagogue, and there was the Flodden Wall, solid and visible. He would think of the panic building of the wall in that distant September of 1513, and of the lost Flowers of the Forest. How doth a city sit solitary, that was full of people! how is she become as a widow! she that was great among the nations, and princess among the provinces, how is she become tributary! These words from the Book of Lamentations, Kinot, so familiar to him from their ritual recital in Hebrew when Jews remembered the destruction of the Temple, seemed a sort of Hebrew Flowers of the Forest. And on *tishah be-av*, the ninth day of the month of Ab, anniversary of the Temple's destruction, they recite in shul other keening poems of remembrance. *Ziyon, halo tishali lish'lom asirayich* . . . Zion, will you not ask after the peace of your captives, who seek your peace, who are the remnant of your flocks? Years later he was to produce a verse translation of this long lament by Jehudah Halevi for Zion destroyed. As a youngster he learned it secretly by heart, reciting it to himself in bed at night, glorying in the fact that his people could make great poetry out of their sorrows. Jehudah Halevi wrote much longer after the destruction of Zion than Jane Elliot wrote after Flodden, yet the Hebrew poet felt even more personally involved with the tragedy he commemorated. At the same time, his poem was not merely a lament, but concluded on a note of hope, restoration, and renewal of youth. Flodden was an episode of the bad old days, to be sighed over with other old, unhappy, far-off things and battles long ago. But the destruction of Zion was still a part of living history, Jewish exile continued, restoration was still expected, was indeed round the corner. And he, walking by Flodden Wall to join in laments for Zion in the Graham Street synagogue, was he at home or in exile? At home, surely; this was his city and he espoused its memories fiercely. Those ancestors of his, ancient Israelites with a perpetual tendency to backslide, that temple worship with its sacrifices and ceremonies, had they really anything to do with him? Yet they were his ancestors, and among them were scholars and poets and kings. Like Jane Elliot, he had high aristocratic notions, which he took no pains to conceal. He was even capable of telling his schoolmates that their ancestors were painting themselves with woad while his were inventing their religion. And they believed him; no one ever questioned it. Wasn't it true, after all? His past was a background to enrich the present, to give it piquancy, to enable him to play a role. And he knew it. He did play a role. Sometimes he frightened himself by asking himself what he REALLY was. He would look at his face in the mirror and try to find out what it meant. And sometimes, alarmingly, upsettingly, when he was alone in the bath, he became aware of himself from the outside, as someone else as it were; he was aware of himself being aware of himself, and there was a terrifying difference between the self that was aware and the self that that self was aware of. Whole minutes would go by in this strange state, and in panic he felt himself accepting it, accepting this exclusion from his own self. He would jump out of the bath and dry himself hastily, anxious to seek the company of others and restore his normal self by exposing it to ordinary interaction with others. He once tried to describe this experience to his mother, but could not. Words, he learned, had their limitations.

But words could create identities. The message boy from Cameron's the grocer would refer to an uncouth and frightening character called the Gaggies Man, and for years he saw this man as a hairy giant waiting in a side-street to make a violent entrance. Years later he read about Big Aggie's man and realized that the Gaggies Man, so clearly visualized by him, had been a mishearing for a very different phrase with a very different meaning. And those Lorders you got at the post office – naturally called Post Lorders because they were for sending by post. A Lorder was a rectangular piece of paper representing a sum of money. And it LOOKED like a Lorder. Yet, accustomed as he was from earliest childhood to hearing languages other than English spoken by visitors to the house, and having learned to read Hebrew perhaps before and certainly no later than he learned to read English, he knew that words had no unique and natural connection with their referents. At the same time shabbos was different from the sabbath, shul was a warmer and more familiar building than formal gentile-used synagogue, *frum* was certainly not the same as pious, and a *yomtov* was something other than a festival. The Hebrew for word, *davar*, also meant thing and event. The book of Deuteronomy was known as *d'varim*, words, from its opening: These are the words which Moses spoke unto all Israel. Yet the Hebrew title for Chronicles, which was also the regular word for history, was *divrei hayamim*, which did not mean words of the days but events of the days. For the Israelites words were the most important events, and the words given to Moses on Mount Sinai marked the central event in history. Words could be sacred, and books and scrolls containing sacred words were also sacred. The scroll of the law read from each shabbos was sacred, and men kissed its exterior as it was carried round before and after the reading. It was a disturbing thing to drop a Bible or a prayer book, which had to be kissed on being picked up.

Here, in the realm of books, there really was a distinction between sacred and secular. But all books were good things; in his house reading in general was a good; and there was no expectation that he would read only sacred books on sabbaths and festivals. Those were the days, in fact, when, after the substantial midday meal consumed on the return from shul, he would ransack the bookcases in his father's study for a nineteenth-century novel or book of poetry with which he could settle down all afternoon, lost for hours in another world. Even school-books had their appeal, at least when they were examined for the first time. He would go to Thin's with the list of that year's required books, instructed always to buy second-hand copies if they were available, for that reduced the formidable bill. How happy he was when no second-hand copy was available and he got a brand-new book, which was opened and examined on his return home with a special kind of excitement. Thin's itself was an enchanting shop, and he could spend hours just walking about there looking at books. Some boys got their books at Baxendine's, but his father had an account at Thin's, a bookshop which he considered far superior because of its greater size and greater variety of books displayed. Later he would browse among the open stalls of second-hand books at John Grants in George IV Bridge, and pick up old copies of Nelson's classics for twopence or threepence a volume. He would pass Nelson's building on the way to Arthur's Seat, and the thought that that was where books were made was powerfully exhilarating. Books: he would cut up sheets of paper and sew them together, then invent a title to inscribe on the outside sheet and write anything that came into his head on the inside. He was making books. He would make in this way pocket diaries and dictionaries (one once got as far as the letter C) as well as collections of verses and even of advertisements. He wondered how books actually got printed and wondered if it would ever be possible for him to print his own books himself. He learned in school that the first printing press in Scotland was set up in Edinburgh by Walter Chepman and Andrew Myllar by licence of King James IV who fell at Flodden six years later. 15 September 1507. To all and sundry our officers, lieges, and subjects whom it concerns, to whose knowledge these our letters shall come, greeting. Know ye that, forasmuch as our loved servants

Walter Chepman and Andrew Myllar, burgesses of our burgh of Edinburgh, have at our instance and request, for our pleasure and the honour and profit of our realm and lieges, taken on them to furnish and bring home a press, with all stuff belonging thereto, and expert men to use the same, for imprinting within our realm of the books of our Laws, Acts of Parliament, chronicles, mass books, and portuus after the use of our Realm, with additions and legends of Scottish saints now gathered to be eked thereto, and all other books that shall be seen necessary, and to sell the same for competent prices, by our advice and discretion, their labours and expenses being considered; we have granted and promised to them, that they shall not be hurt nor prevented therein by any others to take copies of any books forth of our realm to cause imprint the same in other countries, to be brought and sold again within our realm, to cause the said Walter and Andrew lose their great labour and expense.

Since then Edinburgh had been a city of printers. R. and R. Clark, T. and A. Constable, the Ballantyne Press, Morrison and Gibb, Turnbull and Spears. And among Edinburgh publishers he knew besides Nelson the names of Blackwood, Chambers, and Oliver and Boyd who published so many of his school text-books. W. and R. Chambers had started from nothing, first establishing separate book-selling businesses of the most humble kind, then W. branching into printing and publishing and R. into writing. W. described his first press as constructed to stand on a table; it consisted of a wooden sole, with a carriage, in which the forme of types was to be laid; and this carriage, or movable part, required to be pushed forward and drawn out as you would push and draw out a drawer. The power consisted of an iron screw hung on a cross beam, sustained by two upright supports. The handle was attached to the upper and projecting end of the screw, and had to be turned about twice with a smart jerk before the pressure could be effected. The working of the machine was slow and imperfect. Owing to the unsteadiness of the structure, the impression was far from perfect. When the screw was brought to the pull, a jangling and creaking noise was produced, like a shriek of anguish, that might have been heard two houses off. The impression being so effected, the screw had to be whisked back to a state of repose. His first printing venture was a pocket edition of the songs of Burns. 'I think', he wrote, 'there was a degree of infatuation in my attachment to that jangling, creaking, wheezing little press. Placed at the only window in my apartment, within a few feet of my bed, I could see its outlines in the silvery moonlight when I awoke; and there, at the glowing dawn did its figure assume distinct proportions. When daylight came fully in, it was impossible to resist the desire to rise and have an hour or two of exercise at the little machine.' The little Burns volume sold either in single copies at a shilling, or wholesale to other stall-keepers at a proper reduction. He cleared nine pounds in all. Edinburgh was full of booksellers in the early nineteenth century: the principal ones, says Cockburn, were Bell and Bradfute, and Manners and Miller, in the Parliament Close; Elphinstone Balfour, Peter Hill, and William Creech, in the High Street; and William Laing in the Canongate. Constable began as a lad in Hill's shop, and – unlike either Chambers – hardly set up for himself when he reached the summit of his business. He took possession of the open field. Abandoning the old timid and grudging system, Constable stood out as a general patron of all promising publications, and confounded not merely his rivals in trade, but his very authors, by his unheard-of prices. Ten, even twenty, guineas a sheet for a review, £2,000 or £3,000 for a single poem, and £1,000 each for two philosophical dissertations, drew authors from dens where they would otherwise have starved, and made Edinburgh a literary mart, famous with strangers, and the pride of its own citizens. Our hero learned in school of Scott's involvement with Constable and with Ballantyne and of the eventual crash. Books could be dangerous, they could tempt to ruin. But that only confirmed his view that they were the most exciting things in the world.

He was suspicious of Wordsworth's suspicion of books, though he saw his response to nature as absolutely right. Why the alternative?

> Books! 'tis a dull and endless strife,
> Come, hear the woodland linnet,
> How sweet his music; on my life
> There's more of wisdom in it.

He himself was enchanted with the idea of roaming the countryside with a book in his pocket, to be read when the fancy took him on the hillside or on the bank of a stream. He had a particular delight in small books, pocket editions. He liked the World's Classics and the King's Treasuries Series better than Everyman, because they were small and more easily pocketable. He came across once, while idly thumbing through a collected Wordsworth that belonged to his mother, a startlingly bad poem on Rob Roy's grave. He knew Rob Roy only through books and the theatre, and so it seemed paradoxical to him that Wordsworth should use Rob in his anti-book campaign.

> Said generous Rob, 'What need of books?
> Burn all the statutes and their shelves:
> They stir us up against our kind;
> And worse, against ourselves.'

But why equate books with statutes? And why bring in the shelves? To find a rhyme for ourselves, he suspected. It was easy to mock Wordsworth; he was the first great poet whose lapses seemed to him absolutely blatant. But he knew he was great in spite of this.

> No nightingale did ever chaunt
> More welcome notes to weary bands
> Of travellers in some shady haunt,
> Among Arabian sands:
> A voice so thrilling ne'er was heard
> In spring-time from the Cuckoo-bird,
> Breaking the silence of the seas
> Among the farthest Hebrides.

The last two lines of this stanza sank into his mind with total enchantment. Yet – Cuckoo-bird? Then why not Sparrow-bird or Nightingale-bird? Chaunt, though he knew it was there to rhyme with haunt, he accepted: it had an antique and magical sound. But he kept puzzling over Cuckoo-bird. Had Wordsworth got away with it?

> All night he heard, until they ceased,
> The growlings of the tiger-beast.

> All day he watched, with glowing eye,
> The flutterings of the butter-fly.

No no, that way lay Lewis Carroll, the bread-and-butter-fly. Anyway, Wordsworth couldn't have written

> A voice so thrilling ne'er was heard
> In spring from the cuckoo.

He needed a line of the same shape and rhythm as the previous one, as well as the rhyme. You couldn't rhyme cuckoo anyway. The nearest you could get to it would be look you or took you. It certainly shook you, that song of the cuckyoo. No, he would not mock. He loved the poem. He decided that Wordsworth had got away with it on this occasion. But sometimes he didn't. Sometimes he seemed so interested in his mood or his message or his anecdote that he failed to notice exactly how his language was working. Great poet though he was, he could be insensitive to what was happening verbally in a poem of his. What are words worth, William?

51

4

SOMEHOW 'The Cloud' found its way into a school reader he used in the term that began just after his seventh birthday, and for long he remembered the teacher reading and explaining the poem. He pored over it, and noted that it was said to be by P. B. Shelley. Peebee Shelley. In December 1919 the Chief Rabbi of the British Empire was visiting Edinburgh, and was entertained at his father's house. The Chief Rabbi, Dr J. H. Hertz, was proud of his familiarity with English literature and of his literary taste. In the course of a conversation over tea in the drawing-room he mentioned Shelley, and the little boy interrupted the grown-up conversation to ask: 'Do you mean Pee Bee Shelley?' The very reverend gentleman was much struck at this evidence of precocious familiarity with a great romantic poet, and the next week, as a Chanukah present, there arrived in the post for him a fat World's Classics edition of *Selected Poems of Shelley* bound in red leather. On the flyleaf the great man had written an inscription to him – to himself, by name – and signed it JHH. He realized that you had to be very distinguished before you could sign your name with your initials only. He also felt that he had won the book by false pretences. For 'The Cloud' was the only poem by Shelley he had ever heard of, and the only fact he knew about Shelley other than that he had written this poem was that he was Pee Bee. He tried to remedy his ignorance but found the task daunting. The first poem in the book was entitled 'The Daemon of the World, A Fragment' and had an introductory Latin quotation before beginning

> How wonderful is Death
> Death and his brother Sleep!

Mmmm. He wasn't sure about that at all. And when, a few lines further on, he came to

> Hath then the iron-sceptred Skeleton,
> Whose reign is in the tainted sepulchres,
> To the hell dogs that couch beneath his throne
> Cast that fair prey?

he found himself bewildered. He skimmed through 'Alastor' and the dedication of 'The Revolt of Islam' and 'Rosalind and Helen' and 'Julian and Maddalo' with increasing disappointment and confusion. In 'Prometheus Unbound' he was struck by Semichorus I and Semichorus II, and thought he would like to write a poem introducing Semichoruses though he had no idea what a Semichorus was (a kind of fairy, he suspected). The end of 'The Cenci' disturbed him strangely: he had not read the play through properly nor followed the action but he was aware that Beatrice was going to her death and read in almost frightened wonder

> Here, Mother, tie
> My girdle for me, and bind up this hair
> In any simple knot; ay, that does well.
> And yours I see is coming down. How often
> Have we done this for one another; now
> We shall not do it any more. My Lord,
> We are quite ready. Well, 'tis very well.

Later, in earliest adolescence, he re-discovered Shelley, and memorized the final chorus from 'Hellas' – The world's great age begins anew – before imitating it in a chorus of Hebrew captives in his epic poem on Judas Maccabeus. He was moved by 'When the lamp is shattered', and stirred by 'Adonais'. Later still, he succumbed to 'The Mask of Anarchy'. But 'The Cloud' remained his favourite all his schooldays, and seemed to him to represent the original Peebee. And the vision of Shelley as a poet who wrote one splendid weather poem which was seen against a background of strange melodramatic outbursts, cryptic mutterings, oracular Semichoruses, and uncanny funereal calm was never completely ousted by a more sophisticated view. Behind everything was JHH with his black beard and his interrupting self asking Do you mean Pee Bee Shelley? He was touched and impressed by the gift that resulted from his innocent question, and memory of it remained to soften his view of JHH in later years, when he became increasingly aware of the deep unspoken rivalry between JHH and his own father, and of course he took his father's side. JHH was a proud and opinionated man, who regarded himself as a Jewish Archbishop of Canterbury and dressed accordingly, except for the gaiters. (There seems to have been an unspoken assumption that gaiters were not kosher.) The tapes on his silk hat were especially intriguing. The Edinburgh rabbi, who was the unchallenged Jewish authority in Scotland, looked with some suspicion on the grandiose imperial title adopted by JHH and the Anglo-Jewish establishment behind him, considering it both pretentious and unreal. He also considered himself superior in diplomatic skills to the official representative of British imperial Jewry. JHH was a combative personality: it was said of him that he never despaired of finding a peaceful solution to any problem when all other possibilities had failed. Our hero heard him preach, and noted with disapproval that he did not take his text from that sabbath's portion of the Law, as his father always did, and he believed the story that, since he had no permanent pulpit of his own and travelled about giving the occasional single sermon in others' pulpits, he had only half a dozen sermons, which he continually repeated. When the Edinburgh rabbi published a book of essays entitled *Aspects of Judaism* he naturally sent a copy to JHH, who replied with a letter of thanks saying that the book was beautifully printed. This presumed damning with irrelevant praise was regarded as a sign of jealousy in Edinburgh. But the gift of Shelley had happened before any of this emerged, and remained as an ameliorating memory.

The Edinburgh Jewish community was removed in more respects than geographically from the Anglican Jewish establishment in the south, with its inter-marrying high families seasoned with titles and money. If the posh London Jews were Church of England Jews the poor Edinburgh Jews were Church of Scotland Jews. And the posh London Jews had just the same provincial attitude to Scotland as their Christian opposite numbers so often displayed. For years the Edinburgh rabbi protested against the title English Zionist Federation, which included the Zionist societies of Scotland and Ireland. At meeting after meeting in London he protested that he, as the Edinburgh rabbi representing a Scottish constituency, could not logically be a member of an organization whose title proclaimed itself purely English. The English Zionists had become accustomed to the letters EZF and answered the Edinburgh rabbi – as he contemptuously told his family on his return home from one of their meetings – that it was unthinkable that EZF should be changed to BZF, British Zionist Federation. BZF, they said, didn't sound right. In the end, however, the name was changed to Zionist Federation of Great Britain and Ireland, a great triumph for the only Scottish Nationalist rabbi in history. That the Scottish rabbi was also a passionate Zionist did not seem to him or anyone else illogical. The provision of a national home for the Jews in Palestine, not only as a refuge for the persecuted and a source of recognized diplomatic representation for Jewry that would carry weight with the governments of the world, but also as a centre of a regenerated spiritual and religious Jewish life that would flow from Jerusalem throughout the diaspora, was unquestioned by the rabbi and his family. For from Zion will go forth the law and the word of the Lord from Jerusalem. This prophecy, uttered confidently every sabbath, was felt to be near fulfilment, as a result of the Balfour Declaration and the subsequent British mandate in Palestine. Palestine was regarded as a land which, once flowing with milk and honey, had through centuries of neglect fallen into a parched and barren state, sparsely inhabited by nomadic Arabs who could only benefit from the re-fertilizing of the country by idealistic Jewish endeavour. The majority of western Jews would remain as contented communities in the countries where they had settled, loyal and patriotic citizens, while at the same time benefiting spiritually from the new currents that would flow from Zion. Bliss was it in that dawn to be alive, though to be young, like our hero, was hardly heaven. Zion restored by means of a penny a week put into the blue collecting box of the Jewish National Fund, which stood on the chimneypiece of his father's study, was a splendid ideal to work for; but meantime here was Edinburgh with its own insistent and continuous demands. Edinburgh, like Jerusalem, had once been the proud capital of an independent nation and had lost that status, though by more devious means than the loss of a war of independence. Joshua, Judas Maccabeus, William Wallace, Robert the Bruce, were heroes of the same kidney. There was no Jewish community in Edinburgh before 1816, but this was no obstacle to his feeling a sense of identity with the city and its history and with the country of which it was still the capital. He knew for a fact that the posh English Jews couldn't pronounce Hebrew properly, drawing out their vowels into diphthongs with a sort of Oxford accent. Roash ha shoh-noh. Ugh! Robert ben Bruce would have known better. And wasn't Joseph's coat of many colours the original tartan?

He joined the school pack of wolf cubs because he liked the idea of swaggering in a sort of uniform, but as they met in the early evening on Fridays it was only in the late spring and summer, when the sabbath did not come in till late, that he could attend; so cub meetings were always for him associated with the arrival or the imminence of summer. He lost continuity that way, but he read the literature, and had no difficulty in picking up the jargon and all the curious imitations of animal and primitive human behaviour. He once attended a massive cub rally at Murrayfield, where cubs from all over the world attended, with a most wonderful variety of colours in their kerchiefs. The contribution of his own pack in this great show was to form a circle and utter ceremonially certain sounds said to represent the ritual of Australian – or was it New Zealand? – aborigines. His father was astonished to hear this, and inquired what object such behaviour was designed to promote. He had difficulty in finding a satisfactory answer, even for himself, since he realized that a lot of the cubs' goings-on was quite daft. It was mixed up in his mind with Kipling's Jungle Books, but he was never really convinced that imitating animals was a justifiable pursuit. A – kee – la – we'll – do – our – best! It was a bit embarrassing really, but he enjoyed the uniform and he enjoyed winning proficiency badges that his mother could sew on his sleeve. A few years later a Jewish troop of boy scouts was formed, and met in the damp basement synagogue hall. He joined this, already a veteran because of his wolf-cub experience, and sported the purple shoulder ribbon of the tiger patrol. (Animals again.) They went to Blackford Hill and cooked kosher meat in billycans to demonstrate their fitness to fend for themselves in the great outdoors; they tracked each other; and they passed messages verbally down a long line to find that they invariably emerged garbled. The scout-master – a man called Jacobson who had served in the navy during the war and was now an income-tax official in Edinburgh – told them of a message that had been passed on verbally from the front-line trenches to the rear some time during the war. It had started as, We are going to advance, send reinforcements, and finally emerged as, We are going to a dance, send three-and-fourpence. The Jewish troop competed in an all-Edinburgh inter-troop competition, held in a little room somewhere in the Cowgate. They had to tie knots and answer questions involving hypothetical chimney sweeps having to attach a rope to a chimney with one hand. They didn't come top, but achieved an honourable placing. Someone from scout headquarters came to the synagogue hall once to teach them wrestling, but was inhibited by the fact that the bare wooden floor was not a suitable ground on which to try out falls. If we had some mattresses, the instructor said, stressing the word mattresses on the second syllable, I'd demonstrate to you, and he stressed the word demonstrate on the second syllable. The thought of him demonstrating on mattresses gave great pleasure to our hero and his friends. Whit dae ye think o' ma tresses? asked Rapunzel as she let her hair down out of the window, justifiably proud. They learned semaphore signalling with flags and the morse code with dots and dashes, and would signal to each other across the synagogue hall, communicating with great difficulty over a long space of time what they could have told each other in a few seconds. The brim of his scout hat wouldn't stay stiff, and before each meeting he would have to damp it with sugared water and then iron it. The end of his knotted kerchief would fall into his soup on those days when he had dinner before going to an evening meeting. Gradually he found the uniform less and less exciting, and eventually he dreaded having to go upstairs to the cold linoleum-floored bedroom in the winter time to change into his scout clothes before an evening meeting. None of the proficiency badges he won represented a proficiency that had any reality in the life he led. In the end he began shirking meetings and eventually dropped out. But he always remembered the joy he once had in attaching a whistle and his scout knife to his belt. He never had occasion to use the whistle, and even the knife was more of a decoration than anything else: it had a marlin spike, and he was never able to employ that for any purpose whatever. His scout pole proved a troublesome accoutrement, and once in his bedroom he inadvertently hit the electric light bulb with the end of it, with the result that the bulb was smashed and the function of the pole became more problematical than ever. A dirk stuck in the stocking, now, that would have added some panache to the uniform. He admired the dirk stuck in the stockings of kilted pipers; you couldn't really have a dirk without a kilt. The Jewish scouts of Edinburgh were not a kilted troop, as some Edinburgh troops were, but perhaps they could have worn the Gordon tartan, since Gordon was a Jewish as well as a Scottish name and there were two Jewish families called Gordon in Edinburgh. There were many great Jewish Gordons: Aharon David Gordon, Hebrew poet and philosopher of the Zionist labour movement; Judah Leib Gordon, Hebrew poet of the Jewish Enlightenment; Jekuthiel ben Leib Gordon, the eighteenth-century cabbalist; and L. Gordon, breeches-maker (Edinburgh). The Gordons were all Russian Jews, at least originally, and it was said that Jews in Russia adopted Gordon as a surname in honour of the Scots-born Russian general Patrick Gordon whose popularity with Peter the Great enabled him to influence that monarch in favour of better treatment of his Jewish subjects. The ancient, noble and illustrious Scottish house of Gordon comprises no fewer than one hundred and fifty seven main branches. George Gordon fourth Marquess of Huntly was created Duke of Gordon in 1684. The mad Lord George Gordon, a younger son of the third Duke of Gordon, converted to Judaism shortly before being committed to Newgate prison, where he died in 1793. Another George Gordon, Lord Byron, wrote a book of poems entitled *Hebrew Melodies*. Isaac Nathan, son of the Jewish cantor at Canterbury – the Canterbury cantor, in fact, which might well have been but was not the name of a dance – announced in the *Gentleman's Magazine* for May 1813 that he was about to publish *Hebrew Melodies*, all of them upwards of 1,000 years old and some of them performed by the Antient Hebrews before the destruction of the Temple, and the following year appealed to Byron to supply words for them. 'Oh,' wrote Byron to Annabella on 20 October 1814, 'I must tell you one of my present avocations. Kinnaird applied to me to write words for a musical composer who is going to publish the *real old undisputed Hebrew melodies*, which are beautiful & to which David & the prophets actually sang the "songs of Zion" – & I have done nine or ten on the sacred model. Augusta says they will call me a Jew next.' Of course it was nonsense about the real old undisputed Hebrew melodies, but Byron acted in good faith, and wrote

> Oh! weep for those that wept by Babel's stream,
> Whose shrines are desolate, whose land a dream;
> Weep for the harp of Judah's broken shell;
> Mourn – where their God hath dwelt the Godless dwell!

to say nothing of The Assyrian came down like the wolf on the fold, which he learned at school, together with the poem by Browning that they laughingly called How they brought the good news from Aches to Pains. (I galloped, we galloped, you (singular) galloped, you (plural) galloped, he she or it galloped: it was great fun all the same, but he always felt frustrated at not knowing what the good news was.) There was obviously some inbuilt sympathy between Gordons and Jews, and L. Gordon breeches-maker sitting in his top hat in the wardens' box in shul looked, with his massive side-whiskers, like a Victorian minister of the kirk. James Gordon, minister of Rothiemay in the seventeenth century, produced his famous bird's eye view of Edinburgh, reproduced in all books on the city. Jane, the beautiful Duchess of Gordon, held Edinburgh captive in the 1780s. 'It is really astonishing', wrote a troubled Edinburgh advocate in February 1786, 'to think what effect a single person will have on public manners, when supported by high rank and great address. She is never absent from a public place, and the later the hour, so much the better. It is often four o'clock in the morning before she goes to bed, and she never requires more than five hours' sleep. Dancing, cards, and company occupy her whole time.' Oh, there was much to be said for the Gordons, the gay Gordons. Some of the numerous Gordons associated with Edinburgh were less gay. Sir Adam Gordon, Sir John Gordon, Gordon of Cluny, Gordon of Earlston, Gordon of Ellon (the rich Edinburgh merchant from Aberdeenshire whose two sons were murdered by their reverend tutor whose mind had been affected by reading too much about predestination), Gordon of Haddo, Gordon of Kindroch, Gordon of Lesmoir, Gordon of Letterfourie, Gordon of Newhall, Gordon of Pitlurg . . . L. Gordon breeches-maker held his head up proudly among these:

> The Cohens are braw,
> The Goldstones an' a',
> But the cockie wee Gordon's the pride o' them a'.

There was a clothier called B. Hyam who had a shop near the corner of Nicolson Square, and once advertised in a huge poster on his window a clearance sale of trousers. Hyams trousers coming down, come and have a look! the poster beseeched. The breeches made by L. Gordon showed more pride: they were never displayed, but were kept discreetly within doors, awaiting the discriminating individuals for whom they were tailored. Less discreet and less discriminating was the Jewish tobacconist C. Lawrence, who displayed an advertisement reading: 'See Naples and die. Why not rather C. Lawrence and live (every smoking moment)?' You can't do that, he said to himself, you just can't do that: see, Lawrence?

Shelley wrote an ode to Naples; it was in the selection given him by JHH. It contained epodes, strophes and antistrophes, each mystically numbered, but it seemed pretty vaporous none the less.

> Naples! thou Heart of men which ever pantest
> Naked, beneath the lidless eye of Heaven!

He really couldn't take that pantest. Pantest and lidless came together in his mind to suggest pan-lids. Every year a man would come to the house with pan-lids for sale. Twice he answered the door on such an occasion, and the man delivered an identical speech: Is your mother in sonny? Will you tell her I'm the man who sold her the pan-lids last year? As his mother never bought pan-lids from this man, the announcement was puzzling. Another annual caller was a knife-grinder, whose services were regularly employed to such effect that the dinner knife always used in his household as a carving knife (for some reason no carving knife as such ever appeared there and for long he did not know that there existed such a separate species of knife) grew annually narrower in mid-blade. He used to use it for sharpening pencils, for the other dinner-knives, which did not enjoy the knife-grinder's services, were too blunt. These were fleischig knives, used only for meat and poultry; the rigid distinction between milchig and fleischig foods, each with their separate dishes and utensils, was taken for granted in the rabbi's family, though he sometimes wondered why the biblical prohibition of seething a kid in its mother's milk should be carried to such lengths. It was quite right to prohibit such seething, which in any case sounded much worse than boiling; the pagans who, he was told, engaged in such an unfeeling practice were clearly inferior to the more sensitive Israelites to whom it was properly forbidden. But a question sometimes rose in his mind. Were the things so expressly forbidden in the Bible specifically forbidden because the Children of Israel would otherwise have shown a natural tendency to do them, or did the prohibitions indicate a natural revulsion on the part of the said Children against the prohibited activities? If they hadn't thought of doing some of the things anyway, wouldn't prohibiting them just put ideas into the Children's heads, like the mother who before leaving home told her little boy not to put peas up his nose when she was out – something he had never thought of doing but which, his curiosity aroused, he now promptly did? Did a prohibition suggest that something was tempting, but should be resisted, or that something was revolting and should therefore of course never be contemplated? He could not imagine a kid seethed in its mother's milk being a special delicacy, but then he knew about *de gustibus*, and didn't some people think raw shell-fish delicious? He used shell-fish as bait in catching fish from the rocks on the Fife coast, and could not conceive of them as human food. Shell-fish were naturally prohibited food, but there was no prohibition against using them as bait or against looking at them, handling them, or indeed doing anything with them except eating them. Why then go to such extraordinary lengths to remove the possibility of seething a kid in its mother's milk? Not only did you have to have different dishes and cutlery for meat dishes and milk dishes; you couldn't even eat or drink anything made with milk for at least three hours after having eaten any meat or poultry. And with the ultra-orthodox it was six hours. Yet for some reason you could have a milk dish just before a meat dish, though not just after one. And then poultry. You couldn't seethe a chick in its mother's milk if you tried. He was moved reluctantly to the conclusion that a kid seethed in its mother's milk must have seemed so fantastically tempting to the Jews of old that every conceivable barrier had to be set up against the remotest possibility of their ever coming within a million miles of consuming such a delicacy. Still, all this meat and milk differentiation seemed wholly natural to him. To put butter on bread you were eating with roast beef or with chicken seemed to him an impossible practice. Buttered bread went with fish and with eggs, the latter of which could range freely on both sides of the barrier. A fish meal was a milk meal; finnan haddock seethed in milk was delicious as well as morally quite untainted; there was some divine purpose in haddocks not having been created mammals. As for gefillte fish, it was inconceivable as part of a butterless meal. Friday night was generally a fish night, a milchig night. Every week his mother would ring up Mrs Kerr the fishmonger in South Clerk Street and ask what had been landed. Mrs Kerr catered well to the Edinburgh Jews and their fish-eating habits, and owed her rise in fortune to their solid patronage. After some years, from running a small shop with just an errand boy to assist her, she opened a larger and more luxurious fish emporium. By that time many Edinburgh Jews had discovered the glories of Mr Bryson and were less dependent on Mrs Kerr, who now appealed to a more ecumenical clientèle. Young Mr Bryson, who had to be distinguished from Mr Bryson *tout court*, was renowned among a section of Edinburgh Jews for having personally demonstrated the physical impossibility of eating a pigeon a day. It was the domineering and garrulous Mrs Sherwinter who had told the story, at tea before the drawing-room fire one winter afternoon. Fixing his father with her fierce eyes she announced that the doctor had ordered young Mr Bryson to eat a pigeon a day and he tried, but HE COULDN'T DO IT. It remained a mystical fact that the human frame is so constituted as to be unable to absorb a pigeon a day. An apple a day, however, was not only possible but desirable. There were always plenty of apples in the house, and no limits were set on their consumption. Jonathans, Snows, Delicious, Russets, Newton Pippins – he recognized them all, and munched with discrimination. Rankins was the fruit-shop they most often went to. Mr Rankin had started out with a small shop – or was it a barrow? – in Portobello, and then had opened a shop in Clerk Street or perhaps Nicolson Street, but anyway near enough to the Jewish shops and in the Jewish area bounded by Buccleuch Street and St Leonards. He then opened a third shop in the same area. Each shop looked a bit more prosperous than the last. And each contained its proportion of buxom Rankin daughters, of whom there seemed to be a limitless quantity. Later Rankins burgeoned more and more to become eventually perhaps the best-known and most numerous of Edinburgh fruit-shops. But, like Mrs Kerr, Mr and the Misses Rankin were first set on their way by their Jewish customers. For fruit was a food free of all Jewish food regulations. It was neither milchig nor fleischig; it could be eaten with anything at any time and in any place: an apple in a grocer's shop surrounded by sides of bacon remained a Jewishly edible fruit. Even on Passover ordinary fruit bought in ordinary gentile shops could be eaten at will by the most orthodox. Apples and oranges and nuts were incorruptible. On Rosh Hashanah, New Year's Day, one would ceremonially eat a piece of apple with honey and pray for a sweet new year.

As the years moved on, novelties appeared. Grapefruit took their place in the fruit-cupboard, and eventually a message reached them from the great world of society about the desirability of grapefruit spoons. Messages of another kind were coming in too – by wireless. For in 1923 the Edinburgh wireless station 2EH was set up, with its curiously shaped aerial just at the top of his street. In a fever of enthusiasm he and his brother persuaded their father to finance the purchase of a small rectangle of ebonite, a variometer, a cat's whisker with an appropriate detector, a hertzite crystal, and the cheapest obtainable pair of headphones. These were bought at a garage at the foot of Argyle Place, and the two brothers who ran it were obliging enough to drill holes in the ebonite to enable the various instruments to be mounted on it. The rabbi shared the boys' enthusiasm, to the point of agreeing to have an aerial erected on the roof. And so wireless entered his home. On the headphones he could hear music and talks s.b. – simultaneously broadcast – from 2LO in London. Edinburgh had its own children's hour, with Auntie Molly, and it was she who initiated his literary career by reading out over the air a poem he had sent in, having first rung up the rabbi to make quite sure that the poem was the boy's own work. Experiment raged. After the first crystal set there was one with a valve amplifier. Then they built a two-valve set, with a detector valve and an amplifying valve, and tried to make a loud-speaker out of an old horn mounted on one earpiece of the headphones. This was not a success, and eventually a proper loud-speaker was bought, another amplifying valve added, and the dining-room filled (faintly) with the strains of the Savoy Orpheans or Henry Hall and his dance orchestra. They took in the *Radio Times* and selected programmes. And the pages of *The Family Entertainer* carried mock wireless programmes, including The Chief Rabbi: Songs at the Piano (the first of which was entitled Can a Kosher Cat Cut Capers?), a concert of sparrow songs s.b. from Aberdeen, and Weather Guess, and Talk to Flea-Keepers by Mr Keating. In the issue of January 1927 it was announced that there would be a broadcast from Rome of the seventh attempt on Mussolini's life. He knew nothing about Italy except a few vulgar facts. Marconi was a wireless pioneer, he knew. Macaroni was an Italian dish that was long and worm-shaped, but they never had it at home. Lokshen, narrow noodles, was the Jewish pasta, and they had it in chicken soup. Macaroni was a subject for jokes. She opened the window and in flew enza. The doctor ordered macaroni but it didna mak 'er ony better. There were Italian ice-cream men in Edinburgh, and some of them established dynasties. Our hero and his family used to go to Di Rollo's in Port Seton the year they holidayed there: an ice-cream after bathing in the Firth of Forth, a sort of homeopathic treatment, driving out cold with cold. It was a far cry from Di Rollo to that other Italian in Edinburgh whom he learned about in school, David Rizzio, musician, adviser and favourite of Mary Queen of Scots, who was dragged from her and murdered in the outer room of her apartments in the palace of Holyrood on 9 March 1566. John Knox approved the deed, writing later that that poltroon and vile knave Davie was justly punished, but it was a deed that posterity regarded with an even greater shudder than they afforded the murder a year later of one who was deeply involved in Rizzio's death, Darnley, the Queen's husband. This too was an Edinburgh murder, done at Kirk-of-Field, and the details of the blowing up of the building where Darnley lay convalescing from smallpox were part of the city's lore. It was in the controversies surrounding Mary Queen of Scots and John Knox that our hero felt most his ancestral remoteness from the actors, and so was able to preserve a certain impartiality. Mary was of course the more attractive character, but Knox had his own kind of fascination, and his house in the High Street could still be seen. There were more than Scottish-Jewish paradoxes involved in his attitude to history. He was, like his schoolfellows, always for the Scots and their allies the French against the English. Yet he was for

Elizabeth and Sir Francis Drake against the Spanish Armada. The emphasis shifted in school history teaching as the boys grew older. First they learned only Scottish history: Edward I of England was a wicked man, the enemy of the noble Wallace and Bruce, and Elizabeth was a shadowy figure whose significance lay only in the role she played in relation to Queen Mary and in dying unmarried so that James VI of Scotland inherited her throne. But later the boys learned English history, and were shown Edward I as a great English king. They could never accept his virtue, though, as they did that of Elizabeth who, in spite of having ordered Mary's execution, was clearly a heroine with heroic subjects. He had special Jewish reasons for hating Edward I, for he expelled the Jews from England in 1290. There were no such anti-semitic acts staining Scotland's record, as the rabbi took pleasure in recalling. The first British university to grant degrees to Jews was Marischal College, Aberdeen, where Scott's Dugald Dalgetty studied and where Jacob de Castro Sarmento was awarded a medical degree in 1739. De Castro Sarmento was Portuguese-born and had written a discourse for the Day of Atonement in Portuguese in 1724 after emigrating to London, where he later published a number of medical works. If he had lived early enough to have been able to attend Darnley, perhaps that unfortunate man would have survived longer, for De Castro Sarmento was an expert in smallpox inoculation, and if Darnley had not been ill with smallpox he would not have been convalescing at Kirk-of-Field and so given his murderers their opportunity. Our hero liked to bring together in his imagination historical characters of different periods and to meditate on what might have happened if they had actually met.

He had difficulty with his own smallpox vaccination, when he had it done at the request of the school during a smallpox scare. The scar stayed for weeks, and in the end left a permanent blob like a jellyfish. When he was nine he had scarlet fever with a great variety of complications which resulted in his being in the Edinburgh fever hospital for over two months. He was carried feverish and confused into the children's ward where complete pandemonium reigned. Children shouted, threw things, jumped on beds, and said rude words. As he improved and was able to take proper notice of his new environment he realized what a totally new society this was. It was different in not only being non-Jewish; it was also socially different, for it seemed to him that most of the children in the ward were keelies. Their language was astonishing and educational. They had no respect at all for the nurses, and he soon found himself echoing their mock-abusive language. Not that the nurses seemed to mind. It was all very rough and ready. Something was wrong with his ears, and every day they would be painfully syringed. Doctors in white coats lectured over him to students with a pointer. On Sundays a minister came with a portable harmonium and sang hymns, jumping up and down as he played, so that the children called him Jumping Jesus. Dr Matheson visited him every day, and it was a comfort to see his familiar face. One or other of his parents came daily too, but they were not allowed inside the ward, and he could only wave to them as they stood at the entrance. His neck swelled up, and he had to have it swathed in a special kind of bandage. When after many weeks he finally had it taken off one of the children asked him why he wasn't wearing his collar. There was a terrible moment when he was first allowed proper food and he was brought a plate of mince. Earnestly he explained to the nurse that he couldn't eat it, as he was Jewish. The nurse, genuinely surprised, asked what kind of meat Jews could eat, and he tried to explain about the special method of slaughter and the removal of the blood, but he was confused himself and made the nurse even more confused. So he went back on slops again, until his mother brought some kosher steak to the hospital which was presented him the next day fried to an absolute cinder: they were taking no chances on the blood. He crunched the charcoal in his mouth and swallowed it with difficulty: he couldn't bring himself to complain. He was in hospital over Christmas, and they decorated the children's ward with red shades on the lights. It was the first Christmas he had ever celebrated. He was gratified to find that every child in the ward received a present – nothing expensive, but thoughtfully chosen. His was a book of postcards to be painted. Months later he learned that his mother had presented the presents to the ward, and that they were not therefore due to the generosity of the hospital, as he had thought. He coloured the postcards with crayons and wrote several to family and friends, giving them to a nurse to post. But, as again he learned later, they were never posted. Nothing in fact that came to the hospital ever went out: it was thought that it would spread infection. So the numerous books he received from various relations had to remain forever in the ward. At Christmas Jumping Jesus conducted a carol service, and he felt he had to sing with the other children, even when the carols were theologically offensive, as he did not want to seem arrogant or surly. The worst part of the carol service, however, was not any offensive sentiments in the carols but the fact that it lasted so long and it was impossible to obtain a bottle or a bedpan from a nurse while it continued. Many of the children besides himself were in agony with a desire to relieve themselves. At last one of the nurses passed round an almost full bottle for the use of the boys; each time it was passed to another bed some of the urine slopped out on to the bedclothes. He reflected that he would have been better off away in a manger.

When at last he was allowed out of bed he found to his astonishment that he could not walk. He was allowed to put his own clothes on again, which was a great luxury, and he staggered about the ward, already by far the oldest inhabitant among the patients there. They used to give him his meals alone on a little table at the top of the ward, to which they would encourage him to try to walk. At last the time came when he was told he was to leave the next day. That night he spent in another part of the hospital, in a room by himself. He was given a reeking pink carbolic bath before supper. The next morning his mother called for him in a taxi: he was still unable to walk properly. He had come from a strange land of which his parents knew nothing, a land of noise and violence and disorder and rude language and the most extraordinary casualness about natural functions. Somehow he knew that that land was the real world, more real in a significant way than the genteel world he normally inhabited. He kept his knowledge secret, but from that time on he was conscious of being the only one of his family who was aware of certain truths about life. He had even eaten treife food, for he had consumed beef soup which he knew was made with meat for there were actual bits of meat floating about in it. He scrupulously left these bits of meat untouched, but he knew that the soup was nevertheless treife, non-kosher. He knew also, however, that in time of sickness normal dietary rules could be waived, so he was committing no sin. He was struck by the fact that the soup tasted like any other soup. He could have refrained from eating it, but as he avoided meat (the experiment of cooking kosher steak brought by his mother was not repeated), this would have reduced his diet fairly stringently, so he took it. Later he explained to his father that he had carefully removed the bits of meat, but the rabbi only smiled faintly and said that it made no difference: the soup was still treife. He knew that already, but he hoped for a somewhat more encouraging remark. The soup was not on his conscience, though. What had been at stake in that ward was survival: he had adapted, and survived.

He never once thought of Peebee Shelley during those many weeks in the fever hospital. But when he got home and refamiliarized himself one by one with the details of the domestic scene, he found his copy of the poems given him by JHH with its red book-mark at the last page of 'The Cloud'.

> I pass through the pores of the ocean and shores;
>   I change, but I cannot die,

he read. Like me, in a way, he thought. I have changed, and now I'm here again, still here. Things looked the same, yet different. He turned back the pages, and his eye fell on the last line of the 'Ode to the West Wind'. If Winter comes, can Spring be far behind? He felt a surge of energy. I think I know what Shelley means, he said to himself aloud.

PART TWO

Israelites

5

ABRAHAM, *avraham avinu*, Abraham our father, why did you do it? Why did you leave the comfortable and sophisticated civilization of Mesopotamia – when was it? Nearly four thousand years ago? – with all home comforts, law, literacy, administrative efficiency, flourishing agriculture, lively architecture, to wander westward and southward to God knows where? God did indeed know where. Was that it? Get thee out of thy country, and from thy kindred, and from thy father's house, unto a land that I will show thee. *Lech lecha*, get thee out, said the Lord. Now what an extraordinary thing. Had Abraham (he was called Abram at that early stage in his career, but no matter) done anything special to be given such a message? For I will make of thee a great nation, and I will bless thee, and make thy name great. But why? As far as we know, there was no damn merit about it. History just picked on him. Or was it he who picked on history? Did he hear voices because he wanted to hear voices? Had he become suspicious of comfort, wary of civilization? For God's sake, did this archetypal Jew WANT to become an exile? Apparently, and for God's sake. He dropped out, for God's sake! He was no chicken either: seventy and five years old he was, says the good book, but we take this *cum grano salis*; there was a lot of salt by the shores of the Dead Sea (as the wife of his nephew Lot was to learn to her cost), which was the direction in which he was heading, and it was liable to get into numbers in considerable grains. Anyway, this no longer young man left home with his wife and his nephew and all his household and moved south-west to the land of the Canaanite. And between Bethel and Hai he built an altar and called on the name of the Lord. And then he kept on going south. What was he looking for? What did he hear from on high apart from the simple call to Go west old man? To go from urban security to roam in nomad's land was hardly an act of prudence. Of wisdom, then? Was there something rotten in the state of Babylonian culture, in Mesopotamian progress, in the well-built city of Haran? Was he hungry for something he couldn't get there? Did he find prosperity threatening? Was he critical of the materialism of modern civilization? Sarah (she was called Sarai at that stage, but no matter), Sarah my dear, there's no use arguing: when you gotta go you gotta go. But Abraham, just when we've had the new bathroom put in? And the new dining-room carpet! It's no use, my dear: I heard the Lord say to me, Leave your new bathroom and your dining-room carpet and go to a land that I will show thee. The Lord said that. He used the familiar form of the second personal pronoun. I think you're crazy, she said. No matter, said Abraham, I'm the boss. So they went, with all the souls they had gotten in Haran. It's better, said Abraham, to be an ancestor than a descendant: I now know that my métier is to be a patriarch.

Patriarch: father or ruler of a family or tribe. But in Hebrew it is simply *av*, father; a patriarch is simply a father *par excellence*. Yet it was this man, who chose fatherhood as a profession, who agreed, though in agony, to sacrifice his son Isaac to the Lord. Of course the Lord substituted a ram at the last minute, just when Abraham had stretched forth his hand and had taken the knife to slay his son. Lay not thine hand upon the lad, neither do thou anything unto him: for now I know that thou fearest God, seeing that thou hast not withheld thy son, thine only son, from me. So it was all right, then? God had only been testing Abraham after all. The angels, whom we must assume to have known what God had in mind, presumably looked down cheerfully, knowing that God was only testing, testing. But did that diminish Abraham's agony? If he had got so far as to stretch out his hand with the knife, did it really matter what happened after that? Agony is irreversible, and happy endings can come too late. Each year, when this biblical passage was intoned on the second day of Rosh Hashanah, our hero felt his flesh creep. Surely, he thought, a sacrifice demanded by God as proof of obedience must have some moral end other than demonstration of blind obedience? To kill a son and offer him as a burnt offering? To offer himself, perhaps; a man has a right to sacrifice himself. And what of Isaac's trauma? Behold the fire and the wood, he said to his father, but where is the lamb for a burnt offering? And Abraham replied, thinking he was lying but in fact telling the truth, My son, God will provide himself a lamb for a burnt offering. But the moment came when Isaac saw that his father intended to slaughter him and no lamb. What, the boy wondered, squirming in his hard seat in the Graham Street shul, what was going on in Isaac's mind when he watched his father's arm with

72

the raised knife? As for God's purpose, it was an odd business. When he gave his order to Abraham about sacrificing his son, he emphasized, with a leaning on the words, that Isaac was the old man's only son and his beloved son – take now thy son, thine only son Isaac, whom thou lovest, *et bincha, et yechidcha, asher ahavta*. But God was nervous, surely, for he used an expression that he never uses elsewhere in all the Bible in giving an order to a mortal man. He said, Take, please, thy son (the old translators rendered it 'now', but the word used, *na*, is a particle of supplication). Take, I pray thee; please, please, do it. As though he had had a bet on, as he had, in a manner of speaking, on a later occasion with the Satan about his servant Job. What a testing for Abraham and Isaac both, what a training for the first two patriarchs, the first two of the three founding fathers of the Jewish people. Yet neither they nor their descendants ever bore malice, and they considered this macabre test as a mark of divine favour. Generation upon generation of Jews continued to be called Abraham and Isaac, and Christians used the names in fiction or satire or humour as quintessentially Jewish names. Any semitic-looking man with a beard could be jocularly referred to as Father Abraham, like the Edinburgh professor who was so addressed in high alcoholic comedy by a couple of students who met him on the street, but the professor deftly substituted another biblical character: No, he said, I am not Father Abraham, but Saul the son of Kish, who went out to look for his father's asses, and lo I have found them. The name could be affectionately yiddishized into Avrumkele or vulgarly abbreviated into Aby or Abie, which suggested flashy young men in the Palm Court of a 1920s hotel. There was a song called 'Abie my boy', and a Jewish matron once approached the orchestra leader in such a hotel and said, Play Abie my boy. Certainly, Madam, replied the dark-moustached fiddler, and what would you like me to play? Our hero heard fragments of the song, but was never sure whether it was the real song or a parody:

> Abie, Abie, Abie my boy
> What are you waiting for now?
> You promised to marry me
> One day in June,
> It's never too late
> And it's never too soon . . .

There was also the story of little Abie in the museum being shown a statue by his foreign-born mother: A B C D F E G, which any know-

73

ledgeable youngster knew meant, Abie, see the effigy. *Quantum mutatus ab illo*, changed utterly from the questing patriarch with his desperate search for spiritual duty. It is a long road from Abraham's Sarah to Abie's Irish rose, that appalling comedy to which his father had been sent free tickets and to which he took his family, to sit in frozen horror while stalely debased American Jewish and Irish jokes were presented as a comically saving truth about the relation between Jews and Catholics. How he resented this, as he resented all the lowering images of Jews and the savagely diminutive versions of grand biblical names. Ikey Mo. The two images farthest removed from each other which can be comprehended under one term are, I think, Isaiah, – 'Hear O heavens, and give ear, O earth!' and Levi of Holywell Street – 'Old clothes' – both of them Jews, you'll observe. So Coleridge wrote, unaware of his own guilt in forcing the difference, ignorant of the transformation of Levi of Holywell street to Levi the father welcoming the sabbath over candles on Friday night. When the great Coleridge found himself sitting opposite a poor Jew in a coach, he addressed him thus: Son of Abraham! thou smellest; son of Isaac! thou art offensive; son of Jacob! thou stinkest foully. So the fragrant Coleridge, stuffed with Christian charity and opium, mocked the characters and language of the Bible. It's odd about the stinking, though, since Jews were fanatical about cleanliness, and had to wash ritually before partaking of any food, making the appropriate blessing during the process. It was – he was actually told this at school by Dr Brydon, the history master – the Christians who made dirt into godliness, wearing hair shirts which they never changed so they could be tormented, for their souls' good, by the dirt and the insects underneath. After Thomas Beckett was murdered, Dr Brydon said, they found a hair shirt under his splendid vestments, a shirt that had not been changed for years, and beneath it was a thriving colony of lice. That proved him saintly. But to Jews cleanliness was if not next to godliness at least a condition of godliness. Cleansing rituals of all kinds were built in to the Jewish religion. If a Jew was dirty and stank, it was poverty not principle that forced him to it: my poverty and not my will consents. The caricaturist's Jewish nose was long to indicate, surely, that the Jews were particularly sensitive to smells. On Saturday night, after the sun had set and at least three stars had appeared in the sky, the rabbi would sniff at a fragrant silver spice-box, and then pass it round the family to be sniffed by each member, so that the pleasing scent would console them for the departure of the Princess Sabbath. As he sniffed, the rabbi recited a Hebrew blessing: blessed art thou O Lord our God, King of the universe, who createst divers kinds of spices. He that planted the ear, shall he not hear? He that formed the eye, shall he not see? And the Psalmist might well have gone on to ask: He that formed the nose, shall he not smell? And shall he not allow his creatures to enjoy divers kinds of spices? Yet schoolboys suspected scent, and a perfumed lady French teacher at school was known (and our hero never dissented from the appellation) as Stinky Davidson. When he was ill, his mother spread lavender water about his bedroom, and sometimes rubbed his fevered brow with an icy stick of solid eau-de-cologne. He relished that. Blessed art thou O Lord. Yet the Lord also created sulphuretted hydrogen, which was contained in stink bombs that boys occasionally let off in school, and there were other bad smells, some of them human, about which boys were conversing loudly and rudely outside Henry John Findlay's classroom when Bill Anderson, the science master, passed by and said briskly: Keep your minds pure, boys, keep your minds pure. But the smell of growing seaweed on the seashore was the best smell of all, reminiscent of summer holidays and rock pools and the undulating sea itself, and it was easy to believe that God was responsible for that. Divers kinds, because they were to be discovered in the depths of the sea. They made a sweet out of seaweed, called carrageen, which he once tasted in a hotel in Mallaig when his family was on holiday at Glenuig in Moidart, where he spent most of his time catching cuddies and mackerel, as well as the occasional unwanted dogfish which however was found appetizing by Lord Elgin, who was living in the big house further along the shore: he would present the evil fish to the peer, who gleamed and said Ah, dogfish pie, and rubbed his tummy in a joyous schoolboy gesture. Oddly enough, the Hebrew for fish was *dog*.

In Edinburgh he would often see Newhaven fishwives, with their picturesque striped skirts, and baskets of fish on their backs. Once he was in a crowded tramcar in the Bridges and rose to give his seat to a large and brawny fishwife. She looked down on him and his offer, saying peremptorily, Sit doon, son. Yet he was not offended: she was a force of nature, and he settled down comfortably in his seat secure in the knowledge that the universe would have him there. His mother bought a book of Scottish songs with a tartan cover and would sit at the piano and play and sing 'Caller Herrin' ', a song that he always associated with the harbour at Anstruther and the sight of the fishing boats leaving or coming home.

> Wha'll buy my caller herrin'?
>   They're bonnie fish and halesome farin';
> Wha'll buy my caller herrin',
>   New drawn frae the Forth?

The lines that sent a frisson down his back were

> Wives and mithers, maist despairin',
>   Ca' them lives o' men.

There were also fishwives from Fisherrow, which was now really part of Musselburgh which you could reach by tramcar from Edinburgh. 'There the Fish-wives, as they are all of one class, and educated in it from infancy, are of a character and manners still more singular than the carriers of greens, salt, &c, and particularly distinguished by the laborious lives they lead. They are', continued the Reverend Alexander (Jupiter) Carlyle in 1795, 'the wives and daughters of fishermen, who generally marry in their own cast, or tribe, as a great part of their business, to which they must have been bred, is to gather bait for their husbands, and bait their lines. Four days in the week, however, they carry fish in creels (osier baskets) to Edinburgh; and when the boats come in late to the harbour in the forenoon, so as to leave them no more than time to reach Edinburgh before dinner, it is not unusual for them to perform their journey of five miles, by relays, three of them being employed in carrying one basket, and shifting it from one to another every hundred yards, by which means they have been known to arrive at the Fishmarket in less than ¾ths of an hour.' The reverend gentleman added in a footnote that 'it is a well attested fact, that three of them, not many years ago, went from Dunbar to Edinburgh, which is 27 miles, with each of them a load of herrings on her back of 200 lb. in 5 hours. They sometimes carried loads of 250 lb.' He and his brother once walked the twenty-five miles to North Berwick, via Musselburgh, Prestonpans, Cockenzie, Port Seton, Aberlady and Gullane, along the hard main road all the way, to flop down wearily on the beach at North Berwick where they lay waiting for the blisters to rise. Walking there was all right; it was getting about after a rest, with blistered feet and stiff legs, that was painful. He had covered more than that over hills and plains, but tarmacadam, as he discovered, was another matter. John Loudon McAdam was the hero and villain of this adventure, for he it was who discovered how to make hard roads of broken stone. On a good well-drained soil a thickness of 6 in. will make an excellent road for ordinary traffic, and McAdam's opinion that 10 in. of well-consolidated material was sufficient to carry the heaviest traffic on any substratum if properly drained has proved to be correct. McAdam absolutely interdicted the use of any binding material, leaving the broken stone to work in and unite by its own angles under the traffic. In 1819 he published his *Practical Essay on the Scientific Repair and Preservation of Roads*, followed, in 1820, by *The Present State of Road-making*. In pursuit of his investigations he had travelled over thirty thousand miles of road and expended over £5,000. Parliament recouped him for his expenses and gave him a handsome gratuity, but he declined a proffered knighthood. McAdam was an Ayrshire man, and died at Moffat, Dumfriesshire, in 1836. Tar macadam came later. The tar ought to be boiled, and if too thin, a little pitch may be added to it, though not enough to make the heap consolidate. All this might seem to take the romance out of roads, but no, the sight of a road rising and then dipping out of sight never failed to excite in him a lust for adventure. To put on his shoulder a stick with a bundle at the end and set out for no particular destination, just following the road, had been a dream of his almost from infancy. He never actually carried a burden in that way, and when he grew old enough to start serious hiking he had to make do with a rucksack, but the symbolic figure of the tramp never lost its appeal. From the moment when he first read at school the last stanza of Horace's ode about Regulus he was haunted by that picture of his setting out on his last journey:

> quam si clientum longa negotia
> diiudicata lite relinqueret,
>   tendens Venafranos in agros
>   aut Lacedaemonium Tarentum.

He wrote an essay trying to explain why those last two lines, which consisted of little more than place-names, names in themselves of no interest, should be so inexpressibly moving, but his explanation satisfied neither himself nor his Latin master. Regulus's was the ultimate setting out, the road taken for the last time. Roads had divine sanction. The voice of him that crieth: In the wilderness prepare ye the way of the Lord, make straight in the desert a highway for our God. (He knew from the punctuation and structure of the Hebrew that the wilderness did not belong to the voice crying, but to preparing the way – prepare a way in the wilderness, make a highway in the desert – and he used to smile on hearing people talk of a voice crying in the wilderness, for he knew it was a mistranslation. He was a great one for mistranslations. Later he learned how to deal with intrusive evangelists quoting biblical texts at him: It's a mistranslation from the Hebrew, he would say dismissively; you had better look at the original.) A desert highway: he saw its endless ribbon winding through the sand, a symbolic biblical road, a tar mac-Adam, a ben Adam, who was Abel, and who is more able than a roadmaker? He remembered the song about Adam and Eve: their life it was a happy one and peaceful in the main, until they had a baby boy and started raising Cain. Cain was sentenced to be a fugitive and a vagabond for killing his brother; he became the first tramper of roads. The extraordinary thing was that he eventually settled in the land of Nod, on the east of Eden, and a book of very childish poems that he had acquired when he barely knew how to read had made it clear that the land of Nod was a teasingly childish phrase for dreamland, falling asleep. Now you go off to the land of Nod, he would be told, having settled down for the night. And then to discover that that is where Cain landed up! Did it mean that he finally forgot his guilt in sleep? It couldn't, though, for Nod in Hebrew had nothing to do with nodding off to sleep. It simply meant wandering. So nobody knew what happened to Cain, he rationalized, and when they said he settled in Nod they must have meant that he kept on wandering. Like Felix the cat, in that ridiculous song that suddenly swept the country. Miles up in the air he flew, he just murmured toodeloo, landed down in Timbuctoo, and kept on walking still. The reason for the cat's insistently peripatetic activities eluded him. But Felix's way of walking was something he recognized: with his hands behind him you will always find him – exactly as you would find Mr Lurie, Mr Plantsy and other Edinburgh Jewish worthies who, when they were walking and not talking, kept their hands behind their backs. *Felis* or *feles*, he knew, was Latin for cat, hence presumably Felix the cat. But *felix* meant happy, and were cats by nature happy? It amused him to construe *felix* as meaning Felix the cat in certain Latin passages. *Felix qui potuit rerum cognoscere causas*, wrote Virgil of Lucretius, happy the man who was able to perceive the causes of things. Or, Felix, who was able to perceive the causes of things. A perceptive cat, and a cat who kept on walking still,

> tendens Venafranos in agros
> aut Lacedaemonium Tarentum.

A learned cat, keeping on walking to Venafran fields or Lacedaemonian Tarentum. That really was the sublime and ridiculous together. What made him explore these combinations?

Felix
As he licks
His fur,
Meditates CAUSAS
Reflectively miauws as
His thoughts become surer
DE RERUM NATURA.

Fur was Latin for thief, so it would be advisable to keep a cat rather than a dog to protect your house from a *fur nocturnus*, since a cat would be adept at licking the fur.

Sed haec hactenus. Satis superque habet. Enough. Genug. Dai. Dayenu, we have had enough. It struck him as grammatically odd that this Hebrew word *dayenu*, enough for us, our sufficiency, was used in a conditional sense in the Passover Haggadah, when during the Seder they recited the blessings wrought by God for his people in a list of conditional sentences: If God had brought us out of Egypt and not wrought judgment on the Egyptians, it would have been enough for us. *If* he had done this and not that, that and not the other, the other and not then something more, *dayenu*. If he had brought us to the land of Israel and not built us the Temple, *dayenu*. We would have considered it enough. What an effortless way to deal with the conditional tense, just to ignore it and let the context suggest it. When he thought of his struggles with conditional tenses in Latin and Greek, unfulfilled conditions in the past tense *et hoc genus omne*, he marvelled at the genius of a language that could ignore the whole thing. The ancient Hebrews were a religious but not a philosophic people, and they did not split hairs with pluperfect subjunctives or even bother very much about tenses, which in Hebrew could not be reduced to any logical and temporal scheme of the kind found in Latin and Greek. The only Greek exercise where he got almost all the verbs wrong was the very last one in North and Hillard, which was an exercise in mixed past and future conditionals. The Greek master, who used a key supplied by the publishers, changed every one of the verb forms he had used to something else; yet even the master didn't seem certain that his own was right, for he said something about a good effort and didn't mark him down for all those erroneous verbs. Purpose clauses were easier, especially in Latin: he once had a dream in which he saw UT walking down Melville Terrace with the subjunctive. He was in fact fascinated by grammar, and didn't understand why most boys thought it a bore. He liked the structure of such sentences as *bis dat qui cito dat,* where because the 'he' was implied in the first *dat,* the *qui* acted as a he-who bridge. In English you had to have both the 'he' and the 'who'. The only English prayer in the regular Sabbath morning service was the prayer for the royal family, which the rabbi recited in stentorian tones. It began: He who giveth salvation unto kings and dominion unto princes. Mr Peterkovsky (whose name later became shortened to Peters and whose daughter was reputed to be the first Jewish girl in Edinburgh to have her hair cut in an Eton crop) once arrived very late at the service and asked our hero, Has the HE-WHO been yet? On the other hand Mrs Levinson, who spoke a strong Yiddishized Scots, once told off her maid for not cleaning the mirrors properly. You had to breathe on the mirror and then rub it with a soft cloth, she explained. 'Mak a hoo,' she said. 'Didn't you know that to clean a mirror *you must mak a hoo*?' And she made a hoo, breathing on to the mirror, showing the maid. Unlike Abraham's wife, Mrs Levinson did not offer her maid to her husband as a concubine, on whom he could beget a child. Sarah herself had as yet no child. But when Hagar the maid conceived, Sarah grew jealous, and ill-treated Hagar so that she fled into the wilderness. But there an angel of the Lord appeared to her, telling her to return, and promising her great things. Behold, thou art with child, and shalt bear a son, and shalt call his name Ishmael; because the Lord hath heard thy affliction. Ishmael, God heard. And he will be a wild man; his hand will be against every man, and every man's hand against him. But he, too, like Abraham, was to be the father of a multitudinous people. Then at last, in old age, Sarah herself miraculously produced a child, Isaac, and this time she grew jealous of Ishmael and insisted that Abraham cast him and Hagar his mother out. Abraham strongly objected, but God intervened. It's all right, he said. Let it not be grievous in thy sight because of the lad, and because of thy bondwoman. Of the son of the bondwoman will I make a nation, because he is thy seed. And this time God himself appeared to Hagar in the wilderness and said, Arise, lift up the lad, and hold him in thine hand; for I will make him a great nation. And God was with the lad; and he grew, and dwelt in the wilderness, and became an archer. So Abraham became the patriarch of two peoples, the Jews and the Arabs, both sponsored by God. A strange story, our hero thought, and if only Sarah hadn't been jealous, Isaac and Ishmael would have grown up as brothers: perhaps Ishmael would have been the second Jewish patriarch instead of Isaac? Poor Isaac: he was never to get over his almost being sacrificed by his father. He remains a passive figure in Genesis, whose real heroes are not Abraham, Isaac and Jacob, but Abraham, Jacob and Joseph; those are the three round whom the great stories of Genesis are woven. Isaac's descendants would have to come to terms with Ishmael's later, much later: presumably God knew what he was doing in making each of them the ancestor of a great nation.

Ishmael dwelt in the wilderness. There was much talk of wildernesses in the Pentateuch: the children of Israel wandered in the wilderness forty years – forty years! – after the exodus from Egypt. What was a wilderness really like? Barren, of course, but with what sort of landscape? The man in the wilderness he asked me how many strawberries grow in the sea. It was a magic word, really, with no very specific content, a locus for strange events. I would not have given it for a wilderness of monkeys, said Shylock to Tubal of the turquoise ring that he had from Leah when he was a bachelor and which his daughter Jessica stole from him when she eloped with Lorenzo. Our hero supposed that Shakespeare introduced the wilderness to give a semitic stamp to Shylock's speech: he clearly had not the faintest notion how Jews talked, and invented a weird quasi-biblical speech. A wilderness of monkeys was not a Jewish concept, though it is true that a monkey figured in his Hebrew reader: the first story, *hakof ve-hamishkaphayim*, the monkey and the spectacles, was very risible. But a wilderness of monkeys, with or without spectacles – an extravagant image, indicating perhaps Shylock's disturbed state of mind. It was a disturbing play for an Edinburgh Jewish schoolboy for whom Shakespeare was god-like and anti-semitism unalloyed evil. He could not accept the romanticizing of Shylock's character, though he accepted that Shakespeare had humanized it. In fact he found no character in the play particularly attractive. He especially disliked Bassanio, that lightweight fortune hunter, and Lorenzo, who had no interest in human feelings other than his own. There was something gravely wrong with Antonio too. Jessica was silly and shallow. But Shylock, he saw, was no hero: he had to be accepted as Shakespeare presented him. The school dramatic society put on the play once, and Henry John Findlay, the English master, asked the class to write an essay reviewing the performance. He thought the performance terrible, particularly the acting of the boy who played Shylock, who spoke throughout in a supposed semitic accent and waved his arms about as he talked in supposed semitic gestures. He was indignant, and trounced the actor, whose name was Barger, in his essay. But Henry John did not understand his indignation and for once he was not complimented on his essay. He was always top in English, and was astonished to be told by one of his school rivals that this was because he had had to learn English as a foreign language and that was why he worked so hard at it and was so good at it. English a foreign language! It was HIS language, his mother tongue, his loved speech that he could shape to his desires, that he knew he would one day do wondrous things with. Hebrew was for reading, not talking, and for writing only in exercises. Yet when the boy Mitchell made this strange remark to him, some pride in him, some desire to suggest, All right, I'm different from you, I'm an outsider, I'm BETTER, made him accept the charge, and he remained silent, and the simple truth that English was his native language and his only one remained unuttered. His pride was fed later that same term when Henry John asked the boys to write a poem on Christmas but suggested that, being Jewish, he might like to write one on another subject. He wrote a poem on winter dawn over the Meadows, and Henry John read it out saying that he was the only boy in the class who knew how to write a poem, who knew about metre, who knew how to shape language in verse. A foreign language indeed! Yet the next term Henry John read out to the class a form letter he had received from an Edinburgh money-lender offering to lend money without security, using a fake Jewish accent, and then warned the boys against Jewish money-lenders. Our hero choked with indignation and misery, and even more with astonishment that so perceptive a teacher could be totally unaware of what he was inflicting on one of his pupils, and one of his most admiring pupils at that. This business of Jewish money-lending troubled him deeply. He knew that in the Middle Ages Jews had been forced into money-lending because they were not allowed into any of the trade guilds nor were they allowed to own land, and, further, they needed all their possessions to be readily portable for they were liable to be expelled from their homes and countries at any time. But now? He wanted all Jews to be scholars or poets or pioneer farmers, and winced at the thought of Jewish financiers, and most of all at Jewish money-lenders. His father had founded the Edinburgh branch of the Jewish order of B'nai Brit, sons of the covenant, and the order simply would not accept a money-lender as a member. They were determined to stamp out this blot on Jewish history. He thought of this as he sat in his place of honour in the back seat of the English classroom, red with indignation, deeply hurt, bewildered, as Henry John read out the Shylock letter. It was only afterwards that he realized that nobody in that classroom, from Henry John himself to the most perceptive (and the most imperceptive) of the boys, appeared to have any inkling that he might be hurt by what was going on or that he was involved in any way at all in what the English master was saying. He slowly began to see the meaning of Some of my best friends are Jews. The other side of that was that some of *his* best friends were non-Jews, yet this could not be counted on to prevent them from displaying, in a quite general way, antisemitic prejudice. This serpent in his Eden arrived quite late in his schooldays. A lady teacher he had had long before, when he was seven, had shown a rather special kind of respect for his religious views. She had been telling the boys about Abraham, how God made him two promises, firstly that his descendants would be a great nation and secondly that from his descendants Jesus Christ, the redeemer of mankind, would be born. For that, she said, was the meaning of God's promise to Abraham, in thee shall all the families of the earth be blessed. When the time came for her to ask the class what were God's two promises to the patriarch, she had no difficulty in eliciting the first one, but though she went right round the class she found nobody who remembered the second. Except our hero, who put up his hand and duly informed Miss Smith that God also promised Abraham that through him all the families of the earth would be blessed. Quite right, she said, *but you shouldn't have said that*. She knew perfectly well that Jews repudiated the Christian interpretation she had given and was uncomfortable at leading the small boy away from his ancestral faith. Our hero understood this, and appreciated it. He knew perfectly well that Miss Smith's interpretation of the second promise was wrong, and he cunningly gave his answer by using the biblical phrase and not her explanation of it. The main thing, though, was that he was not going to be cheated out of demonstrating his knowledge. It was all a kind of a game anyway: he did not go to school to be told about his own Bible. Some years later, when Greek was one of his subjects, there were optional lessons in New Testament Greek and a special prize awarded to the boy who came first in the examination in it. It was taken for granted by the Greek master that he would not be a candidate, and he felt that he was in no position to insist that he should, though he wanted to learn New Testament Greek: the idea of reading the Christians' own gospel in the original language appealed to him. As much of the teaching of the subject was done in parts of regular Greek lessons, he did in fact learn quite a bit, and ended that year with an ability to recite the Lord's prayer by heart in Greek, *pater hemon ho en tois ouranois hagiastheto to onoma sou*; he took pleasure in seeing how easily the Greek phrases went into familiar Hebrew, *avinu she-bashamayim mekadesh sh'mecha*, which proved to his satisfaction that Jesus was one of our own Jewish boys working with traditional Jewish material and not a Christian at all. He found nothing wrong with the Lord's prayer except the bit about God forgiving our trespasses as we forgive those that trespass against us. What did this mean? That God was to take a lesson from man, and forgive men as men forgave their enemies? That was a laugh. Or perhaps it meant that God should forgive men in proportion as they forgave those that trespassed against them, that the reward of man's being forgiving was that God would be proportionately forgiving? That made more sense, but it was an odd sort of bargain: surely God should consistently behave better than man.

He was driven to precocious theologizing by his awareness of the religious difference between himself and his school environment. He knew precisely the differences between Jewish and Christian theology; he understood the Christian doctrines of the atonement, the incarnation, the trinity, and marvelled at all this complicating of the relations between God and man. He could define the essentials of Christian belief better than most of his Christian contemporaries. He had to be able to in order to survive as a friendly Jew in a Christian society. He could see what Christian theologians had made of Jesus, and was sure that Jesus himself would have been absolutely astonished if he could return and find out. His Jewish monotheism winced at the idea of God's having an only begotten son, which he considered the purest paganism; at the same time, he felt that if Jesus (he would not call him Christ) was also God, as Christian theology asserted, then it was mockery to pretend that by living as a man on earth and dying in agony he was suffering the way mortal and unknowing man suffered in such circumstances. No suffering like my suffering? Many thousands were crucified by the Romans as well as Jesus, and they must have suffered at least as much; and as for the torturings, burnings at the stake, hangings and drawings and quarterings that went on throughout the Christian centuries – well, who would want to compile a table of degrees of suffering? Then there was this matter of saving one's soul. The rabbi always maintained that keeping divine ethical commands kept a society healthy and ensured its salvation, but personal salvation was another matter. On Yom Kippur, the day of atonement, they prayed all day, fasting, for forgiveness of sins, but never for just their own sins, always for those of the whole community. Never peccavi, always peccavimus. When our hero protested to his father that he had to plead guilty to a long list of sins some of which had never even entered his head and most of which he had not committed, he was told that this was because confessing sins was a communal and never a personal act. *We* have sinned; forgive *us*. He looked through the Yom Kippur liturgy and found that in every case the confession and appeal were in the first person plural: *al chet she-chatanu lefonecha*, for the sin we have committed before thee. And another point: the *imitatio Christi*. How could Jesus be someone whose way of life people should imitate when he repudiated his mother and his family, remained unmarried, and acted as though he believed he was the Messiah? How could you proclaim that Christianity believed passionately in family life and yet ask Christians to imitate the life of someone who rejected family life? Judaism rejected the doctrine of *imitatio*. The Hebrew Bible contained no perfect men whose lives were held up for imitation. Even Abraham, *avraham avinu*, Abraham our father, the man of faith who set out from Haran on a spiritual quest, the man who spoke with God, was far from perfect. Twice – once in Egypt and once in Gerar – his behaviour is presented in the Bible as contemptible: on each occasion he told the king that Sarah was his sister and not his wife, so that they would not kill him if they wanted her. Fortunately, though both Pharaoh and king Abimelech of Gerar tried to take Sarah, they were prevented, and on discovering that she was really Abraham's wife they honourably sent her back to the patriarch, reproaching him for deceiving them. Not very nice. And look at other biblical heroes – Jacob, King David, frail and fallible both. There was some pretty seamy stuff in the Hebrew Bible. Man even at his best was not God and could not be God. Perhaps Abraham the patriarch and Abraham the old clothes dealer were more alike than Coleridge thought.

6

JACOB HAD TROUBLE from the beginning. He clashed with his brother Esau while in his mother's womb: Rebekah felt the struggle of her two unborn sons within her and asked the Lord what it meant. And the Lord said unto her, Two nations are in thy womb, and two manner of people shall be separated from thy bowels; and the one people shall be stronger than the other people; and the elder shall serve the younger. Genesis is full of antagonistic brothers. In the beginning Cain slew his brother Abel; then there were Isaac and Ishmael; now Jacob and Esau; and later there were to be Joseph and his brothers. The Jewish people was founded on fraternal quarrels, yet they held aloft the ideal of fraternal love. Behold, how good and how pleasant it is for brethren to dwell together in unity. It is like the precious ointment upon the head, that ran down upon the beard, even Aaron's beard. Even Aaron's beard! *Z'kan aharon*. Our hero had been taught about similes and metaphors quite early in his schooldays. But this was something rather special. Brotherly amity was like ointment on the head that ran down upon the beard, even Aaron's beard. Aaron had a special significance as the first priest, the founder of the Jewish priestly order. His beard thus had a special significance as the beard of the first priest. The ointment which dripped down on to his beard thus had a special significance as the ointment on the beard of the first priest. But how did it illuminate the nature of brotherly love to compare it to the ointment on the beard of the first priest?

> There was an old man with a beard,
> Who said: A strange truth has appeared.
>   The oil that drips down
>   To my chin from my crown
> Is like brotherly love. Ain't it weird?

It was strange that beards, symbols of age and dignity, were also inherently comic. One would say BEAVER on seeing a bearded man in the street and add it to one's competitive collection. Beards were not then common on the streets of Edinburgh, and those that could be spotted showed no visible signs of having been anointed. Hairiness was not in itself a sign of holiness even in the Bible, for while all the patriarchs doubtless wore beards, Esau is the only character specifically described as hairy, and he was no moral hero. Jacob emerged from the womb after his brother, and his hand was on his brother's heel. Esau grew up as the outdoor extrovert, Jacob as the indoor introvert. Esau the hunter fed his father venison, and Isaac liked that. Jacob stayed indoors and meditated on the patriarchal heritage, which Isaac had stopped thinking about very much. And when Esau, ravenous from the hunt, came in to find his brother cooking a lentil stew, he asked for some peremptorily. Jacob, still thinking about the patriarchal heritage, said: All right, in exchange for your birthright as the elder brother. What is the use of my birthright when I'm starving to death? Esau replied, and the transaction was completed, physical food in exchange for spiritual assurance. Jacob now knew that he had inherited Abraham's special relationship with God. Was he a bit of a crook, perhaps? Did he trick his simple extrovert hungry brother? Perhaps; but he knew it was his destiny to be the last of the patriarchs, he wanted the job, and Esau never even thought about it. Jacob was going to wrestle with God and wrest a blessing from him, and in so doing change his name to Israel, he that prevails with God. He was working with history, and knew it. Even when he played that really nasty trick on Esau by pretending to his blind old father that he was the elder brother and so fooling Isaac into giving him the elder brother's blessing, he was doing what he had to do. That did not excuse him; Jacob, who brooded about God as his grandfather had done and thought about the meaning of life and time and destiny, was in some respects a rather shady character, a bit unscrupulous. Impulsive men of action like Esau, attractive though they may often be, cannot work with history or change man's sense of the divine; it takes a bit of shadiness to give a new dimension to morality. Yet our sympathies are all with Esau when he discovered that he had been tricked out of his eldest son's blessing (he had forgotten that he had sold his right to it long before) and cried with an exceeding bitter cry unto his father, Bless me, even me also, O my father. And Isaac said, Thy brother came with subtilty, and hath taken away thy blessing. And Esau lifted up his voice, and wept. Jacob was sent back to his grandfather's old home in Mesopotamia to choose a wife, as his father had been sent back before him, and on his way there, to match wits with his uncle Laban who was to prove a formidable opponent, he dreamt of a ladder reaching from heaven to earth with angels of God ascending and descending on it and the Lord himself standing above it to bless him and renew the promise. He was incorrigible. God of Abraham, God of Isaac, God of Jacob, the Hebrews prayers repeated, but it was Jacob who had really pursued God and got him on his side. So, as he had supplanted his brother Esau, in a sense he supplanted his grandfather Abraham too, for the people promised to Jacob as descendants became the Children of Israel, not the Children of Abraham, and even the promised land was called by Israel's name. The Jews were Jacob's people, the original Jacobites. Jacob's name was changed to Israel, and, our hero reflected, Israelites might have reversed the process and changed their name to Jacobites. Or Jacobeans? Or Jacobins? How ubiquitous his name had become, in all its forms. Jacobus, James, John, Jack, all going back to old Jacob, Ya'akov the supplanter. English Puritans of the seventeenth century liked to identify themselves with the biblical people of Israel, but in a later generation the Jacobites were on the other side; one would not have found many text-quoting Calvinists on the side of Bonnie Prince Charlie in 1745. Nor many Jews, the original Jacob-ites, either. But in Edinburgh there was Jacob's Ladder, a footway descending Calton Hill to the north back of the Canongate in two mutually diverging lines, each by a series of steep traverses and flights of steps. This was one of many descents and ascents in that precipitous city, replete not with God's emissaries going up and down but with turnings and corners: not angels but angles. Edinburgh was not however lacking in reminders of the patriarchs. God's covenant with Abraham and the Jewish people's considering themselves B'nai Brit, sons of the covenant, were remembered by those Protestant B'nai Brit, the Covenanters, who first signed their *brit*, their covenant, in Greyfriars churchyard in 1638. It was later placed for signature in an old mansion in the narrow street that henceforward took the name of Covenant Close. The words Britain, British, Brittany, were Celtic in origin, though at least one minister of the Church of Scotland saw the 'brit' element as the Hebrew word for covenant, and even went so far as to explain British as Hebrew *brit*, covenant, and *ish*, man, so that a Briton was a covenant man. Nonsense, said the rabbi briskly, when this etymology was put to him by an eccentric Scottish philosemite, and nonsense indeed it was. But it was a nice idea, our hero thought, and when the teacher in class 6 Upper Junior waxed eloquent over the heroic behaviour of the Covenanters he would have liked to be able to say, Yes, B'nai Brit they were, our chaps really. And when he read of the Highlands being referred to as sons of the mountain and glen, he thought of the Hebrew *ben*, son, and thought how right, Ben Nevis, Ben Lomond, son of Nevis or of Lomond, or even (since mac was the exact Gaelic equivalent of ben) Ben Macdhui, grandson of Dhui. Then the different clans would have to be called B'nai Nevis, B'nai Lomond, B'nai More. My heart's in the highlands, my heart is not here, my heart's with B'nai Vorlich a-chasing the deer.

B'nai, sons of. Ben, son of. Jacob's little Benjamin, *ben-yamin*, son of the right hand, his favourite after the disappearance and presumed death of his beloved Joseph; little Ben, who was sent by his father so reluctantly to Egypt on the demand of the great governor who turned out to be the long-lost Joseph himself. And when Joseph saw his little brother, while he himself still remained unrecognized by his brothers, he said to the others, Is this your youngest brother, of whom ye spake unto me? And he said, God be gracious unto thee, my son. In spite of everything, he could not continue to act the public role he had planned, and had to retire into his room to shed tears: and he entered into his chamber and wept there. Overcome by his love for Ben, he went ben the house. Gae ben the house, says Jamieson's *Dictionary of the Scottish Language*, to go into the inner apartment. Joseph did not at that stage want to show himself too familiar, to be ower far ben, with Ben, so he left the but, the outer apartment of the house, and retired alone to the ben, the inner apartment. The whole marvellous story would go so well in Scots, he thought. And Joseph was wae for the loon, and lookit for a place tae greet, and he gaed ben the hoose and grat there. Joe and Ben, Jacob's two youngest, his only children by his loved Rebekah for whom he had to labour another seven years; the others were Leah's sons. An extraordinary ménage, an impossible household. But from these brothers and half-brothers were descended the twelve tribes of Israel. Except for little Ben, they were all dubious characters in one way or another, even Joseph, who had been a sly one from childhood and clearly enjoyed teasing his brothers with his dreams of glory. But like his father Jacob, he knew from the first that he had a destiny.

That was the thing, to hold your head high whatever happened and know that in the long run you would be more than an anonymous face in the crowd. But could one really know? Why was it one felt oneself different, special, and was certain that the strange things that went on in one's mind were quite unique? Sometimes he was frightened by this conviction, thought that perhaps he was going mad. Other people were all normal, they did the usual and proper things, their responses were the expected ones. Once when he was about seven he was walking home from school across the playground with another boy, to whom he was explaining something that had happened to him in a lively and even excited manner. Suddenly he saw the other boy looking at him strangely, as though wondering why he was carrying on so, and almost in the same instant he saw himself from the outside, flushed and extravagant and worked up about nothing, a bizarre performer, arousing puzzled withdrawal among his fellows. In moments like this he did not want to be different and special, and longed to be ordinary like the others, so that he would never have to worry whether he would provoke wonder or bafflement among the other boys. It never occurred to him that others had his kind of self-consciousness, his kind of conviction that what went on inside his mind was uniquely odd. Some nights he would wait for a voice from God, trembling with conviction that he had a divine mission, but the voice never came. On other nights he had terrible nightmares and would wake up screaming. Often this was before his parents had gone to bed, and one or other of them would rush up to soothe him. They grew used to the experience. Sometimes his parents would be having a late supper alone, and rush up to his attic bedroom with their mouths still full of food. Once his father came up with a plate of fish, and finished it by the washstand in his bedroom while waiting for him to go back to sleep. For someone had to stay with him till the terror passed. He could never explain what the terror was. Once he had a dream, which he never forgot, that ought to have been terrible but wasn't. He dreamt that he was standing at the top of his street, which was a blind alley, and a cart, pulled by two horses, passed across the bottom of the street. On the cart were several men, one of whom had a bow and arrow, which he pointed at him and shot. The arrow pierced his breast and he fell, dead. Years later when at last he told this dream he was informed that no one ever dreamt that he was actually killed: one always woke up before that moment. But he had dreamt it. It had not been painful, but a sudden soft access of blackness. Not that he thought about death, at least his own death: he had the usual child's conviction that death was for others. But he had a morbid fear of an encounter with the dead. The notion of seeing a corpse haunted and frightened him – even if it was a simulated one, on the stage. When the school dramatic society performed *Hamlet* he sat with fearful anticipation awaiting the entry of the bier on which the dead Ophelia would be borne. He had a history book which contained a realistic picture of a dead king in his shroud, and he found the picture both fascinating and upsetting. He knew that his parents would die some day, and he counted up the years to reassure himself that they had a long, long time yet to go. He knew that before you were fifty you were still far away from old age, and all through the 1920s he clung to the fact that his father, who was ten years older than his mother, was still in his forties: he knew he had been born in 1880. Once a boy, whom he knew only slightly as he was not in his year, was killed when he fell off the banisters down which he was sliding in one of those tall Edinburgh flats where the stairs and the floor below are stone. Some-one came into the classroom where he was, to collect contributions to a wreath, and he tried to imagine what it was like to have died in a fall from the banisters. But deaths in literature, unless he actually saw them on the stage, did not bother him. Mark Antony speaking over Caesar's dead body was not only perfectly acceptable; it was one of his favourite scenes in Shakespeare. Once when he was eleven his class was asked to write the autobiography of a dog or other household pet. One boy wrote the autobiography of a West Highland terrier and ended with the dog telling how at last it grew sick and though the family sent for the vet 'it was too late: I grew steadily worse and died that night'. The master, the redoubtable W. W. Anderson whom generations of boys called Dub-Dub, was overcome with contemptuous mirth at the notion of a dog describing his own death, and read out the conclusion of the essay to the class in scornful hilarity. But the poor boy who had written it never understood what he had done wrong. If Dub-Dub accepted that a dog could write the story of its life, why couldn't he also accept that it could describe its own death? Was one possibility more absurd than the other? But you CAN'T write the story of your life once you're dead, roared Dub-Dub. But it's a dog, protested the boy. What difference does that make? sneered Dub-Dub. A dog can't write the story of its life even when it's alive, explained the boy. Our hero tried to formulate in his own mind why, though both master and boy were right, each in his own way, there was a sense in which Dub-Dub was more right. It had something to do with the way you write a story, and nothing to do with whether dogs, alive or dead, could really write. He was struggling with some such notions as literary convention and levels of probability and what Henry James called the donnée of a work, but he had no vocabulary in which to express his ideas, and the point puzzled him for a long time. A living dog is better than a dead lion, said the preacher, and he thought of this during the argument about the dead autobiographical dog. He failed to see the point of the observation. Was any sort of dog, however scruffy, mean-spirited and nasty (he posed this for the sake of argument only, for he liked dogs) better than even the noblest lion just because the lion had died and the dog was still alive? What did the preacher mean by better? Is a living bluebottle better than a dead poet? Is it a disgrace to be dead? But Shakespeare was dead, and Shelley. So were Abraham, Isaac and Jacob, long dead. It struck him then that ALMOST EVERYBODY in the history of the world was dead, long long lists of prophets and kings and poets and innumerable ordinary people. He looked back up the long line that linked him with his biblical ancestors, generation after generation, back (he was told) to Judah ha-Nasi and King David, and marvelled that just the tiny little group at the end were still living – his paternal grandparents, his parents, himself and his brother and sister. In history he learned people's dates. He had seen in poetry anthologies the occasional poem by a living poet whose dates were incomplete, 1865–   . It must be terrible, he thought, to see your name printed with an incomplete date like that, the date of death waiting, waiting. At the same time, only men of distinction had dates. He would have dates some day.

In the French class they had to write letters in French, and write out the date in French at the top. He had to give up French, after three years of it, to continue with Greek, so that the last French date he ever used was 1927. For years that mille neuf cent vingt-sept rolled off his tongue as the year in French; for him time came to a stop in France in that year. He bitterly envied the boys who kept on with French, but he could not give up Greek, which was the only condition on which he could have continued. He enjoyed learning languages, and learning French had been quite simply a pleasure. When Mr Brown, who replaced Miss Ida Smith as his French teacher in his third year, took to the very un-Scottish practice of dealing out a hundred lines to boys who talked in class, he found himself on several occasions visited with this punishment; but he didn't mind; he wrote comic short stories in French, each one entitled Cent Lignes pour M. Lebrun, and eventually Mr Brown would find reasons to set him a hundred lines to see what he would do. There developed towards the end of that year an unusual relationship between master and boy. Received with thanks and returned with contumely, wrote Mr Brown at the foot of one set of lines, acting like a schoolboy himself, though our hero had to look up contumely in the dictionary. Two years later, when they were doing mediaeval European history, the history master told the boys that the best text-book in the subject was in French and prescribed it for the boys who were still doing French. Our hero was indignant that it was assumed that he could not read French, and insisted on using it too, instead of the pallid English alternative. So he went to Thin's and bought *L'Europe au moyen âge 475–1328* par G. Dupont-Ferrier and read it with enormous conscientiousness. In buying it he discovered that other people had their pride too. He breezed into the bookshop and asked the assistant for the book, then said briskly: I'll write the title down for you. There is no need, said the young man coldly, I understand what you said. Which was perhaps surprising, for the title had been pronounced in a far from perfect French accent. He had never been to France, and never heard French spoken by a Frenchman; his French was fluent but badly pronounced. Not that he shared the general attitude of the boys, that it was cissy to try to speak French in a real French way, but he was so keen on speed and fluency that he just didn't think much about pronunciation. He had an obsession with speed, especially in anything to do with languages. Once, in a three-hour Latin exam he thought he saw a boy make a move to hand in his paper, as though he had finished, after an hour and a half. He was annoyed that anyone should have finished before him, though in fact it was a false alarm and the boy had only been going to get some more paper. But the incident filled him with such anxiety to finish the exam first that he rushed through the rest of the translation and triumphantly handed in his paper an hour before the exam was over, to the utter astonishment of the invigilator. Later, he discovered many careless mistakes that he could have corrected if he had taken time to read over carefully what he had written.

Speed was his downfall, impatience his undoing. He apprehended things impulsively and resented any necessity to refine or perfect. Genius was an infinite capacity for taking pains, Henry John had reported Carlyle's dictum to the class, and he thought how dull, what a plodding pedestrian view of genius, which should flash out spontaneously. Shakespeare never blotted a line, he would be the same, running along the page at speed, demonstrating his fluency. Sometimes at an exam he misread a question and saw in anguish afterwards that he had not answered what was asked. Once, coming out of a history exam, he asked a classmate which of two alternative sections he had chosen. What an easy exam it was, I could easily have done both sections, he rattled on. You mean you didn't do both? the boy replied coldly. You should have. They weren't alternatives. You were supposed to do both. He looked at the question paper in his hand and froze with bitter horror when he realized that this was true. Something in his hasty and excited misreading of the questions had led him to believe that there were alternatives when there were none. No one understood his pain. He tried to relieve it by pouring out his frustration in words – it would have been so easy to do both parts, he had great trouble deciding which to do, he really misunderstood the instructions – but no one was interested. The boys turned away from his flushed explanations. You should read the questions, they said. This was nemesis for his pride years before when as a small boy in a class learning to read he rushed through his reading at high speed and thought with contempt of the slow stumblers who moved painfully from word to word. It was the same with the Hebrew prayers: he could get through them in record time. He never cheated, he never missed out words or sank into an undifferentiated mumbling blur as some people did: he said every word, just as he could say The Leith police dismisseth us with six thick thistle sticks very fast without mixing up the consonants. Sometimes in playing allegro on the piano he would unwittingly keep speeding up the tempo and his piano teacher would shout Stop, stop, you're going faster and faster and she would start to beat time for him to keep him at an even pace. When he was not stopped the constant acceleration defeated itself, for he soon reached a speed which tripped him up and the piece crashed into fragments. When he played piano duets with his mother she held him to the proper tempo. He enjoyed those sessions: Beethoven's fifth symphony arranged for two pairs of hands – they would take turns doing the treble and bass – and the overtures to William Tell and Poet and Peasant and Semiramide. He learned about the different instruments from Herbert Wiseman's lecture-concerts for children at the Usher Hall. Walking to school he would compose symphonies in his head – the soaring violins, the plaintive woodwinds, the massive tutti, with winning melodies alternating with resounding chords and cunning transitional passages. It all seemed so easy if you did it impressionistically in your head. He would mess about on the piano too, improvising pretentiously, but the left hand was always sketchy. Ben-yamin, son of the right hand, his compositions might have been called. He would pick up popular dance tunes by ear and thump happily away, Drifting and dreaming, Bye-bye blackbird, Stay out of the south, The birth of the blues,

Lullaby of the leaves, he learned them from the wireless and would never dream of buying the sheet music. Sheet music was for real music by real composers like Mozart and Beethoven. He would parody the more sentimental ones, and sang regularly at parties his parody of A Russian Lullaby:

> The moon is blue, the clouds are too,
> The sky is fresh and clear.
> What would I do if I'd not you
> My love, my dove, my dear?
> The wind is gently sighing
> Among the leafy trees;
> The stars above are spouting love
> And humming melodies.

It was a dialogue. The girl replies that she will love him if he has money –

> But if you've spent your final cent
> I love another man.

He reassures her in the last part of the final stanza:

> No problem, dear, with money,
> So cheer your saddened soul:
> Each week, my pet, some cash I get
> For I am on the dole.

But though he could parody sentimental popular songs he could also compose plaintive melodies of his own and croon them over to himself until he felt his eyes fill with tears. He was never quite sure whether he made up these tunes or whether he was recollecting airs he had once heard. Some of the tunes sung by the chazan as he intoned Hebrew prayers affected him deeply, and he found especially moving the song he sang standing alone facing the ark after he had replaced the *sepher torah*, the scroll of the law, at the conclusion of the sabbath morning's reading. *Ki lekach tov* . . . For I have given you good doctrine; forsake not my law. It is a tree of life to them that grasp it and those that hold it shall be happy. Its ways are ways of pleasantness and all its paths are peace. And then the marvellous last sentence: *Hashivenu adonai eilecha* . . . Turn unto us, O Lord, and we shall return: renew our days as of old. Though he knew perfectly well what the Hebrew meant, the tune was so pleasing-melancholy that he imagined it as a lament for a lost love. *Chadesh yamenu ke-*

kedem, renew our days as of old, the chazan plangently pleaded, his voice rising in the minor melody, and our hero invented a scene of deep love-tragedy to go with the sad chant. Plaintive numbers: he always thought of the chazan singing that part of the service when he read that phrase in Wordsworth's poem. The Friday evening service, to welcome the sabbath, was short and sweet, really sweet: he loved the way the chazan would sing the last two verses of each of the six psalms that opened the service, coming to rest each time on the same cadence, moving from the perfect fifth to the tonic and leaning in a special way on the third on the way down. Then there were the special Yom Kippur tunes. *Anu malei avon ve-atah malei rachamim* . . . We are full of iniquity, but thou art full of mercy; our days are like the shadow that passes, but thou art changeless and thy years have no end. The chanting of the law was done in a special minor melody on Rosh Hashanah and Yom Kippur. The normal sabbath tune for this chanting was not exactly gay, but had less of an oriental wail about it. He knew the method of chanting the law from earliest childhood; somehow, at home after dinner on Friday nights singing the next day's portion of the law with his father, he picked up the meaning of the tiny signs above and below the words to indicate the way the tune went and soon learned to sing any portion at sight. The portion from the prophets went to a quite different chant, a more interesting one really, and he used to sit with fretful impatience in shul as some doddering old man with a cracked voice, no ear and a poor understanding of Hebrew stresses, croaked and stumbled his way through the passage he had been called up to read, when he himself could have done it so marvellously. For while the chazan, the cantor, read from the law it was always a member of the congregation who read from the prophets. Most of all he liked the concluding Friday evening hymn, *yigdal*, and the way in which the tune died away at the end of each verse: in winter especially, with the tiny congregation (not many came to the Friday evening service) singing in the four-fifths empty Graham Street synagogue, he felt the singing of this hymn as an act of assertion, of identity, of continuity with the Jewish past; at the same time, walking out into the early dark of an Edinburgh winter, he thought it very much an Edinburgh winter song, and as he crossed the Meadows with his father and brother with the strains of *yigdal* still ringing in his ears, the Hebrew hymn seemed to him bound up not only with Jewish history but also with Edinburgh Castle and the Vennel and that whole northern shore on which after so many centuries history had cast his family.

Through what adventurings and accidents they had reached here! A picture of his great-grandfather hung in his grandfather's study. He wore a fur cap and looked as much Russian as Jewish. He was *dayan* and *rosh yeshivah*, head of the rabbinical college, in Kovno. He had died in 1891, and never saw England or Scotland, never conceived, probably, that his son would settle in England and his grandson in Scotland, distant gentile territories far from the warmly enclosed yet constantly threatened ghetto Jewish life of eastern Europe. An ancestor of his had married the beautiful and accomplished daughter of David ben Aryeh Leib of Lida (in Belorussia) who later became rabbi of the Ashkenazi community in Amsterdam in 1671, a kabbalist known for the controversies into which his aggressive character kept drawing him. Other ancestors included the great eleventh-century biblical and talmudic scholar Rashi, a French Jew of Troyes who made the rabbinical schools of Champagne and northern France famous throughout Jewry, and Judah ha-Nasi, the Prince, compiler of the Mishnah early in the second century and himself descended from King David. Judah ha-Nasi had lived in Palestine, and so the link from Scotland to the land of Israel was complete. He could see his ancestors, like the lines of kings shown to Macbeth, in a long row stretching back from Eastern Europe through the Rhineland to France to the Middle East. Nearly two thousand years in Europe. They were more European than the Europeans, then: his father had told him that Jews had settled in the Rhineland centuries before there were any Germans there. And in France there were Jews from the sixth century. Sur le pont d'Avignon. Ancestors of his may well have known that bridge, for there was a flourishing Jewish community at Avignon in the Middle Ages, and when the Popes were at Avignon they treated the Jews well. Gregory XI's bookbinder was a Jew. He learned at school that this Pope ended the Babylonian captivity at Avignon by removing to Rome in 1376: the echo of Jewish history in this name for the papal exile was clear enough both to master and pupils, but who in that classroom except himself knew the real significance for the Jews of that episode in the history of the Christian church? In 1374 in Avignon 87 of 94 textile dealers and 41 of 62 timber merchants were Jews. *Ir hagefanim*, city of grapes, they called Avignon in Hebrew, and they welcomed the sabbath in a blessing over glasses of côte de Provence. Blessed art thou O Lord who createst the fruit of the vine, *borei pri ha-gafen*. Bookbinders, textile dealers, timber merchants, and of course rabbis and scholars innumerable: they lived the Jewish life happily in southern France. Jews were settled in Provence in the first century, and he liked to think that his own ancestors had come there from Palestine and lived there for some generations before moving north. Provence was a nest of rabbis and scholars, David Kimchi of Narbonne, Judah ben Moses of Arles, Kalonymus ben Kalonymus, Isaac ben Abba Mari of Marseilles, Nissim ben Moses of Marseilles, marvellous names all. When they talked at school about the auld alliance between Scotland and France he thought of that aulder connection and forged in his mind a triple alliance, Judaeo-Franco-Scottish, working now in Edinburgh in the year mille neuf cent vingt-sept. In David Kimchi's Hebrew commentaries on the Bible he occasionally introduced a vernacular word, a *loaz*, but it was not French, it was Provençal. And that was rather like an Edinburgh Jew speaking in Scots rather than in English, identifying himself with the local culture. But some Scots was French: gardyloo, watch out for the water, they had cried from the windows of the high flats of Edinburgh when they emptied their unsavoury slops over unwary passers-by in the street below; Dr Johnson was not the only visitor to find the practice offensive. *Tsei u-l'mad*, go out and learn, the rabbis used to say, and many an unsuspecting visitor to Edinburgh in earlier times had gone out and learned about gardyloo to his cost. The Scots were in some respects a coarse people, but then so they were in England too in the eighteenth century. Sir Robert Walpole was a coarse man, Dr Brydon told them at school, adding, with a twinkle through his rimless glasses, or rather not so much coarse as COORSE if you know what I mean, boys. Of coorse they knew what he meant. A coorse ba (bah? baa? he had never seen it written down) was Edinburgh schoolboy for a dirty joke. Which of course was different from a fit ba', which was a football. Fit audience though few did not, however, mean a meagre audience of footmen. When he first heard about promenade concerts in London (in Edinburgh you always sat down in proper seats at concerts) he said that in Edinburgh the audience would be called a fit audience. Nobody exploded into fits of laughter. Punning for him was a way of exploring the idiosyncrasies of language; he found it a constant source of wonder and delight that the same or similar words could mean radically different things. At a pantomime once there was a parade of characters each representing a different newspaper; one was a small tottering kilted figure and the audience was asked to guess what paper he represented. It was of course the *Weakly Scotsman*. Robinson Crusoe was not alone on the island: there was a big swell on the beach and a little cove running up the sand. In school stories he had read boys shouted cave to give warning of the approach of a teacher or other intrusive adult, but not in Edinburgh; in Edinburgh you kept shote, kept a look-out, and shouted shote when you spied someone coming. Shote! Yon's the parkie! – a familiar cry in the Meadows when the park-keeper hove in sight to castigate boys for climbing over railings. There was a continuous warfare between schoolboys and the parkie, with his peaked cap and spiked stick for picking up paper, but it was a friendly warfare. The parkie never did anything more than blow his whistle and occasionally shout. There were things you weren't supposed to do in the Meadows, and these were listed in a large printed sheet on several notice boards: Bye-laws relative to public parks. When he first read it he read the bye as by and thought relative was stressed the same way as relation, so he scanned it rhythmically: By LAWS reLAtive to PUBlic PARKS, and he danced across the grass chanting the meaningless line of poetry to himself, By LAWS reLAtive to PUBlic PARKS, By LAWS reLAtive to PUBlic PARKS. You could be related by laws to Public Parks, and that would be a purely legal relationship, or on the other hand you could be a real blood relation. You can't do that to me, I'm a relation of Public Parks. (His younger brother, Private Parks, went into the army. He never understood, though, why a soldier who was not an officer should be called a private: an ordinary soldier conscripted into the army to fight for his country was surely more public than an officer who bought his commission or got it through influence or social position. It was the latter, surely, who was the private. There were many such usages that puzzled him. It was long before he appreciated why illegitimate children were called natural: surely the natural thing was for children to be born to a married mother, and it was illegitimacy that was unnatural. It took him some time before he came to doubt the naturalness of human institutions. The phrase 'natural son' was often used in Victorian novels, and he pondered deeply over it.)

Edinburgh was much involved with parks. There were the Meadows, Bruntsfield Links, Inverleith Park, and King's Park at the foot of Arthur's Seat. There were Hope Park Terrace and Warrender Park Road and Park Place. Over hill, over dale, Thorough bush, thorough brier, Over park, over pale, Thorough flood, thorough fire. He used to climb over pale into the Meadows – high spiked palings they were – even though there were many open entrances, because it was the thing to do. Once when the people next door were away on holiday and the house was empty he and his brother climbed over the iron railing into their garden to play luxuriously in this alien territory. But a man who lived across the street spotted them and said he would call the police. In panic our hero climbed back into his own garden, but caught his blazer on a spike and ripped it. He had to be somewhat inventive in explaining the accident to his mother. Inventiveness of that kind came easily to him, and never troubled his conscience. It was, of course, quite different from telling a lie. Expansion, modification, decoration, alteration, exaggeration of truth were not only sometimes necessary to present an adequate picture of the real significance to oneself of what had happened, but also represented legitimate art. When he first met the phrase poetic licence he understood it at once and claimed it as his own. And when he first heard Pooh Bah talking about corroborative detail intended to give artistic verisimilitude to an otherwise bald and unconvincing narrative his heart leapt with recognition. He was rather glad, all the same, that the ten commandments contained no prohibition of lying. He mentioned this once to his father, who took pains to point out that lying was specifically prohibited in other parts of the Pentateuch. But the patriarchs had lied: Abraham had lied to Pharaoh and to Abimelech and Jacob had lied to his own father, and these were not artistic lies, poetic licence, but deliberate lies told for the purpose of self-interest. But if you know that your destiny is divinely ordained for a glorious purpose, then pursuit of your own self-interest becomes meritorious. A doubtful argument. But Jacob paid for his deviousness. When they brought his beloved Joseph's bloodstained coat to him, he said, It is my son's coat; an evil beast hath devoured him; Joseph is without doubt rent in pieces. And Jacob rent his clothes and put sackcloth upon his loins, and mourned for his son many days. And all his sons and all his daughters rose up to comfort him; but he refused to be comforted; and he said, For I will go down into the grave for my son mourning. *Va-yevk oto aviv*: and his father wept for him. But Joseph was not dead, but carried off by the Midianites to be sold as a slave in Egypt to Potiphar, an officer of Pharaoh's, the captain of the guard. He was a born Lucky Jim, and in spite of misadventures rose to be governor of Egypt. And at the end of the day he sent for his aged father and all the rest of his family to settle in Egypt. Jacob's name was Israel now, and the children of Israel settled in Egypt under Joseph's protection and under the protection of the Pharaoh that Joseph's providence had saved. But Jacob died, then Joseph died, then a Pharaoh arose who knew not Joseph, and the children of Israel became slaves in Egypt. *Avadim hayinu le-Pharoh be-mitsrayim*, slaves we were to Pharaoh in Egypt, they recited at the Seder service on Passover. But redemption came, and with the exodus from Egypt the children of Israel became a nation, for God remembered his covenant with Abraham, with Isaac, and with Jacob. A strange way to set about building a nation. A peculiar people indeed! And what a strange part in the story had been played by the man whose name the people took, the human, fallible, devious yet God-intoxicated patriarch Jacob.

7

MOSES, Moshe rabbenu, Moses our teacher, strangely emerging from an Egyptian background to lead the Jewish people into freedom and obtain the Law for them from God, what were you really like? He survived Pharaoh's edict that all male infants should be killed through his mother's stratagem of leaving him in an ark of bulrushes by the river's bank. And Pharaoh's daughter found him and adopted him and brought him up. Were the suspicions of the irreverent student song justified?

> Moses was a baby whom his ma one day forsook,
> Was found by Pharaoh's daughter as she took her morning dook;
> She brought him in to Pharaoh, said she'd found him on the shore,
> But Pharaoh only sighed and said, 'We've heard that tale before.'

It was strange that the rabbi laughed merrily at that song, while passionately devoted to a belief in the centrality of Moses in Jewish history and the absoluteness of the revelation on Mount Sinai. That tractate of the Mishnah known as Pirke Avot, Ethics of the Fathers, of which one chapter was read every sabbath afternoon during the summer months, summed up the rabbi's position in its opening sentence: Moses received the Torah on Sinai, and handed it down to Joshua; Joshua to the elders; the elders to the prophets; and the prophets handed it down to the men of the Great Synagogue. Where did Moses get his ideas from? asked a languid young man during question time at a meeting of the Edinburgh Jewish Literary Society at which the rabbi had spoken on Jewish ethics. Surely he must have got them from the Egyptians, among whom he was brought up? The rabbi was horrified at the suggestion. Moses was a quintessentially monotheistic Hebrew, the archetypal Jewish teacher, conscripted by God to be the receiver and transmitter of the divine Law. He was a reluctant prophet. When the Lord called him, he replied, O Lord, I am not eloquent, neither heretofore, nor since thou hast spoken unto thy servant: for I am slow of speech, and of a slow tongue. But the Lord would not let him off. Who hath made men's mouth? the Lord said unto him. Or who maketh a man dumb, or deaf, or seeing, or blind? Is it not I, the Lord? Now therefore go, and I will be with thy mouth, and teach thee what thou shalt speak. Getting his ideas from the Egyptians indeed! And yet, and yet . . . A strange name, Moshe, unparalleled among Hebrew names; can it really be explained as Exodus explains it? She called his name Moshe and said, Because I drew him out of the water, Moshe being taken as a participle from the Hebrew verb meaning to draw. Some connected the name with the Egyptian mes, mesu, meaning son, and even sacrilegiously alleged that it may have originally been coupled with the name of an Egyptian deity, as in Ra-mesu and Thoth-mes, which was later dropped under the influence of Hebrew monotheism. Or was it the final element in names such as Ptah-mose, Ptah is born? And then this business of his being a castaway who grew up to be a hero: were there not myths of this kind all over the Middle East? Doesn't Herodotus tell the same story of Cyrus, and what of the Egyptian myth which tells how the infant god Horus was concealed by his mother among marsh reeds to protect him from Seth? Or the birth story of Sargon of Akkad? Avaunt, profane speculation. Moses is ours, Moshe rabbenu, the lawgiver who died of the kiss of God on the anniversary of his birth, the seventh day of the month of Adar. What God revealed to Moses at Sinai was not only the ten commandments and the whole of the Written Law, but also the whole of the Oral Law developed in discussion by later generations of Jewish teachers. As he spent forty days and forty nights on Mount Sinai with God, this was not improbable. There were the ten commandments, of course, which he brought down graven on the two tablets of stone, but also what a lot of precepts and statutes and prescriptions and prohibitions and injunctions! As the chazan rolled them out in reading the sections of Exodus known as *mishpatim*, judgments, and *terumah*, offering, and *tetzaveh*, thou shalt command, our hero marvelled at the extraordinary mixture of the sublime and trivial, the high ethical and the arbitrarily ritual. Some bits he thought very fine. If thou meet thine enemy's ox or his ass going astray, thou shalt surely bring it back to him again. If thou seest the ass of him that hateth thee lying under his burden, thou shalt surely release it. The rabbis said you must always feed your domestic animals before you sit down to a meal yourself. They were good about animals. But what was one to make of offerings of rams' skins dyed red, and porpoise-skins and acacia wood; of the fifty loops on each of the curtains of the tabernacle; of the pomegranates of blue and of purple and of scarlet round about the skirts of the robe of the ephod? Strange stuff, fascinating in its way, but not really relevant to anything at all. As for all the details about sacrifices, he preferred not to dwell on them.

Yes, Moses was the man who brought the Law, and the Law was central: it's what you do, not what you think or how you feel that matters. Orthopraxis not orthodoxy was what Judaism required, the rabbi always said, and the notion that believing rather than doing was what God chiefly wanted of man was not a Jewish notion at all. One cannot anyway control one's belief by an act of will, our hero often reflected, and as for *credo quia absurdum*, that was a very quia announcement indeed, surely God didn't give us minds so that we should flout the evidence they provide us. As a small boy he had been answered when posing awkward questions of adults by the single word 'because', and though that was frustrating it was also in a way satisfying, for all answers, all explanations, ought to begin with because – because that is the meaning of an explanation. Therefore was an equally important word. Once when he had spots and a temperature Dr Matheson had examined him and professed himself puzzled at the nature of the illness. He heard him say in a singsong voice that long stayed in his mind, ticking off each item on a finger: 'It's not measles, it's not scarlet, it's not diphtheria, it's not mumps – THEREFORE . . .' There was quite a pause before the doctor concluded quickly, 'Let's call it German measles.' *Al-ken nekaveh*, therefore we hope in thee O Lord our God, was the beginning of the second paragraph of the central Hebrew prayer *alenu*. It was the logical inference from the statements about God made in the first paragraph. The statement about God that he liked best was the one that Moses himself had uttered when he was on Mount Sinai and the Lord descended in a cloud and stood with him there. It was sung three times on festivals when the scroll of the Torah was being carried from the ark. The Lord, the Lord, God gracious and merciful, slow to anger and abounding in lovingkindness and truth, keeping lovingkindness for thousands, forgiving iniquity and transgression and sin. *Erech apayim ve-rav chesed ve-emes*. He liked that phrase *erech apayim*, but it was strange, long of anger it meant, but also oddly enough long of face for the Hebrew word meant both anger and face: it also meant nostrils and that must have been its original meaning because its form was a dual plural, the kind of plural used when you had only two of something like arms and legs and eyes. He supposed that in anger your nostrils flared so that if you were slow of nostrils you were not easily roused to wrath. He was disappointed to discover that this fine declaration about God's nature was an incomplete quotation from Exodus 34 and that the biblical text went on immediately to add something about what God would do to the guilty. Still, whoever chose that passage for the prayer book had chosen to break off the quotation in such a way as to emphasize God's lovingkindness and mercy and that surely meant something important in the history of the Jewish religion. He once heard a schoolmaster say that Judaism was the religion of the God of wrath and Christianity the religion of the God of love and this upset him very much for he thought it was much more a sign of a religion of wrath to believe in a God that destined untold numbers of his creatures to eternal punishment in the next world not only for what they had done but even for not being able to bring themselves to believe in something. The Jews at least settled for punishment in this life and did not see God as pursuing a man into the next. As for being punished for believing or not believing or any notion that believing or not believing had anything to do with goodness or badness, he thought that was both illogical and nasty. The psalmist said that if you didn't believe in God you were a fool, not that you deserved eternal punishment. Of course if you didn't believe in God you would be more likely to behave unjustly and wickedly and you would be rightly punished for that. When in his teens he learned of the existence of just and benevolent atheists and agnostics he was troubled, but at least it emphasized the importance of orthopraxis over orthodoxy. The important thing remained what you did.

Yet of all those laws, multiplied, particularized, codified, elaborated, some surely had little enough to do with goodness and badness. Build a fence round the Law, the rabbis had said, meaning that the central things enjoined and prohibited ought to be protected by all sorts of minor injunctions and prohibitions in order to make sure that nobody would get within miles of disobeying anything central. So you had separate dishes for milk things and meat things and never carried anything on the sabbath and just before Pesach springcleaned the house and put away all the usual dishes to bring out a complete set of dishes used only for one week in the year so as to make sure that nothing *chometz*, nothing leaven, was remotely present during that passover week, even by association. Had Moses intended that when he led the children of Israel out of Egypt? True, the first of the commandments he brought down from Sinai asserted the identity of the Lord who had brought the people of Israel out of the land of Egypt, out of the land of bondage. The festival in memory of that liberation was surely central. Yet to go so far as to cancel the milk from Pettigrew's dairy and have special passover milk delivered from Gerber's the Jewish dairy? How could milk be leaven? Oh he knew all about *kosher al Pesach*, about certifying Passover food free from the slightest the most notional contact with anything leaven and the total change of diet on Pesach was genuinely exciting, but is that really what Moses meant or for that matter what God meant? Yet there was something to be learned from this way of fencing the law, for the special *kosher al Pesach* Fry's cocoa was a fawn colour instead of the usual dark brown and the kosher butter from Holland was absolutely white. It was thus that he discovered how many foodstuffs were normally artificially coloured, for with the prohibition of any artificial additives in Passover foods their real colour emerged, fawn cocoa, white butter, a whole new chromatic range. But milk was the same colour and he couldn't really see that it made any difference where you got it from so long as it came from the cow. Still, it helped Gerber der milchiger, the kosher dairyman, though it was doubtful if he needed help. When the rabbi had first come to Edinburgh to take up his position there he had been taken round the Jewish shops by the chazan and when they passed Gerber's dairy chazan Levinson had remarked (in Yiddish which was his native tongue) that Gerber was a rich man. What, exclaimed the rabbi, from milk? 'Nein', replied the chazan laying a finger on his nose, 'fun vasser,' from water. This was probably folklore, for all dairymen were accused of watering milk as all grocers were accused of sanding sugar, and though the rabbi repeated the story with a chuckle he never really believed it. Gerber certainly never watered the rabbi's milk. He drank a glass of it warm on Saturday nights as part of the ritual announcing the departure of the sabbath.

Oddly enough, though Moses was instrumental in bringing the children of Israel out of Egypt he played no part in the Seder ritual that celebrated that exodus. There it was all ascribed to God alone. After the youngest child had asked the prescribed four questions about the significance of this special night, the answer was given, Our ancestors were slaves to Pharaoh in Egypt, but God brought us forth from there with a strong hand and an outstretched arm. And it was God who gave the Torah to Israel, not Moses. Blessed be almighty God who gave the Torah to his people Israel, blessed be he, the Passover Haggadah pronounced, and every sabbath after the Torah was taken out God was similarly praised for giving it to his people, though here it does say by the hand of Moses. Why this apparent depreciation of Moses? Neither the psalmist nor the Hebrew prophets are much concerned with him either, and he largely fades out of the Bible after the book of Joshua. Moshe rabbenu, the only man who spoke with God face to face, the leader, liberator and lawgiver of Israel, is not the man who will reappear to usher in the Messiah. That role is reserved oddly enough for the minor biblical figure of Elijah who plays a strange and haunting part in Jewish folklore. But our hero knew no Jewish folksongs about Moses. Go down Moses way down in Egypt land, tell old Pharaoh let my people go, that was a Negro spiritual and a very fine one too and there was nothing like it in Hebrew song. It was a question of dividing the honours, was almost how the rabbi explained it when faced by our hero's puzzlement, because although Judaism is based on the Law as revealed on Sinai through Moses yet Moses was only a man not in any way divine, not a Jewish Christ or man-god of any sort, a great but fallible man who made mistakes. His tomb was left unmarked and unknown so that it would not become the centre of a cult. The priesthood was assigned to his brother and his successor as leader was Joshua who was no relation at all and the purpose of that is to remind us that we are all human and limited however gifted or favoured by God. Moses was well rid of the priesthood, certainly, our hero thought, for all that priestly ritual so meticulously laid down in the Torah was something deeply alien to him and he did not know what he would have done if he had lived in the days of sacrifices and the officiating of priests. He was the son of the rabbinical and not the priestly tradition, with an ancestry of scholars and teachers not priestly celebrants and he resented the special place in certain parts of the synagogue service still reserved for *cohanim* and doubted very much whether in any case the name Cohen really meant direct descent from the original *cohen* Aaron. He sensed his father's similar views on this, though the rabbi was never explicit about it. The Law was a rational thing, intended by God to enable men to live in peace and order and dignity, and its purely ritual aspects were surely concessions to primitive frailty. Of course some rituals were splendid and moving, but these were not the prerogative of the *cohanim*.

Go down then Moses down into history and into geography too with your crossing the Red Sea and marching in the wilderness and climbing the holy mountain, your people have left you there, horns of light on your head (rays really, not horns, it was the Christian interpreters who misunderstood *keren*, meaning horn or corner or peak or ray of light or strength, so that painters showed Moses horned like a devil) and the tables of the Law on your arm, go down Moshe *rabbenu*, you were too much for the people you led out of bondage into freedom, they went in for backsliding as soon as your back was turned and well you knew they would again after your death for you prophesied it, go down with honour and awed respect but dare we say it not with wholehearted affection for though the Law you gave brought life and not death, freedom and not slavery, it was a hard load for a folk to bear through the generations, a burden as well as a privilege, and not to kindle a fire in thy habitation on the sabbath could mean a damn cold Saturday in later ages and other climes. There were plenty other Moseses after the original, like Moses of Coucy the first itinerant preacher among French Jews who publicly disputed about the Talmud in Paris in 1240 with that terrible apostate Nicholas Donin who turned Franciscan and bitterly persecuted his former brethren. But the greatest of the later Moseses was Rambam, Moses Maimonides, who flourished in the twelfth century in the golden age of the Jews in Moslem Spain and produced an Aristotelian Jewish philosophy over half a century before Thomas Aquinas produced his Aristotelian Christian philosophy, which showed once again how the Jews were the pioneers, thus giving our hero great comfort. In a later age Moses Mendelssohn who was a great friend of Lessing brought the secular philosophy of his age into his philosophy of Judaism, which was splendid because our hero's father the rabbi was doing the same thing in his century but it was disturbing too for Moses Mendelssohn's enterprising bringing together of Jewish and modern wisdom, so right so enlightened so encouraged by the rabbi who had written a book on David Hume and essays on Kant and yet was a Talmudist and upheld the Law, began a slide towards total loss of Judaism so that Mendelssohn's grandson grew up as a Christian. He thought of this as he practised the Songs without Words out of the bright red music book and played them for Miss Brown during his weekly piano lesson. Later Moseses still became Moss or Moser and perhaps Moss Bros who let out dress suits and morning coats were originally a couple of Moseses, brothers like Moses and Aaron. Was the Moss – no first name ever recorded – who delighted Edinburgh audiences on the stage of the Theatre Royal at the end of the eighteenth and beginning of the nineteenth century originally Moses? He was certainly an outstanding Shylock. Moss, wrote Donaldson in his *Recollections of an Actor*, 'caught the inspiration from the renowned Macklin, whose Jew, by Pope's acknowledgement, was unrivalled, even in the days of David Garrick, and he bequeathed to his protégé Moss that conception which descended to the most original and extraordinary Shylock of any period – Edmund Kean.' And what about this name-changing, was it cowardly, was it treason to your ancestors? Well, our hero reflected, Moses wasn't the real name anyway, but a Greek or Latin alteration, and Moss was as like the Hebrew Moshe as Moses was. There was an Edinburgh Jewish family called Cowen, and Cowan was a common Scottish name, which was very comfortable for the Cowens, but a boy at school, where young Cowen was a fellow pupil of our hero, said that it should be Cohen and that it was dishonest to change it. But our hero explained that the vowel rendered as O in Cohen was pronounced OW in the Ashkenazi pronunciation of Hebrew in use by Edinburgh Jews so that Cowen really reflected their Hebrew pronunciation of the word more accurately than Cohen. But why all these flowers and mountains and fields and precious stones in Jewish names, he wondered. Rosenberg, Rosenfeld, Edelstein, Blumenthal, Rosenbloom – these names were clearly quite unJewish in origin, they had been picked up in Germany or elsewhere on the Continent, just as all those Jewish names ending in ski and witz had been acquired in Russia or Poland. So why not change Rosenberg to Montrose when you had settled in an English-speaking country, for it was the exact equivalent, or (he thought this one up himself and was rather proud of it) Rabbinovitz to Clarkson? His own surname was unique and special and to most people mysterious and there would be no question of changing that. But Stein could legitimately be changed to Stone. A rolling stein gathers no moses becomes a rolling stone gathers no moss. He always thought that Solway Moss, that sad battle of 1542 where the Scots were defeated by the English so that James V died soon after in despair, could be an adaptation of a very Jewish name, Solomon Moses. But no Scottish Jew would want to call himself Solway Moss, the associations were too tragic.

Even if Moses was an Egyptian name, he reflected, that need not prevent him from being regarded as a Jewish national hero who led his people to liberation, for was not Robert the Bruce himself, who so gloriously defeated the English at Bannockburn and thus restored Scotland's independence, the descendant of Norman knights bearing a Norman name? And the original Stuarts were Bretons: Walter the

Steward, whose marriage to Marjory Bruce founded the Stuart dynasty, was descended from men who had held the office of steward to the archbishops of Dol in Brittany. And the Irish nationalist leader De Valera had a Spanish father and a Spanish name. And the kings and queens who sat on the thrones of Europe were all at least half foreigners. Kingships of foreign countries were doled out as prizes even as late as Napoleon's time, while kings nearly always married into foreign royal families so that their children were very mixed up. Consider the kings of England, Danish or French or Dutch or German, not to mention the queens they married. From King Canute to George V they were a pretty mixed bunch. He took pleasure in these reflections, for they reinforced his combination of pride in his Jewish ancestry and relish of his Scottish environment. The rabbi once met George V (whom he prayed for weekly in his synagogue) at a garden party in Holyrood and remarked afterwards that his face appeared to be heavily made up with artificial sunburn. Le roi soleil, Charlie Brydon had told them, was what Louis XIV was called, but King George was a sun king of a different kind. He had a bearded face of expressionless dignity, rather like the chief constable of Edinburgh who was firmly believed by the boys at school to be an illegitimate son of Edward VII and so King George's half brother. King Edward's widow was still alive, and was also prayed for in the synagogue: the rabbi used to roll out the names: Our sovereign lord King George, our gracious Queen Mary, Edward Prince of Wales, Alexandra the Queen Mother, and all the royal family. May the supreme king of kings in his mercy put a spirit of wisdom and understanding into his heart and into the hearts of all his counsellors, that they may uphold the peace of the realm, advance the welfare of the nation, and deal kindly and truly with all Israel. In Russia presumably they had similarly prayed for the Tsar, and perhaps they prayed now for the communist party or for the proletariat? German and British Jews had prayed equally for victory during the Great War, a disturbing fact, but then wasn't the Kaiser a cousin of King George or something like that? Jews were enjoined to be loyal to the country in which they lived, to seek the peace of the city where they dwelt, but to be loyal sometimes meant to seek war and to fight fellow Jews who in turn were being loyal to the country where history had landed them. Anyway, with the League of Nations there weren't going to be any more wars, and that solved a whole range of dilemmas.

The question of sides was a teasing one. He was taught all about the struggle of the Greeks against the Persians and the glories of Thermopylae and Marathon and Salamis, and he rejoiced in the overthrow of the despotic oriental Persians by the enlightened and civilized Greeks. But shouldn't he really have supported the Persians? Hadn't Cyrus let the Jews return to their own land after he had conquered the Babylonians who had originally carried them off? And wasn't Persian civilization more like ancient Jewish civilization than either was like Greek? Was it? The Greek master presented Socrates as a sort of honorary Christian, but our hero saw him as an honorary Jew: after all he was a monotheist and talked about *ho theos*, the god, not about the gods. All the same he was puzzled by Socrates' remark about owing that cock to Asclepius. Would the history of the world have been better if the Persians had won against the Greeks? The master posed the question in a lesson on Greek history. Everyone in the class instinctively answered no, but had he a right to do so, was he perhaps betraying something in Jewish history in doing so? Yet he couldn't help thinking of ancient Persians as he thought of ancient Egyptians, stiff, stylized, monumentally cold and death-like, not warmly human like Jews. But perhaps this was historical nonsense. What would he think of Moses if he could see him now as he really was in his lifetime? A stiff bearded Egyptian? Not a very sweet-tempered man, he imagined, but presumably a man with a divine mission could not afford to relax. Perhaps that was why Moses didn't figure in the Haggadah, for the Pesach festival was one of relaxed enjoyment while Moses was a stern lawgiver who might cast a shadow over the feast. He thought of him when reading Wordsworth's 'Ode to Duty', which Henry John had them memorize: Stern Daughter of the Voice of God. Thou, who art victory and law. Stern Lawgiver. That was him.

A sort of Jewish John Knox. Or rather Knox was a sort of Scottish Moses. His beard was even longer than any Jewish beard our hero had seen, and he wore a flat sort of hat, which though not exactly a *yarmelka* showed that he kept his head covered in the Jewish manner. Chief among the venerable fabrics of the old town of Edinburgh is the singularly picturesque building terminating the High Street towards the east which has been assigned by long-accepted tradition as the mansion provided at the expense of the town for the lodging of its first parish minister, the great reformer, John Knox. He was indebted to the liberality of individuals for the support of his family. Not really like Moses: more, perhaps, like the prophet Nathan who castigated King David for his behaviour with regard to Bathsheba or like Elijah who confronted King Ahab and was persecuted by the wicked Queen Jezebel. Knox certainly had it in for Mary Queen of Scots, but was she a Jezebel as the belligerent reformers maintained? If there be not in her, Knox wrote, a proud mind, a crafty wit, and an indurate heart against God and His truth, my judgment faileth me. His judgment probably did fail him. The First Blast of the Trumpet against the Monstrous Regiment of Women was a wild and silly outburst: it hath blown from me all my friends in England, Knox admitted, and that was a sad thing for him since he was pro-English and anti-French and might have landed up happily with a high position in the Church of England if his blast against female rule had not made him, as he said, odious in the eyes of Queen Elizabeth. His wife was English and his two sons were educated in England and became clergymen of the Church of England. So John Knox, seen by the world as the very epitome of an ingrainedly Scottish Protestantism, in fact rejected the deepest traditions of the Scottish nation. He even saw the shameful Scottish defeat at Solway Moss as the work of God. Worldly men may think that all this came but by misorder and fortune, as they term it; but whosoever hath the least spark of the knowledge of God may as evidently see the work of His hand in this discomfiture as was ever seen in any of the battles left to us by the Holy Ghost. For what more evident declaration have we that God fought against Benhadad, King of Aram, when he was discomfited in Samaria, than now we have that God fought with His own arm against Scotland? Because Knox was on the side of the English Protestants against the Scottish Catholics he was sure that God was on his side. But our hero, who was in some respects the beneficiary of the Scottish Protestant identification of themselves with the people of the Bible, was pretty sure that God remained neutral as between Protestants and Catholics except in such matters as the inquisition and the burning of heretics where God must have been against the inquisitors and burners. As for Mary, brought from gay France to reign over a turbulent people in a bleak northern climate, one couldn't help being on her side, confronted by Knox and his beard, fought over, bullied, trapped, imprisoned and in the end executed. He had seen Rizzio's bloodstains on the floor at Holyrood. 'If we turn to Holyrood, what visions and memories must arise of Knox, standing grim and stern before his queen, in his black Geneva cloak, with his hands planted on the horn handle of his long walking-cane, daringly rebuking her love of music and dancing – unbending, unyielding, and unmelted, by either her exalted rank, her beauty, or her tears; and of that terrible night in the Tower of James V, when sickly Ruthven, looking pale as a spectre under the open visor of his helmet, drew back with gauntleted hand the ancient arras as the assassins stole up the secret stair, – and then Rizzio, clinging wildly to the queen's skirt, and dying beneath her eyes of many a mortal wound, with Darnley's dagger planted in his body.' Ah, the melodious rhetoric of the nineteenth-century historian. How different from today's newspapers. KNOCKS FROM KNOX. THE QUEEN REBUKED. Interviewed after her confrontation with the great reformer, the Queen said, I have taken many hard knocks in my time but none so hard as those from that obnoxious man. It seems that when the renowned preacher knocked at the door of the Queen's chamber her lady-in-waiting asked who was there and heard the reply John Knox. John knocks? she repeated. John who? The suspicion that he was being played with did not soften the temper of the world-famous theologian. Our hero was interested in the word obnoxious and even more in the shorter form noxious which appeared in the translation of the Haggadah in the passage describing one of the ten plagues of Egypt as a mixture of noxious beasts. What beasts? he inquired. A variety of beasts, he was told. Mixed beasts? So he changed the phrase to a noxture of mixed beasts, which pleased him immensely. He defined a noxture as a group of harmful persons or animals. Or perhaps it could be a harmful drink, so that instead of reading on a medicine bottle, THE MIXTURE, to be taken three times daily after meals, you might read THE NOXTURE, not to be taken.

But whether Knox was noxious was a matter of opinion, or perhaps a matter of mood, so that his stern reforming moralizing in some moods seemed admirable and in others intolerably narrow and oppressive. He felt a similar ambiguity about Cromwell, shuddering at his behaviour in Ireland yet on the whole admiring him as a man and a ruler. The history he was taught at school was on the whole pro-Cromwell rather than pro-Charles, for it was the covenanting tradition rather than the romantic Jacobite one that prevailed. So on the whole he saw Cromwell as a stout fighter for freedom from royal oppression forced by events to take over the political leadership of his country. Yet he sympathized with the romantic Jacobite tradition too, and was very much on the side of Bonnie Prince Charlie in the next century, as somehow he stood for Scotland against the hated English red-coats, and that view was bolstered by his seeing Rob Roy at the King's Theatre. But he had sneaking sympathies even with seventeenth-century royalists, very much as he could not help being on the side of the French aristocrats rescued by the Scarlet Pimpernel while welcoming the French Revolution as putting an end to the intolerable abuses of an absolute government. There was little logic to it. He detested James VII and II, mourned Monmouth's defeat and execution, and rejoiced in the events of 1688. But he was on the side of James's grandson. Charles II was clearly culpable for his secret agreements with Louis XIV behind the back of his own government. But being a merry monarch he couldn't be taken wholly seriously. There was another point in Cromwell's favour, his attitude to Jews, whom he allowed (though not by any public act of state) to return to the country from which they had been expelled by Edward. (Edward I, malleus Scotorum, the hammer of the Scots, was also malleus Judaeorum, and Jewish and Scottish feelings could reinforce each other beautifully on this issue.) The Edinburgh Jewish Literary Society had regularly on its syllabus lectures about the return of the Jews to England in the seventeenth century, particularly about Manasseh ben Israel's mission to Oliver Cromwell. Manasseh came over from Holland to present humble addresses to Cromwell asking for the return of the Jews, and Cromwell convened a conference at Whitehall to consider the matter, but sensing a lack of sympathy among its members he dissolved the conference and preferred to let the Jews in quietly. So Cromwell was a sort of Jewish hero. He once amused himself seeing how many Olivers he could get into a sentence about Cromwell. When a Jew talked about a recently deceased person he always added after mentioning his name the words *olov hasholom*, peace be upon him, which sounded to our hero's ears like oliver sholom. He imagined a Jew in England recalling being told of Cromwell's death: When they told me it was all over with Oliver Cromwell olov hasholom I was struck all of a heap, which really sounded like, When they told me it was Oliver with Oliver Cromwell Oliver sholom I was struck Oliver heap. It was an odd name Oliver, one of Charlemagne's twelve peers and Roland's friend, Olivier in French and that meant olive tree. Olive was the female equivalent, but why the man should be the tree and the woman the fruit remained obscure. His mother cooked with olive oil, frying in oil being a basic Jewish cooking procedure as it couldn't be an animal fat for fish, the article most fried, and he was fascinated to learn once from the huge many-volumed *Century Dictionary* that stood in a special bookcase of its own in his father's study and was the most absorbing reading that the words olive and oil came from the same root, Latin *oleum*, oil, basically the same word as Latin *oliva*, olive or olive tree, Greek *elaion*, olive tree. *Elaion* = olive? Ah, but he remembered about the lost digamma that loomed like a shadow behind certain Greek words. If you restored that, then *elaion* would be *elaiFon*, which was more like olive. He was delighted to find the lost digamma in the Hebrew word for Greece, *yavan*. You inserted the digamma into Ionia and lo, you got IFonia. *Yevanim nikbetsu alai*, the Greeks rose up against me, they sang in the *maoz tsur* hymn on Chanukah, and if he hadn't been taught at school about that lost Greek letter lurking invisible in such words as Ionia he would never have seen the connection. Of course the Greeks that Judas Maccabeus fought against were not real Greeks, but debased and degenerate hellenists rather than classical hellenes. Ionia was the birthplace of so much Greek art, music and philosophy, he thought it must have been because of its relative proximity to the Hebrew centre of civilization to the south-east. Homer's Greek was Ionic and not Attic. Dr Johnson thought if you lived in an attic your brains would work more swiftly because you would be whirled round faster with the turning of the earth, so perhaps Attic Greek was for the intellectuals and Ionic for the poets. True, Greek philosophy had started in Ionia but it reached its climax with Plato and Aristotle in Athens. Zeus and his fellow gods must have spoken Attic Greek on Olympus, the attic of Greece, its divine top storey. But Homer wrote his divine stories in Ionic Greek.

Jimmy Allan had told them at school that the Greeks believed in learning from suffering and quoted the Greek proverb *ta pathemata mathemata*, suffering is learning. But the boys turned it around and said *ta mathemata pathemata*, learning is suffering. *Mathemata* was the plural of *mathema*, something learned, and it puzzled him why the English word derived from it should be as restricted in meaning as mathematics was. Especially since he considered that mathematics was not so much learning as figuring things out, quite different from history and languages where you learned new things. Euclid now, ideally you could work out every single proposition by logical inference, step by step. He couldn't have done it unaided himself of course for he didn't have that kind of mind, though he wasn't bad at geometry and much preferred it to arithmetic. Algebra, though, was his best mathematical subject, and he found juggling with x's and y's and with a's, b's and c's very satisfying. He was sternly accused of turning all arithmetical problems into algebraic ones, preferring always to work out problems through an equation, let x equal the required number or quantity. But he found that so much easier than those intolerable problems about two trains starting simultaneously from opposite points and going at different speeds. Where would they meet? It made his head spin to consider the question. Yet some boys could work these things out in their heads with astonishing speed. People differed in what subjects they were good at. There was Mr Levi, who had come to Edinburgh as a small boy and still couldn't pronounce the English language. His command of English idiom was perfect, his use of Scottish slang remarkable, but his pronunciation remained Yiddish. The extraordinary thing was that he always pronounced a W like a V and tried so hard not to that he pronounced all his V's W's. He once gave a classic description of his first eating oysters, all the more shocking because oysters, like all shell-fish, were not kosher, not possessing fins and scales. But Mr Levi, who had made his pile in the furniture business, was anxious to emancipate himself from the narrower elements of Jewish law, though remaining faithful in a larger sense, and besides he wanted to enjoy the sports of the gentry with whom he now associated. He had a hard time with his first oyster. At first he makes you vant to womit, he gravely explained. Why he should denominate the oyster by the masculine pronoun was no clearer than his transposition of V and W. Our hero puzzled greatly over this. If Mr Levi could pronounce W after all, why could he only do so when pronouncing a V while remaining unable to pronounce it in its proper place? But there was no accounting for Mr L's accent. When they were building the new Edinburgh synagogue he strongly urged that when planning for the electric lighting they should insist on SONKEN SVITSIS. The phrase flew round the Edinburgh Jewish community, and few indeed there were who recognized immediately that the reference was to sunken switches. Mr L devastated the head waiter at a celebrated Edinburgh restaurant by the simple grandeur of his question after the salmon which he had been assured was caught in the Tay the previous evening turned out, by the test of Mr L's discerning palate, to have been neither Tay salmon nor so freshly caught. Vy did you lie to me? he asked with solemn reproach, and the waiter had no reply. His daughter Violet was generally called Vi but her father called her Wi. There was a kind of cocoa he remembered from his very earliest childhood called Vi-cocoa and the story went that an elderly Jewish housewife went into the Jewish grocer's to ask for cocoa and the proprietor asked Vi-cocoa? She answered, Vy not? Theirs not to reason vy. Theirs not? Yours not to ask, his not to question. Mine not to inquire further into this usage. Someone else's to. Some people used the infinitive with please: please to give me back my cap, a boy pleaded in the playground when some bullies had taken his cap from him. Please to put a penny in the old man's hat. Pleased to meet you, but that was different. He was taught that it was vulgar to say pleased to meet you, it should be how d'ye do. Suppose you met someone on the street and you weren't quite sure if you had met before, and passed without greeting, then looked back and found him looking back? He remembered Bob Merry's song:

> I was looking back to see
> If she was looking back to see
> If I was looking back to see
> If she was looking back at me.
> As I was looking back to see
> If she was looking back at me,
> We both looked back and saw each other
> Looking back to see.

But looking back was what history was about, and it was a long way back to Moses.

8

DAVID, Dovid ha-melech, David the king, son of Jesse the Bethle-
hemite. He was cunning in playing and a mighty valiant man and a
man of war and prudent in matters and a comely person, and the
Lord was with him. So at least said one of King Saul's servants to
him when he asked him to bring someone who could play well. But
we are also told that he was but a simple shepherd with no experience
in warfare and quite unable to wear the armour Saul offered him for
he had never worn armour before. And that was surely right, because
he slew Goliath with a stone from a sling, a most remarkable feat, a
little shepherd boy slaying an enormous tyrannical giant. But what a
strange fate for this humble shepherd, taken up by the King,
favoured and promoted by him, and then, when Saul's evil spirit was
on him, hated by the jealous King and assaulted by him. And then
there was the King's son Jonathan, who became David's best friend,
a type and symbol of friendship, like Roland and Oliver, and when
Jonathan was slain with his father in battle on Mount Gilboa David's
grief was terrible and he lamented in a poem that rolled sadly and
grandly off the tongue. *Ech naflu giborim*, how are the mighty fallen.
Ye mountains of Gilboa, let there be no dew, neither let there be rain
upon you. The lament was for Saul too, for David remembered only
his good moods and forgot those black moments when the tragic King
would throw his spear at him. Saul and Jonathan were lovely and
pleasant in their lives, and in their death they were not divided:
u-vemotam lo nifradu. They were swifter than eagles, stronger than
lions. How are the mighty fallen in the midst of the battle. Our hero
thought of this lament when cadets marched past the school war
memorial on armistice day. He had seen those words inscribed on
another war memorial somewhere. In death they were not divided.
Swifter than eagles, stronger than lions. The flowers of the forest are
a' wede awa'. There was a plaque on the wall of the west wing of the
school recalling that German zeppelins had dropped bombs there,

and there were still holes in the masonry bearing witness to that raid. And on the pavement below they had set a German imperial eagle in brass, which the boys would step on in contempt. Swifter than eagles. This was a strange, stylized, two-headed eagle, and if he hadn't been told it was one he probably would not have guessed. Once when he was very small he woke up in the middle of the night and found himself to his bewilderment on the dining-room sofa with the rest of the family around him. There was a zeppelin raid going on, and his parents had wanted them all to be together if the house was hit. He vaguely recalled a sense of bemusement and excitement. He remembered too seeing wounded soldiers in blue hospital uniforms and once a soldier on leave came to the house in khaki and mended his sister's doll with string. He liked the belts that officers wore diagonally across their chests. He and his brother had marched round the back yard, being soldiers: his brother was to be the highest possible ranking officer and he was to be second. What is the top officer? they asked the rabbi. The King, the rabbi replied, he is the commander in chief of the whole army. This was a very disappointing answer, for they wanted an elaborate and fancy name for an exalted rank and an almost equally elaborate name for the rank just next to it. King seemed very bleak, and besides everybody knew that King George stayed in his palace and didn't go to war in a khaki uniform. Well, he smiled now as he brought to mind those childish fancies and thought of King David leading his men against the Philistines. For in those days kings really did lead their men on the actual field of battle. Into the valley of death rode King Saul and his son Jonathan, and the shepherd boy who mourned them ascended the dead king's throne.

David was the son of Jesse, pronounced in English just like the girl's name Jessie, which seemed a pity, since at school they used Jessie to refer to a boy suspected of effeminacy and cowardice. They would drawl out the first vowel: you're just a big J-e-e-e-e-ssie, with a bleating *ehh* sound. But the Hebrew name was Yishai, which sounded much more masculine. He was the son of Obed, who was the son of Boaz and his Moabite wife Ruth – that Ruth who after the death of her first husband in Moab went with her Israelite mother-in-law Naomi back to the latter's country, refusing to stay in her native Moab, saying to Naomi, Intreat me not to leave thee, or to return from following after thee: for whither thou goest, I will go; and where thou lodgest, I will lodge: thy people shall be my people, and thy God my God. So if Moses may have been Egyptian, King

David's ancestry was partly Moabite, and our hero welcomed this notion as he welcomed all notions of transfusion of cultures producing a stronger patriotism, like Robert the Bruce being Norman. Ruth was a favourite Jewish name, yet she was the proto-proselyte, who chose Israel and its religion deliberately, so that from that time on all female converts to Judaism were given the symbolic name of Ruth. And she was David's great-grandmother. And from David the Messiah would be descended. As the rabbi chanted in Hebrew on Saturday nights after the sabbath had departed: *eliyahu ha-navi*, *eliyahu ha-tishbi* . . . Elijah the prophet, Elijah the Tishbite, Elijah the Gileadite, may he come speedily to us with the Messiah the son of David, *im mashiach ben David*. Messiah, *mashiach*, the anointed: David was anointed too and was also called *mashiach*: O let our eyes behold thy kingdom according to the word that was spoken in the songs of might by David, thy righteous anointed, *al yedei David meshiach tsidkecha*. And in a mystical sense David was always alive. In the strange ritual of the blessing of the new moon (which the rabbi never practised but which our hero found in the rabbi's big old-fashioned Hebrew prayer book, which contained so many more prayers than they ever spoke, with massive commentaries) one recited three times: *David melech yisrael chai ve-kayam*, David king of Israel is alive and well. And after that one had to recite three times, *shalom aleichem, aleichem shalom*, peace be to you, to you be peace. Then a final thrice-repeated sentence whose English meaning was, Good augury and good luck be to us and to all Israel. (Good luck, *mazel tov*, was also what you said to someone to congratulate him: he often wondered why a wish of good luck should be taken to mean congratulation on some special achievement. Surely the recipient of congratulations must have already had the good luck to be in a position to be congratulated.) He puzzled over these strange mystic sentences in that old black-bound prayer book, and concluded that the ritual must have been invented in medieval times by rabbis who wanted to cheer themselves up in an age of persecution. David king of Israel is alive and well. Peace. Good luck.

How could you secure good luck? Everything was uncertain, and if you wanted something desperately there were certain things which suddenly you felt might help you to get them. Such as holding your breath until you had counted up to a very high figure. Or you might say, If I can bounce this ball against the wall twelve times and each time catch it with one hand as it comes back, then the thing I want to happen will happen. Once, the day before an exam result, he noticed two books upside-down in the dining-room bookcase: he made a mental note to put them right way up, but forgot. The next day when the exam result was announced he found that he had done unexpectedly well. Ever after that he regarded the sight of a book upside-down in a bookcase as a good omen, and he considered it prudent to leave it that way. Of course this was nonsense, pure superstition, like Friday the 13th and other sillinesses, but somehow if it was your own nonsense it did matter to you. It was the superstitions he invented himself that he felt bound by. He would give himself challenges – if he could do this, if he could do that, so many times, or in some particular way, or in a certain pattern, then some especially desired event would occur. He never checked to see how many times performing the test was followed by the hoped-for consequence, since nearly all the tests he set himself were thought up on impulse and quickly forgotten afterwards. When he learned at school about the Greek sense of hubris followed by nemesis, he understood at once. It was dangerous to glory in something good that was happening to you. Jews used the Yiddish expression *umberufen* when they praised a baby or made any remark about a state of affairs that might, if fate willed, be speedily reversed. He's a beautiful child, *umberufen* (that is, *unberufen*, not shouted out, not proclaimed from the house-tops). The expression was the Jewish equivalent of touch wood, which he had been told had something to do with the wood of the cross, and therefore not a proper expression for Jews (though in fact he used it quite a lot). There was the Scottish idea of not sinning your mercies, not being unappreciative of such good fortune as you had, for that was just as dangerous as boasting about it. Oh he knew from a very early age that life was a most uncertain business, it might rain on the day a picnic was planned, you might just miss the prize competed for at school, something eagerly looked forward to for weeks might turn out meaningless and miserable. But there were some occasions when a totally unexpected pleasure suddenly presented itself, as on that day early in the summer holidays when his father announced out of the blue that they would all go to Aberdour and spend the day there on the silver sands, and everyone rushed around making preparations, and they took the train across the Forth Bridge, and the weather was lovely, and even the sand that got into the sandwiches (making them real sandwiches, as he pointed out) added to the joy. Why need you never go hungry on a beach? Because of the sand-which-is there. One Sunday a member of the rabbi's congregation who had recently bought a car drove up unexpectedly and took the whole family to North Berwick. Rides in motor cars were enormous treats, and he could hardly enjoy them for anticipating the time when they would come to an end. Yet time moved slowly in those days. When the school session finally came to a close, after what seemed an eternity, the two months' summer holiday stretched ahead endlessly, promising an unbroken series of carefree days. But it was the unexpected treats, punctuating the routine of ordinary living, that were most exciting. Once in the Easter holidays, when his father was in Palestine for the opening of the Hebrew University, his mother suddenly decided that the whole family needed a change and on her own initiative took them all for ten days to Port Seton. In all other years they went away for a holiday only in the summer, and it was with incredulous joy that he heard of this plan. He continually longed for impromptu decisions on the part of those in charge to do quite unexpected things. He would wake up in the morning and think, Perhaps there's some extraordinary news. Perhaps school has had to shut down for a week and we all have to go off to the Highlands for some unknown but compelling reason. The General Strike, which occurred the year after the Port Seton affair, was for him simply a piece of excitement, and he suffered a real sense of disappointment when he watched Willie the janitor pin up a blue-pencilled notice on the main school notice-board, reading STRIKE OFF – OFFICIAL. Not that he didn't worry about the unemployed and about starving coal-miners. Something ought to be done about them, he was sure, but he had no knowledge whatsoever of economics and his politics at this time were simply a vague and watered version of his father's support for the Liberal Party, involving little more than a belief in tolerance and good will on all sides. Conservatives were too conservative and Socialists were too revolutionary, and the kindly, decent, middle way of the Liberals was obviously the best. Besides, Sir Herbert Samuel was a Liberal. It was a good omen that Sir Herbert was High Commissioner in Palestine, for had not the original Samuel anointed both Saul the first king of Israel and then David the second king? Perhaps Mashiach ben David was about to come at last.

King David was a musician and a psalmist as well as a fighting man, and our hero certainly preferred to think of him as playing the harp and composing poems rather than fighting those interminable battles against the Philistines. And those wars against the Arameans and the Ammonites and the Edomites and the Moabites (in spite of his great-grandmother's having been a Moabite), a tedious chronicle, even if these military activities did enable him to establish his kingdom from Dan to Beer-sheba. He captured Jerusalem from the Jebusites and established it as his country's capital. Before that he had reigned in Hebron over Judah seven years and six months and in Jerusalem he reigned thirty and three years over all Israel and Judah. So Jerusalem, for whose restoration they prayed daily, and to which each year at the end of the Passover Seder they looked forward to going the following year, was just about three thousand years old as the central city of Jewish imagination. Abraham had not known of it, Jacob had no connection with it, Moses was unaware of it. Jerusalem was David's city, *Ir David*. And rebuild Jerusalem the holy city speedily and in our days, they implored God in the grace after meals. They still mourned its destruction in an annual fast. Would Sir Herbert Samuel rebuild it, under the authority of the British Mandate? Would he be remembered as III Samuel, after I Samuel and II Samuel? That is what the British Zionists hoped. Zion? Tsiyon in Hebrew. The Jebusite name for the city David fortified and rebuilt as Jerusalem. A strange word. Jerusalem meant foundation of peace, but he had no idea what Zion meant.

Zion was the evocative word, the poetic word, the first word of those laments for the lost land of Israel which they chanted on the fast of Tishah Be-av, the ninth day of the month of Ab, anniversary of the destruction of the Temple. *Tsiyon ha-lo tishali lish'lom asirayich*, Zion, wilt thou not ask after the peace of thy captives, that seek thy peace and are the remnant of thy flocks? The words were by Jehudah Halevi, the great Hebrew poet of early medieval Spain: each year they recited his Ode to Zion, lamented the lost glory, comforted themselves with the hope of restoration. After all, the hope of restoration had been fulfilled before. Each shabbos before the grace after meals they sang the 126th psalm: When the Lord turned the captivity of Zion, we were like those that dream. But that was a strange song, for though it began in wondering joy at the restoration after the Babylonian captivity, it ended with a yearning appeal for the end of captivity, as though it had not occurred. Return us from our captivity, O Lord, like streams in the south, they sang, and ended with a haunting image of sowing in tears and reaping in joy. *Ha-zorim bedima berinah yiktsoru*: they that sow in tears shall reap in joy. Though he goes on his way weeping bearing the store of seed, he shall come back with joy, bearing his sheaves. But the Babylonian exile had only lasted seventy years, and those who sat down and wept by the rivers of Babylon when they remembered Zion really remembered it. If I forget thee, O Jerusalem, they sang, let my right hand forget her cunning. Well, they hadn't forgotten, not after two thousand years, and old men in the rabbi's congregation actually shed tears as they sat in shul on Tishah Be-av and recited the *kinot*, the songs of lamentation for the loss of Zion, Jerusalem, the land of Israel. Yet what was it really like, our hero often wondered, to live in ancient Israel as a member of the peculiar people? There were few vistas of peace and long-continued happy community life in the biblical story, but wars and backslidings and civil strife, and prophets vainly urging repentance and lovingkindness. How nobly the prophets preached, help the fatherless, be kind to the widow, return return return to the ways of love and righteousness and God will revoke his edict of wrath. O Israel, return unto the Lord thy God, for thou hast fallen by thy iniquity, cried Hosea, in the name of God. I will heal their backsliding, I will love them freely, for mine anger is turned away from him. I will be as the dew unto Israel: he shall grow as a lily, and cast forth his roots as Lebanon. And when punishment had fallen, Isaiah preached God's comfort to his oppressed people in the most memorable chapter of all, read in shul on *shabbos nachamu*, the sabbath of comfort: *Nachamu, nachamu ami*, comfort ye, comfort ye my people, saith your God. Speak ye comfortably to Jerusalem, and cry unto her, that her warfare is accomplished, that her iniquity is pardoned; for she hath received of the Lord's hand double for all her sins. Double indeed: two thousand years of exile and persecution, of weeping for the loss of Zion. What sins they must have been, to merit such punishment! And because of our sins we were exiled from our land, they recited on Rosh Hashanah, New Year's Day. But our hero could not really believe this. It was not that the people of Israel had been uniquely sinful, surely, but that they were uniquely responsible, they bore a greater burden; much, much more was expected of a people who had received the Law at Sinai and had been favoured with so many prophets. The trouble was, they didn't want to be a peculiar people, not at all. They wanted a king like other nations, and the prophet Samuel reluctantly granted them Saul and, when he failed, David. You only have I known out of all the nations of the earth and THEREFORE I shall punish you. Would it not have been better to be like other nations, not chosen, not held so strictly to account, not visited for every backsliding, not acting out a moral lesson for history? It was all so strenuous, even when it was not dangerous. Oh he was proud of being Jewish all right, but sometimes – just sometimes – he surrendered to a momentary feeling that life would be altogether more comfortable if he was like the others, the *goyim*, the unconcerned non-Jews who could eat milk with meat without feeling guilt and did not weep annually for a lost past.

Not that there weren't all sorts of joyful occasions in the Jewish year, with cheerful *zemirot*, post-prandial songs, and happy psalms. Make a joyful noise unto God, all ye lands. I was glad when they said unto me. That was an odd way to begin a psalm. He thought of it as sung with a Salvation Army thump in a nonsense hymn:

> I was glad when they said unto me
> Let us go to Mrs Smith's for tea,
> And there we shall partake
> Of bread and wine and cake,
> And return at a quarter past three.

> (CHORUS)

> Oh, glory glory glory hallelujah,
> Glory glory glory hallelujah,
> And there we shall partake
> Of bread and wine and cake
> And return at a quarter past three.

He sang this marching along the beach at Crail to a splendid military tune he invented, banging two big stones together like cymbals and pretending to be a Salvation Army band. It was odd that the rabbi didn't think it blasphemous. He didn't think it funny either, just silly. Still, there was a triumphant kind of feeling in some of the psalms which was not altogether unlike this sort of thing. There were other moods too, all sorts, including deeply tragic ones, like the opening of psalm 22: My God, my God, why hast thou forsaken me? *Eli eli, lama azavtani.* That line was used as the climax of a powerful Yiddish folk song. It came as a great surprise to him to discover that these were Jesus' last words on the cross, only he said them in Aramaic, which was very like Hebrew: *Eli eli, lama sabachtani.* Aramaic was a familiar language to anyone brought up on the Hebrew prayers, for some of these were in Aramaic, as was much of the Talmud (or at least it was in a kind of mixture of Hebrew and Aramaic). Aramaic was the vernacular of Palestine in Jesus' day, and his native language. If his last recorded words were a quotation from the psalms in Aramaic, wouldn't this mean that he was used to reciting them in the vernacular rather than in Hebrew? This was strange. It was strange too that this clear evidence that Jesus was a betrayed prophet (like so many others) rather than an incarnation of God was ignored by Christian theology. How could an incarnation of God ask God why he had forsaken him? He would have liked to ask one of his schoolfellows this question, but didn't have the nerve. He thought this made Jesus more human and more tragic, and he now felt even more strongly that Jesus was one of our boys, a misunderstood and betrayed Jewish prophet, whose last words were a quotation from the Jewish psalms. It was however laid down that a Jew's last words (where he was in a position to determine them) should be an affirmation of faith in the unity of God; the Jewish martyrs in their final tortures exclaimed, 'Hear O Israel, the Lord is our God, the Lord is one' and there is no record of any one of them having given way to despair at the end. Didn't this make this particular story about Jesus all the more convincing, since no one would have wanted to invent an account of his last moments which conflicted both with Jewish tradition and with Christian theology? The other Jewish prophets were reluctant, chosen by God to convey his message to the people and often resisting at first very strongly; but if Jesus had chosen himself, and firmly believed that he had a mission from God, that he was the predicted Messiah, which at the end God refused to confirm, that would account for his despair at the end. Thou shalt love thy neighbour as thyself, he said, and when our hero told the master at the scripture lesson that this was a quotation from Leviticus chapter 19 and not a new idea first introduced by Jesus the master was at first incredulous and had to check with his Bible before he agreed. Similarly, it was Amos who first said to hell with sacrifices and burnt offerings, what mattered was justice and doing good, and Micah too repudiated burnt offerings and said that all God asked of man was to do justice, love mercy and walk humbly before God. And Hosea said, I the Lord delight in lovingkindness and not in sacrifices, just as Isaiah said that God delighted not in the blood of bullocks: Cease to do evil, he said, learn to do well, relieve the oppressed, judge the fatherless, plead for the widow. These were passages the rabbi had him learn by heart in Hebrew. Our hero resented the assumption on the part of so many of his non-Jewish friends that such ideas – love and social justice rather than ritual animal sacrifices – were first introduced by Jesus. The Hebrew prophets should have been given the credit for it. Jesus repeated their message in a different idiom, and when he added to it something quite different, it was end-of-the-world stuff about personal salvation after the final destruction, and that cut no ice with our hero at all. Such problems he meditated in his early teens.

He got no help from the rabbi in these theological speculations. Study your Hebrew, memorize eloquent passages from the prophets, participate in the ordained rituals, and of course listen to my sermons and read my essays, and all will be well. That was the rabbi's implicit message to his children. His essays were well argued explanations and defences of Jewish ethics and Jewish practices. But he never got involved in any comparative discussion. The differences between Judaism and Christianity our hero worked out for himself. Sometimes he talked with his school friends about religion – he had no close school friends, but two sons of two Presbyterian ministers were among the few with whom he occasionally talked of serious subjects in the playground. But mostly they asked him questions about his religion, which he answered. He felt unable to raise any points about theirs which might be considered critical. In the old days people persecuted each other, slaughtered each other, burned each other at the stake, because of differences in their religious views which now they were too polite to talk about. If he himself had been born the son of a Presbyterian minister rather than the son of a rabbi, would not he have adhered to the Christian faith with the same proud tenacity with which (for all his questionings) he vaunted his Judaism? An accident of birth, then, was it? Where does truth come in then? He might have been born a Buddhist or a Hindu or a Copt (he wasn't quite sure what a Copt was, but thought of them as some kind of Egyptian Christians embattled with predatory Moslem tribes in a perpetual game of Copts and Robbers). What you believe to be true depends on the family you were born into. He raised this point with the rabbi one Friday evening, but the rabbi only smiled and said that everyone had a duty to strengthen and hand down his own heritage. Of course heritages were different, that was the result of history, and one ought to be proud of one's history. Kabalah was what was received, masorah was what was handed down: these two Hebrew words for tradition indicated the role of the individual, to receive from his parents and to hand down to his children. Continuity was all. But what did Judah ha-Nasi know about catching sticklebacks in Dunsapie Loch, or watching the fishing boats come into the harbour at Anstruther, or the way in which, coming home after a long walk over the Braid Hills, you let the cold water tap run on and on and on to get colder and colder before pouring yourself a glass of water, desperately thirsty though you were? What did he know of the chalk-and-ink smell of school corridors, of the summer evening sound of boys playing cricket in the Meadows, of the thrill with which you watched the first electric tramcar that came to replace the old Edinburgh cable cars?

Once, unexpectedly, on an ordinary school day, when he had finished his homework, his mother remarked that he had been looking very pale and tired and said what he needed was some sea air, and there and then she took him on the top of an open tram on a ride round the Granton circle – extraordinary, unexpected, bizarre, marvellous. He loved the smell of stale pipe tobacco on the top deck of tramcars (men weren't allowed to smoke on the lower deck), and he always sat in the very front when he could, looking ahead with a proud eye. Did furcapped Aryeh Zvi know about that? Yet they recited the same Hebrew prayers, welcomed the sabbath in the same way, ate unleavened bread on Passover and chanted the same grace after meals. He must have had his own separate world too, skating over frozen lakes (the fur hat suggested this) in Russia or Poland or Lithuania or wherever it was, breathing the cold fresh snowy air, the eye picking out something special to observe and rejoice at. And King David himself had his harp. Could they have communicated through music? *Ani kinor le-shirayich*, I am a harp for your songs, Jehudah Halevi said to Zion, music was the common factor from the time when David played his harp to when the Babylonian exiles hung their harps up on trees, to Jehuda Halevi's singing Zion's song in Spain, to – what? His own playing of Mendelssohn's Spring Song on the piano? David's harp music must have been very different. His own grandfather once said that he loved the violin best of all musical instruments, and the world was full of brilliant Jewish violinists. But a violin was not a harp. You could play schmaltzy Yiddish melodies on the violin, but the harp with its cool strings surely was impervious to schmaltz. Yes, he would have liked to hear the sound of King David's harp, strange ethereal tinklings from a distant world. Psalm 22, My God why have you forsaken me, has a prefatory note: *lamnatseach al ayelet ha-shachar mizmor le-david*, for the chief minstrel on *ayelet ha-shachar*, a psalm of David. What sort of instrument was *ayelet ha-shachar*? Literally, it meant 'hind of dawn', a wonderful phrase. Perhaps it was the name of a song? Chief minstrel, set this to the tune of 'The Hind of Dawn'. What a tune it must have been! Li'l David, play on your harp.

On summer evenings a brass band played in the band-stand in the West Meadows, and at intervals a pipe band took over, marching up and down outside the band-stand in splendid kilted panoply. It was a strange thing, when you were involved in the robust music of the brasses the idea of a pipe band was thin and distasteful, and when the pipes first began to play after the brasses they did indeed sound like a shrill wailing; but it didn't take long before you were absorbed into that music, and now the brass band seemed in retrospect to be vulgar and coarse. Every time it was the same, seduction first by one kind of music and then by another. They had singing at school, conducted by Mr De la Haye. Purse your lips, boys, purse your lips. Deep in the heart of a rose a garden of sweetness lies. I set the bell a ringing when the bride to the altar was led. There is a lady sweet and kind. Shut not so soon the dull-eyed night. Where'er you walk cool gales shall fan the glade. I must go down to the sea again. A mixed collection of songs indeed. And the school song, with its rousing climax, Watson's! Watson's! Watson's forever again and again! It was years later that he discovered that this was set to the tune of another song, 'Hail to the Chief'. Hail to the old school that claims our allegiance, proudly we yield it wholehearted and strong. The school concert ended with this song every year. But when he started playing the violin in the school orchestra he didn't have to sing (though he enjoyed singing) and played the accompaniment instead, from a part written out in ink by Mr De la Haye. The day he joined the orchestra, taking his place among the second violins, they were already in the middle of rehearsing a suite by Handel. He kept hearing the main theme played by the first violins and couldn't reconcile it with the music written in front of him. It took him some time to realize that the second violins were a kind of left hand. The school concert was part of the prize-giving ceremony at the end of the session. The Master of the Merchant Company presided, for Watson's was a Merchant Company school, and generally made a tedious speech. One year the current Master gave them a speech about life, going out into the world after school, etcetera. The major piece of advice he gave was that they should refrain from walking more than two abreast along pavements. Only yesterday, he said, only yesterday I was walking along Princes Street and saw SIX schoolboys, SIX, walking abreast, blocking the way for people walking in the opposite direction. That was BAD MANNERS. Bad manners was being inconsiderate. There needs no ghost come from the grave my lord to tell us this. Silly man. Our hero had no very clear idea as to what the Merchant Company was, or why it should run schools; they had a splendid hall in Hanover Street where he had to go and collect his bursary money for Merchant Company bursaries were awarded to the four or five boys who came top of each year at the end of the session. That meant remission of fees and an amount of cash – £5 or £7 10s. or £10. The money was presented to the fortunate boys by a clerk in an envelope. On one occasion, calling as he had been instructed to do at the Merchants' Hall for his envelope, he was puzzled when the clerk handed it to him with the remark 'found money'. Found money? He hadn't found it, he had won it, in fair academic competition. At first he thought the clerk was asking him a question, as though to say, Have you found any money? Then he realized he had made a statement. The clerk's exact meaning puzzled him all the way home. The money was presented by a clerk in an envelope. Piano for sale by a lady with four carved wooden legs. They learned about this from Henry John, who encouraged the boys to make up examples of ludicrous effects obtained by the wrong positioning of a phrase in a sentence. He once made up a splendid example of zeugma: he caught few fish, a cold, the last train back, and IT from his mother when he got home. Henry John thought the IT was a bit much. But you can say, You'll catch it when you get home. *It* was a strange word. You could say go it or stop it or it's a pity, you could also say hang it or damn it. There was no word for 'it' in French or in Hebrew, where everything was he or she. So in those languages you couldn't make jokes like he came to tea, she came to supper, and it came to pass. And it came to pass was all one word in Hebrew, *vayehi*, and it was. Many things had come to pass since biblical times, and Dovid ha-melech had long since passed away, but his memory was green: in a sense, *chai ve-kayam*, King David is alive and well.

PART THREE

Countrymen

9

THE WINTER DARK was falling and he watched the brisk-stepping lamplighter walk up the street with his pole that bore at the top a flame in a perforated metal protector. He stopped at each lamp-post, pushed up (or was it down?) a switch, and lit the gas that was thus released.

> My tea is nearly ready and the sun has left the sky;
> It's time to take the window and see Leerie going by.

Miss Smith of Class D read them Stevenson's poem at school, and she explained that the lamplighter was called Leerie because leer was what you called the moisture that trickled down inside the glass cover of the street lamp. He never heard such a word, though, and years later he looked for it in vain in dictionaries. Leerie, said Jamieson, the name given by children to a lamplighter, Aberd. Edin. Lanarks. Probably of Welsh extract. C.B. *llewyr*, radiance, *llewy-aw*, to radiate; *llewyrch*, illumination. Isl. *liori*, a window. But how did Edinburgh children know that? He was exactly a month past his seventh birthday when Miss Smith read the poem, and he must have talked about it at home because among his first real books was a beautiful little olive-green volume of *A Child's Garden of Verses* with his name written in his mother's hand on the fly-leaf and the date, October 1919. That was two months before JHH gave him Peebee Shelley. Stevenson's lamplighter came posting up the street with lantern and with ladder, but the one he saw needed no ladder, for he had his long pole. Another difference was that they hadn't a lamp before their door as RLS had (oh yes, Miss Smith encouraged them to call him RLS). But that wasn't important. Clearly RLS knew the smell of Edinburgh winter evenings, the way it got grey before it got black, how you put on the light, drew the curtains and poked up the fire before sitting down to your tea in the cosy knowledge that out-side the lamps were shining in the dark.

For Jews the day began at sunset the previous evening. This was right and proper. The drawing of the curtains on a winter evening was not an end but a beginning; there was something celebratory about it. So shabbos began on Friday night, and all the festivals began in the evening. It was all there in Genesis: *va-yehi erev va-yehi voker, yom echad*, and there was evening and there was morning, one day. God made the evening first. To go out in winter when it was dark, with the shop-windows lit up and a sense of adventure in the air, was quite different from going out in the endless light of a summer evening. In January it was already getting dark as he crossed the Meadows coming home from school, and the establishment of the lit warm interior curtained against the outside dark took place almost as soon as he got home. A pilgrimage was over, the external day confronted and survived. And on Friday night it was the whole week that had been survived, and though the sabbath was the seventh and last day of the week, not the first day of a new one, yet he saw its coming as a sign that the week, the workaday week, had ended and something new had arrived. Hebdomadaire. He had come across that word in one of his French text-books, and he relished it so much more than the feeble weekly, the weakly weekly. There was the English hebdomadal, which he liked less because it was reminiscent of abdominal and abominable. He read once something about the abdominal wall, and thought it was the abominable wall, hateful fence. That's an abominable wall you have round your stomach, the doctor said, we must do something about that. Do you have it all the time? No no, replied the patient, it only comes weekly, it's a hebdomadal wall. It comes from too much riding on a dromedary. How do you get from the golden city of Samarkand to the Persian border? There are no trains, you must take the weekly camel, the hebdomadal dromedary. That abominable hebdomadal dromedary! He thought of the hebdomadal Hebrews, who invented the weekly sabbath and celebrated most of their festivals over the course of a week. Then there was Shavuot, the feast of weeks, which occurred seven weeks after the first day of Passover. It was the first of two harvest festivals, the festival of the first-fruits, and it was also the anniversary of the giving of the Law on Mount Sinai. This was in early summer – our hero supposed that in Palestine the climate made a harvest possible at that time – while Succot, the other harvest festival, was in autumn. Two harvest festivals, and the people had not lived on the land for two thousand years! What tenacity, to cling to their customs and festivals as an agricultural people long after they had ceased to be one (though they were at last becoming one again in Palestine). He thought of the slums and the ghettos and the old-clothes men perambulating shabby city streets, all that long history of being penned up in crowded urban constriction with trade and finance the only possible activities, and then of the two harvest festivals and all the rituals of a farming people on which the Jewish year was based, and wondered at the obstinacy of community memory. And here in Edinburgh they prayed annually for rain, the *tefillat tal*, and from the 4th of December until the first day of Passover even recited daily in the morning prayers, *ve-ten tal u-matar livrachah al p'nei ha-adamah*, Give dew and rain for a blessing upon the face of the earth. He had heard the chazan intoning beautifully the prayer for rain when it was pouring outside. And all because in ancient Palestine the farmers needed rain at this time of the year. He knew the story of the Church of Scotland minister praying for rain in a drought: he had barely finished his prayer when a tremendous thunderstorm broke out with an immense downpour and a gale-force wind, so that the church roof blew off. Lord, Lord, exclaimed the minister, looking upward, dinna be *rideeculous*! He thought it a bit rideeculous to pray for rain at any time in Scotland. But at least the Jews were canny in the way they phrased their petition – they asked for rain to be sent *livrachah*, for a blessing, and not for any other purpose, so if the reply were given in storm and flood they could at least point out that that was not in their original specification. They made the point even clearer in the annual Passover prayer for rain: For a blessing and not for a curse, they pleaded, for life and not for death, for plenty and not for famine, amen. That word amen was used in Christian prayer too, but nobody really knew for certain what it meant. The Ashkenazi pronunciation was omain, and it was heard with great frequency in the synagogue. *Emunah* meant faith-fulness or firmness, and there was a verb *aman* to be firm, so pre-sumably amen had something to do with confirming, as though one said, quite so, absolutely true, so be it. Each week at school Henry John Findlay the English master gave the boys a list of difficult words to look up, with their etymologies, so he became interested in the origins of words. But oddly enough, the rabbi didn't share this interest, though he did require a knowledge of verbal forms, a favourite example being the verb *hishtachavah*, which should really be *hitshachavah*, from *shachah* to bow down, the letters being turned round for euphony. Every time they came across that word in Friday even-ing Bible translation the same question about the order of letters was asked and the same answer expected. But etymologies, no. He could not draw his father into the original meaning of amen. It was strange how the word had been taken up universally in Christian prayer and possessed in English solemn religious associations. Not for the boys at school, though, who chanted a meaningless rhyme:

> Amen
> Straw women
> Dirty kids
> Made out of linen

– about as fatuous a verse as the human mind could invent. He wondered who first thought of it, and why. He learned in history lessons about the mutual hostility between Presbyterians and Episcopalians in Scotland, and heard the rhyme with which the former sneered at the latter for their habit of kneeling at prayer:

> Pisky, pisky,
> Amen.
> Doon on your knees
> And up again.

Pisky was an Episcopalian, and there was an eighteenth-century Episcopalian minister called Cockburn who was known as Amen Cockburn. The piskies counter-attacked:

> Presby, presby,
> Dinna bend,
> Sit ye doon
> On man's chief end.

The question what was man's chief end was the opening of the Church of Scotland catechism, while the Episcopalians, like the Church of England, began simply with, What is your name? He had this difference pointed out to him many times as illustrative of the superior theological seriousness of the Church of Scotland. In spite of Amen Cockburn, he could see no evidence in his own time that amen was associated especially with Episcopalians: it was used often enough by Presbyterian Church of Scotland worshippers, as was clear even at school. How divided they all were! Not only Catholics and Protestants, but Episcopalians, Presbyterians, Methodists, Baptists, and dozens more. The Presbyterian Church of Scotland was itself constantly being split up. The Free Church, The United Free, the Wee Frees, he wasn't quite sure how different these were, but he remembered after the Free Church and the regular Church of Scotland had come together there were enough of the former who refused to join the establishment to enable them to continue under the provocative title of the Free Church of Scotland (Continuing). Jews had fewer schisms. There had been the Karaites, a long time ago, who had believed in the literal truth of the Bible and in nothing else, a sort of primitive Jewish Protestants who rejected all tradition and commentary not contained in the good book, and today there were the Liberal Jews who opposed the strict adherence to Jewish law and tradition of the Orthodox Jews, but that was all. In Edinburgh all the Jews were orthodox, in name at least, and the self-indulgent Liberals had no footing. The rabbi considered that the Liberals simply picked out from Jewish law and tradition those things that appealed to them, which was purely subjective and undermined totally the concept of divinely ordained law on which he maintained Judaism was based. The Free Church of Scotland (Continuing) was an obstinate rump, but orthodox Judaism (continuing) was the central tradition maintaining continuity through the ages in spite of everything. That at least was how our hero was taught to look at the matter. Further, for Jews continuity was bound up with identity, and to break with tradition meant to risk existence as Jews. But why worry about that? our hero once disturbingly asked himself. If the Jews were indeed God's people divinely ordained to survive, then they would survive whatever happened. And if they weren't, it didn't matter much whether they survived as a separate group or not. But was divine guarantee the only true reason for demanding the separate identity and existence of a group? The French, the Germans, the Italians – the Scots for that matter – surely had a right to identity whether God had specially authorized it or not. But Jews were Jews differently from the way in which Scots were Scots, for you could be a Jewish Scot or at least a Scottish Jew. But that wasn't the same as being a Christian Scot or a Scottish Christian, of any denomination, because Jewishness had something to do with community and descent as well as religious belief and practice. It was all very hard. These were not questions he could discuss with his father somehow: no one told him not to, but he felt that he couldn't. They led in too many different directions. It was all so strenuous, being Jewish, you had to think things out all the time, almost every day things came up which forced you to speculate on these matters. The goyim had life easier, they took it as it came. Still, thought exercised the brain, and that must be why Jews as a rule were clever.

Since the loss of their independence as a nation Jews had had no opportunity of putting into practice their own legal code derived from the Bible, so they had spent centuries refining its details to a point where hair-splitting seemed a coarse activity in comparison. When his father started his brother and himself on the Talmud, he looked forward to making acquaintance with this massive work so revered in Jewish tradition. But how different it proved to be from biblical prophecy with its marvellous poetry or from the plangent beauties of Jewish liturgy. The rabbis argued and argued and argued about matters that didn't seem to be of the slightest importance. They began with Baba Metsia, the Middle Gate, plunging into a discussion about finding lost property. *Sh'nayim ochzin be-talis*, two men seize a garment: one says I found it and the other says I found it, one says It's all mine and the other says It's all mine. Then one of them shall swear that his share of it is not less than half, and the other shall swear that his share of it is not less than half, and they shall divide it. If on the other hand one says It's all mine and the other says It's half mine, then the one who says It's all mine shall swear that his share in it is not less than three-quarters, and the one who says It's half mine shall swear that his share in it is not less than a quarter, and they divide it (or the value of it) proportionately. But perhaps one of the men is riding on an animal and the other is leading it, and both lay claim to it (to the animal? yes, that's what it says). Then they shall divide its value. Now that's only the *mishnah*, the main text; there follows the *gemarah*, the commentary, which goes on and on and on. What exactly is the relation between seeing something first and finding it? You can go on for ever on this one. And then there's the commentary on the commentary, Rashi's notes on both *mishnah* and *gemarah*. Two men take hold of a garment? Yes, the text means that they really take hold of it, *davke ochzin*, Rashi explains, both have actually got it in their hands. This kind of discussion did have a certain fascination, but it seemed terribly unreal. The prospect of two men arriving at the rabbi's house each holding a part of a garment and each simultaneously claiming that he had found it and it was his, seemed remote. Still, he could see that the facile rule, finders keepers, wouldn't do in law; you had to have some definition of what constituted finding. Children in fact were always having that kind of dispute. It's mine. I saw it first. Perhaps it was mothers rather than rabbis who should study Baba Metsia. Just a moment, children, while I look it up. Now you Joe swear that at least half of it is yours and you Ruth swear that at least half of it is yours and then you can divide it. But you can't divide a pen-knife! Well then Joe keeps the pen-knife and gives Ruth something that's worth half of it, say what's left of your packet of Rowntree's gums. But they're MY Rowntree's gums. No really, he didn't think Baba Metsia would be of much help even with children, those inveterate finders and claimers of objects. In some ways he thought those old rabbis were children, refining and debating and discussing and discriminating for the sheer love of making distinctions and adding definitions, even though the whole body of law on which they spent their time applied to a way of life which the Jewish people had not led since ancient times. Still, at least the law of lost property was relevant whether one lived in an agricultural society in ancient Israel, in a medieval ghetto, or in twentieth-century Edinburgh. But what about all those complex agricultural laws and their relation to the seasonal festivals that marked the Jewish year? There was something infinitely sad in those old men in their stuffy little rooms going over and over and over reminders of a long lost open-air existence. There was a whole section of the Talmud called *zeraim*, seeds. Whatever falls down at the moment of reaping counts as gleanings and belongs to the poor. But if a reaper lets fall the armful he has gathered because he has been pricked by a thorn, then the fallen armful does not count as gleanings but belongs to the farmer. They thought of everything. If the wind scatters the sheaves you must estimate what gleanings the field would probably have yielded if the sheaves had not been scattered and give these to the poor. There are even detailed instructions about what to do with corn found in antholes. If a fig tree stands in a courtyard and overhangs a garden, a man in the garden can eat the figs in his usual manner without paying tithes on them, but if the tree stands in the garden and overhangs the courtyard he is liable to tithes *unless he eats the figs one at a time*. But suppose a fig tree stands in the Land of Israel and overhangs outside it? Aha, in that case the question of tithing is determined *achar ha-ikar*, according to the position of the root.

He supposed that it was from the Talmud that his father had acquired his knowledge of different grains. Sometimes when they were staying at the seaside in August they would take a family walk inland, by ripening fields of barley and wheat and oats, and the rabbi took pleasure in describing the difference between the ears of each, and would even pause and pluck off an ear and bite the raw grain to eat the pulp within. There were no fig trees and pomegranates in Fife or East Lothian, and the procession of seasons, to which the Jewish religion was so firmly linked, was very different in this northern clime from what it must have been in ancient Palestine. Yet the sense of the proper rewards of each season transcended the differences. When the flood was over, God promised Noah that it would never happen again, and that in future the seasons would roll round inevitably year after year. While the earth remaineth, seed-time and harvest, and cold and heat, and summer and winter, and day and night, shall not cease. RLS had expressed it in his own way:

> Sing a song of seasons!
> Something bright in all!
> Flowers in the summer,
> Fires in the fall!

The differences between summer and winter were much greater in Scotland than in the Holy Land, for here in winter it grew dark by teatime and in summer the evening light stretched on endlessly. RLS expressed exactly his feeling about this, except of course that he used candle-light while they had electricity:

> In winter I get up at night
> And dress by yellow candle-light.
> In summer, quite the other way,
> I have to go to bed by day.

But what RLS didn't know was that in winter you could dismiss the sabbath and move into a secular week as early as five in the afternoon on Saturday, while in summer the sabbath lasted until you went to bed. If you could see three stars in the sky, that was a guarantee that shabbos was out. Although the welcoming of the sabbath on Friday evening was always cosy and looked forward to, especially in the winter, by late Saturday afternoon the restrictions of sabbatical activities had become a bit tedious and it was pleasant when dark came early to be able to face some hours of free secular behaviour before bedtime.

> Twinkle twinkle little star,
> What a cheerful sign you are.
> Just two more and we shall be
> Into week-day liberty.

That was however an unJewish reaction, for Jews were supposed to regard the departure of the sabbath, that oasis in a hard secular week, with grief. That must have been so, he reflected, in poor ghetto households, when the return to normal activities meant a return to fear and privation and grinding toil. But in June in Edinburgh it was hard to have to stay in sabbath peace until bedtime. Sabbath peace, he thought, or sabbath piece. A piece in Edinburgh was a slice of bread or a sandwich, and a slice of bread-and-jam was a jeely-piece. You brought a piece to school with you to eat during the lunch interval. Now bread played a very important part in the sabbath as in all Jewish festivals. Shabbos was ushered in by his father making *kiddush* over wine and then cutting bits of bread from a loaf, which he threw – literally threw, despite his mother's frequent protests – to each member of the family. And each member of the family recited a blessing before ritually consuming his piece. That blessing, praising the Lord for bringing forth bread from the ground, was known as a *motsi*, from the Hebrew verb *motsi*, meaning 'brings forth', that figured prominently in it, and by extension the piece of bread itself was called a motsi. So a motsi was a sabbath piece. The first time he heard the phrase pieces of eight he immediately asked himself, pieces of eight what? The past tense of eat was pronounced eight by some people and et by others. He himself usually pronounced it eight. Pieces of ate. Sandwiches that had been consumed. Once at school a boy was reciting from *Julius Caesar*

With Ate by his side, come hot from hell,

and pronounced Ate eight, to meet with crushing scorn from the English master. Eight, boy, eight, eight what? eight little nigger boys? Or perhaps you're a cockney and mean 'ate? But even then it won't scan. With 'atred by 'is side, come 'ot from 'ell, is that what you mean? Improving on Shakespeare? Eight! Bah! He saw a cartoon somewhere of a couple in a museum or art gallery looking at a painting conspicuously titled JUPITER AND IO, and the lady is saying to the gentleman, Jupiter and ten? Jupiter and ten? Jupiter and ten WHAT? He liked that, because it was a new sort of pun, or rather it wasn't a pun at all but a visual instead of an aural confusion. You could only go a certain length in that direction, though, with Roman numerals. Fifty-four could be liv: Live to be LIV O Caesar. A hundred and fifty-nine could be clix: the strange noises went on through the night, he counted CLIX clicks. But no, there was no real road that way. He often wondered how people were ever able to do sums with Roman numerals. Divide MDCCXLVIII by CXIV. It was plainly impossible. The Romans did make things difficult for themselves. Look at the way they did dates. Kalends and ides and nones, with so many days before or so many days after: fancy having to call the 25th of March *ante diem octavum kalendas Apriles*, the eighth day (counting inclusively) before the kalends of April. What's today's date, Cassius? I'll work it out, Brutus. Let me get out my wax tablets and do some sums. Come back in half an hour and I'll have the answer. Meet it is I set it down. Once when his mother brought in an ashet with roast beef and set it on the table, he murmured, Meat it is, I set it down, and everyone looked at him curiously. *Hupodra idon* as Homer said, looking askance, or, as the classics master insisted, looking upward from under your eyebrows.

Eyes figured strangely in literature. In that powerful last poem that Moses addressed to his people, *Ha-azinu*, Give ear ye heavens and I will speak, there occurs the strange sentence, He kept him as the apple of his eye. *Ke-ishon eino*. At least that is how it was always translated, though *ishon* really meant little man, diminutive of *ish*, so *ishon eino* meant the little man in the middle of his eye, the pupil of his eye. But then pupil was a little man too (or a little woman anyway), the pupil of the eye and the pupil at school came from the same Latin word, *pupillus*, feminine *pupilla*, a little girl, a doll, and the Romans called the pupil of the eye *pupilla* because the Greeks had used the word for a girl or a doll, *kore*, in that sense. Job talked about the eyelids of the morning. The leviathan's eyes were like the eyelids of the morning. Milton in Lycidas had the line

Under the opening eyelids of the morn.

Ke-aphapei shachar, like the eyelids of the morning. Now that was a simile, but it was more than a simile. A simile was when you compared one thing to another, but if you compare the leviathan's eyes to the eyelids of the morning you are comparing it to something that has already been turned into a figure of speech, for the eyelids of the morning is itself a metaphor, not a literal description. If the morning had eyelids, they would be like that. Or perhaps the dawn was what was meant by the eyelids of the morning – but no, you would have to add the word 'opening', as Milton did: dawn was when the eyelids of the morn opened, but what then were those eyelids? The sky? When Shakespeare said, Shall I compare thee to a summer's day? he was inquiring about the feasibility of a perfectly straightforward comparison. But if he'd said, Shall I compare thee to a summer's frown, or something like that, then he would be using two figures of speech at once, comparing (in a simile) a person with a metaphor, which was what Job did with the leviathan – or rather it was really

God himself and not Job speaking in that chapter, though Job had also used the same phrase himself in chapter 3, when he cursed the day he was born and said, Let it look for light and have none, neither let it behold the eyelids of the morning. The fringed curtains of thine eye advance, And say what thou seest yond. That was *The Tempest*. Lift up your eyelashes it must mean. Prospero could be very pompous in his speech. Take out thy handkerchief and blow The twin-formed hollows of thy nose. But one couldn't imagine Prospero telling anybody to blow his nose in that or any other language. Some parts of the body seemed less suitable for poetry than others. Eyes and ears were always all right. Lend me your ears. Ope your eyes. But lend me your noses? No. The organ of smell always seemed slightly ridiculous. People held their noses when they encountered a bad smell, and the word 'smell' itself generally meant a bad smell – if you said someone smells you meant he smells unpleasantly. But a sight wasn't necessarily or even usually an unpleasant sight. The Bible sometimes took a risk and boldly confronted noses in serious vein. Noses have they, but they smell not (the Hebrew has it in the singular, A nose they have, but smell not) said the psalmist of idols of silver and gold. They were supposed to sniff incense and the smoke of sacrifices. But biblical sacrifices couldn't have been intended to placate God by pleasing his sense of smell? That was very heathenish, surely. True, God was said to possess all senses: he that made the eye, shall he not see? But not to indulge in them literally by leaning out of heaven and sniffing smoke and incense. The Homeric gods could take pleasure in that sort of thing, but surely not the true God. He was glad the prophets had been down on sacrifices. The psalmist, too, had said that the most acceptable sacrifice was humility. The sacrifices of God are a broken spirit: a broken and a contrite heart, O God, thou wilt not despise. That's what Kipling was thinking of when he wrote

> Still stands Thine ancient Sacrifice,
> An humble and a contrite heart.

The English word 'sacrifice' was very strange, from Latin *sacer*, holy, and *facere*, to do or make. Something made holy. Hebrew had several words, *korban*, an offering, *minchah*, a present or tribute, and *zevach*, a slaughtering. He preferred *minchah*. The best offering or present was surely song: the idea of God listening to a well-sung psalm, accompanied by harps and timbrels and other properly selected instruments, was curiously pleasing. Yes, the eye and the ear were superior to the nose. After all, there were visual arts of painting and sculpture and architecture and there was music, appealing respectively to the eye and the ear, but what fine art appealed to the nose? The perfumer wasn't in the same category as the artist or composer. A symphony of smells, opus 71 no. 6. The first movement is based on lavender water, and the strong opening whiffs introduce this theme immediately. Smellie was not an uncommon name in Scotland. There was William Smellie the printer who printed Burns's second volume of poems, and there were still Smellies in the Edinburgh telephone directory. Some of the boys at school claimed that they made a practice of ringing up a Smellie from a public telephone box and asking Hello, are you Smellie? And when the person on the other side answered yes, the boy said, What are you going to do about it? He wondered whether anybody actually did this, or whether it was just fantasy. He had no sympathy with practical jokes of this kind and never took part when, for example, boys tied a string between the handles of two opposite doors on the stairway of an entry to flats, rang both door bells, and waited to see the vain attempts made to open both doors simultaneously before running away. It seemed to him a mindless kind of cruelty. Boys could be cruel, and he knew he himself wasn't immune to mass cruelty as sometimes practised in the school playground. Loudon Grant, for example, was an odd boy, impulsive in speech and shambling in gait, whom the other boys enjoyed teasing. Once they surrounded him in the playground during the ten-minute-inty and chanted jeeringly at him until he grew so enraged he drew a pen-knife, opened it, and lunged at one of his tormentors. Our hero discovered to his horror that he himself was one of the ring of boys, and it was only the production of the pen-knife which suddenly made him realize how brutally they were behaving. He slunk away, ashamed, and never knew how the episode finished. It was not only that he knew he was different himself, and they might therefore turn on him some day. He had a sudden clear vision of the moral horror of finding pleasure in that savage kind of teasing. He could identify himself too readily with absolutely anybody; when talking to someone he would wonder what it was like to be that person being talked to by him and adjust the tone of his conversation to what he imagined the person's state of mind to be. It was because he knew he was so different that he could imagine himself to be practically anybody. If he expressed his own true self in these daily encounters with schoolfellows and others they would surely regard him with amazement. He was forced into role-taking, but though he could be good at it he was never really assured, always nervous about whether he was sounding like an ordinary person. At the same time he didn't want to be an ordinary person. He was both overpowered by his own identity and anxious to lose it. He read Rosaline Masson's *I Can Remember Robert Louis Stevenson*, which somehow found its way into the house, and identified himself immediately with the frail Edinburgh boy and the velvet-coated young man. He saw and felt late nineteenth-century Edinburgh, with its carriages and carts and men in frock coats and silk hats (there were still some around) and ladies with long sweeping skirts, and Queen Victoria's face on postage stamps, and boys playing in the Meadows with strange-looking knickerbockers and peaked caps. Rosaline Masson's father was David Masson who was professor of English at Edinburgh University when Henry John, his English master, was a student there. Once when they were reading Keats Henry John told the class how he remembered Professor Masson on a dark mid-winter afternoon reading them

> In drear-nighted December,
>   Too happy, happy tree,
> Thy branches ne'er remember
>   Their green felicity:
> The north cannot undo them,
> With a sleety whistle through them,
> Nor frozen thawings glue them
>   From budding at the prime.

It was so dark, Henry John said, that Professor Masson had to have the lamp lit on his reading desk as he read the poem. It was a gas lamp, and the professor clutched its base with his right hand as he read, swaying to and fro as he intoned the melancholy lines. He saw that picture so vividly, and never forgot it. A moment in the past remembered by one man and transmitted many years later to others. What made it so vivid, so permanent? He knew he would never read that poem again without a vision of Professor Masson clutching the gas lamp on that dark late-Victorian Edinburgh afternoon. It was a vision both melancholy and pleasing. Every past was a present once, and those who lived in past times never thought of their experiences as bound to become moments in history. Those young men sitting in Professor Masson's classroom at the end of the nineteenth century, confident surely in their sense of being on the crest of time, knew nothing of the Great War that was to come so soon in the next century and shatter their world.

When he thought of that shattering he thought of another reminiscence of another of his schoolmasters. This was Wee Paulin, the Greek master, who had studied Greek under the great Professor Mair at Edinburgh and used to regale the class with marvellous anecdotes about him. He would walk into the classroom and see a student in the front row reading *The Scotsman*. He would take the newspaper, open it, turn to the editorial and say: Well gentlemen, what shall I turn the editorial into? Thucydidean prose? Homeric hexameters? Pindarics? The class would choose, and Professor Mair would compose the translation on the spot, writing it up on the blackboard, demonstrating how he accepted or rejected a word, how he built up the style. He often did this when he was drunk. His students, said Wee Paulin, foreswore themselves on more than one occasion when there was an official university inquiry into his alleged drunkenness in the classroom: they all swore that they had never seen him the worse for liquor. But he did drink, for the loss of his students in the Great War had broken him, and he was never the same again. He wrote a poem about it, which Wee Paulin used to quote:

> As one who long has dwelt in alien places
>   Comes to his home at last,
> And mourns to miss the old and friendly faces
>   Known to the dear dead past,
> So when today I pace the old Quadrangle,
>   The old familiar 'Quad',
> I mourn the evil times that mar and mangle
>   All that is young and glad.
> Here, as it were but yesterday, were thronging
>   Students from every clime,
> Thinking the long, long, thoughts of youth, and longing
>   To speed the feet of Time;
> To-day there greet me only ghostly faces,
>   And only ghostly eyes
> Greet me, and ghostly hands, and all the place is
>   A home of memories.

Not a good poem, but a deeply felt one, and moving. Our hero saw so clearly the sad professor walking the deserted quadrangle where once his students had thronged that now lay dead in France or Flanders, and that image summed up for him what the Great War meant. In earlier and gayer mood Professor Mair had turned popular songs into Greek, and Wee Paulin taught them his version of Clementine, whose name had to be changed to Nausikaa before it would go into Greek. Mair also wrote a Greek epigram for the Edinburgh University War Memorial dedication, with the last line

chairet'. aei d' humon mnemones essometha.
Farewell. We shall always remember you.

He did, anyway, except when he stifled the memory with drink. There was a link between Professors Masson and Mair, because the latter translated into Greek Keats's In drear-nighted December. It began, *Makarizomen se, dendron,* We esteem you happy, tree. But Mair's finest poem, which Wee Paulin quoted so frequently that our hero could not help learning it by heart, was the one he wrote in 1908 on Hesiod. Somehow it evoked a Greek rural past that could be put beside the promise of seasonal renewal of the agricultural year that God made to Noah after the flood.

> Death at the headlands, Hesiod, long ago
> Gave thee to drink of his unhonied wine:
> Now Boreas cannot reach thee lying low,
> Nor Sirius' heat vex any hour of thine:
> The Pleiads rising are no more a sign
> For thee to reap, nor when they set to sow:
> Whether at morn or eve Arcturus shine
> To pluck the vine or prune thou canst not know.
>
> Vain now for thee the crane's autumnal flight,
> The loud cuckoo, the twittering swallow – vain
> The flow'ring scolumus, the budding trees,
> Seed-time and Harvest, Blossoming and Blight,
> The mid, the early, and the latter rain,
> And strong Orion and the Hyades.

Those plaintive numbers were too attractive, summer evening music that lulled to a pleasing melancholy, fatal to sport, to sociability, to energy of any sort. Forlorn, the very word is like a bell. One August evening when they were on holiday at Crail our hero was walking along the top of the West Braes and heard through an open window someone playing Chopin on the piano. To surrender to all that was to sink Lethewards, he knew. Rescue came in a way from his violin teacher, who had formed with others the Scottish String Quartet, and insisted on his coming to hear their concerts at the Oak Hall of Crawfords the bakers and restaurant. Persuading the rabbi to give him money for his solitary ticket he went by himself and sat at a little table where you were supposed to order coffee and biscuits in the interval, but he had no money for that. Slowly he built up a passion for the disciplined sound of the string quartet and became familiar with many classical examples of the form. He knew that art was formal, was disciplined, was subdued to the demands of the medium, and that saved him from too long self-indulgence: even the long poem he called Tristia after Ovid which he wrote in the three-penny school notebook he was able to buy from the janitor on the grounds that he needed it for his homework – even that poem of selfish brooding which he composed bit by bit in long summer evenings was written in Spenserian stanzas, and he took pride in manipulating them cunningly. Yes, art was difficult. Every Monday afternoon, when Miss Brown came for his piano lesson, he had to start with scales, a different key each lesson. First three octaves of the major (both hands), then the melodic minor, then the harmonic minor, the scales in each case being played first regularly then in contrary motion where the left and right hands went in opposite directions. Then the arpeggios, major, minor, dominant seventh and diminished seventh. Then the scale in thirds, then in sixths, then double thirds, then double sixths. All this required practice and concentration. But in the midst of it all he could relish the appeal of different sounds, different intervals, like the appealing augmented second of the harmonic minor. *Ars longa vita brevis*, observed his father, who was addicted to Latin and Greek tags. Oddly enough he would hardly ever quote Hebrew tags except in his sermons when he regularly cited Talmudic utterances prefaced by the remark, Our sages say. He would quote Shakespeare to Barmitzvah boys: This above all, to thine own self be true, thou canst not then be false to any man. But wasn't Polonius a silly old fuddyduddy? Were we meant to take his precepts seriously? Our hero worried about this, for he found this particular precept memorably phrased and surely right, yet there was something wrong with the speech in which it occurred. Absent thee from felicity awhile. He jocosely maintained to his schoolmates that Felicity was a girl's name and that Horatio was being advised to stay away from her:

> The girl, Horatio, 's really not your style.
> Absent thee from Felicity awhile.

Like the poet who protested that he needed to love two girls if he was to be able to love one properly:

> I could not love thee dear so much
> Loved I not Honor more.

Faith, Hope, Charity, Constance, were all girls' names. There should be male names like Fortitude and Valour. Frailty thy name is woman. Didn't he mean, Woman thy name is Frailty? Henry John used to quote

> My name is Norval. On the Grampian hills
> My father feeds his flocks

as an example of a ludicrous opening of a play. But it didn't seem to him especially ludicrous, and he felt rather sorry for John Home whose play was universally tittered at without anybody's ever reading it. He himself never read it. Whaur's yer Wullie Shakespeare noo? an enthusiastic Scot had triumphantly called from the gallery on the play's first London production. Mrs Sarah Siddons, when visiting the Edinburgh theatre, always spent an occasional afternoon with Mr and Mrs Home at their neat little house in North Hanover Street, and of one of these visits Sir Adam Fergusson was wont to relate the following anecdote: They were seated at early dinner, attended by Home's old man-servant John, when the host asked Mrs Siddons what liqueur or wine she preferred to drink. 'A little porter,' replied the tragedy queen, in her usually impressive voice; and John was despatched to procure what he thought was required. But a considerable time elapsed, to the surprise of those at table, before steps were heard in the outer lobby, and John re-appeared, panting and flushed, exclaiming, 'I've found ane, mem! he's the least I could get!' and with these words he pushed in a short, thick-set Highlander, whose leaden badge and coil of rope betokened his profession, but who seemed genuinely bewildered on finding himself in a gentleman's dining-room, surveyed by the curious eyes of one of the grandest women that ever walked the earth. The truth flashed first upon Mrs Siddons, who, unwonted to laugh, was for once overcome by a sense of the ludicrous, and broke forth into something like shouts of mirth; but Mrs Home, we are told, had not the least chance of ever understanding it.

History does not recount what the Highland porter did when the truth burst upon him that he had been mistaken for a drink. Perhaps it never did. They were ticked off at school for using the word burst in the popular Edinburgh sense of broken. The word implied breaking with some sudden or explosive force, they were told, not just any sort of breaking. We were the first that ever burst Into that silent sea. Was that explosive? Sudden, perhaps. Nunky Shaw, one of the Latin masters, was fond of pointing out that in Latin you would have to say 'we first burst'. Nos primi . . . So then it would have to be

Nos primi irrupimus
In illud mare silens.

That fitted no recognizable Latin scansion, but he liked it. Another Latin master lent him a copy of *The Wandering Scholars* by Helen Waddell soon after it came out in 1927, and he was delighted to find there and in her book of *Medieval Latin Lyrics*, which came out a couple of years later and which he hastened to get from the library, forms and sentiments in Latin verse that were quite different from the classics. It amused him to turn English poems literally into Latin, especially comic ones. The time has come, the walrus said, to talk of many things. *Tempus advenit, dixit valrus, multis de rebus dicere, de calceis, de navibus, de cera, de brassicis, de regibus.* He found somewhere the report of a speech in Latin given by the British owner of a yacht which had been driven by bad weather into an Icelandic port: the owner was entertained to dinner by an Icelandic ecclesiastical dignitary, and as their only common language was Latin, he made an after-dinner speech in that language beginning, *Insolitus ut sum ad publicum loquendum.* A ludicrous construction. There were two words for unaccustomed in Latin, *insolitus* and *insolens*, and the latter could also mean insolent. How? Soleo, I am accustomed. In-solens, not accustomed, unusual. But why should unusual behaviour be insolent behaviour? Solent ought to mean accustomed: some people are solent to public speaking, others are insolent to public speaking. The Solent was the stretch of water between the Isle of Wight and the mainland. The small dog swam into the water off the Isle of Wight: it was an insolent puppy. But if the dog was unaccustomed to swimming? It would be doubly insolent.

The isles of Greece the isles of Greece where burning Sappho loved and sung. Shouldn't it be sang? And he didn't think much of burning as an adjective. Was Byron trying to find a more vivid word than ardent? Heather was a girl's name, but suppose you said

The Kyles of Bute, the Kyles of Bute,
Where burning Heather loved and sung!

That would hardly be an opening to set the heather on fire. With passion I'm burning with love I am yearning, O do not reject me I can't abide spurning; My feelings are churning, at last I am learning the meaning of burning and yearning and churning. You will not accept me? My suit I'm adjourning. I'll not be returning. (He missed out discerning, concerning, sojourning.) To press a suit had two quite different meanings, to make advances to a woman and – well, to press a suit. Presumably you could do the former better if you had first had the latter done: your chances in pressing your suit would be greater if you had already had your suit pressed. With knife-edge creases down the front of the trousers. The way to make more money out of a single pound note is simply to fold it: when you unfold it you find it in-creases. Pound was a unit of money and also a unit of weight. And a verb, to pound something. Perhaps instead of saying to beat time you could say to pound notes? Two pound notes. Take care of the pence and the pounds will take care of themselves. Penny wise pound foolish. Too many cooks spoil the broth but many hands make light work. All hands on deck. He had a vision of a row of sailors standing on their hands with their feet in the air. Handsome is as handsome does. He thought that a handsome cab was a carriage that made a brave show until he discovered that it was spelt hansom. He once saw a hansom cab when he was very small, and he saw plenty of ordinary horse cabs. He had been in them too and loved the sensation of standing on the springy metal step to enter and the mixed smell of leather and horse. What is the difference between a chestnut horse and a horse chestnut? Are you hoarse? Neigh! Oh you are horse. Fifty thousand horse and foot going to Table Bay. A horse's height is measured in hands. A horse of how many hands? No hands, only four feet. Then if fifty thousand horse and foot are going to Table Bay there will really be two hundred thousand foot, four for each horse. For each bay horse. But of course if the foot are separate from the horse they will just be boots boots boots boots marching up and down again, with no bodies attached. Marching in rhythm, metrical feet.

> It's funny the way in which things can be put.
> Now isn't this rather neat?
> An army consists of horse and foot
> But never of horses and feet.

And of course an army marches on its stomach. But what about the rear? And those who ride in the van? But the general rides ahead on his doughty war horse, his hors de combat. Com-bat, battering together. Come into the garden Maud for the black bat night has flown. He found that poem in the *Golden Treasury* and he loved its rhythms and imagery and mood – but why was the night a bat? Twinkle twinkle little bat, how I wonder what you're at. Like a tea-tray in the sky. He once wrote an essay on the moon for Henry John and said that sometimes he thought it flapped in the sky. This bizarre observation was not appreciated, and he couldn't himself tell why he had an image of the moon flapping, for it was absurd enough and he never saw it that way again. As for bats, he had never seen any (except the cricket kind) but he would be quite prepared to believe that they looked like tea-trays in the sky. And wherever I went was my poor dog Tray. When he first heard this he thought the poet was speaking of a dog-tray, like a dog-sleigh, and he envisaged a large tray mounted on runners and pulled by stout dogs. Then he discovered that Tray was a common name for a dog, like Fido but with less apparent reason. With a cargo of Tyne coal, road-rail, pig-lead, firewood, iron-ware, and cheap tin trays. He loved that dirty British coaster, saw it clearly in his mind's eye looking like one of the trawlers that came into Anstruther harbour. The quinquireme of Nineveh was just words, a poet's trick that's all, but the coaster was real and splendid. Not that he was sure what pig-lead was. He'd heard of pig-iron, but pig-lead? Never mind, it was clearly some dirty industrial lumps. A little pig was a piglet, a little island was an islet, but a cutlet? Not a little cut. A martlet? Not a little mart or market. A violet? Not a small viol, which was a medieval musical instrument. But why violoncello and not violincello? A diminutive was not the same as an abbreviation, for generally the diminutive form was the longer. Cab was short for cabriolet but didn't mean a small cabriolet. Taxi was short for taxi-meter. It was also short for taxicab. So the full word was really taximetercabriolet. Boy, call me a taximetercabriolet. All right, you're a taximetercabriolet. He had heard of taxi dancers, girls who danced with paying customers in cabarets. In taxicabarets? Surely the girls should be called cab dancers.

> All night have the roses heard
>   The flute, violin, bassoon;
> All night has the casement jessamine stirred
>   To the dancers dancing in tune;
> Till a silence fell with the waking bird,
>   And a hush with the setting moon.

Ah, that was beautiful. Some day he would fall in love with a girl that way with music and roses and moonlight. He had to look up jessamine, though, and found it was the same as jasmine, any of the fragrant-flowered shrubs constituting the oleaceous genus Jasminum. So Tennyson simply meant the jasmine by the window. That was a nice phrase too, the jasmine by the window, though it wouldn't fit into the pattern of this poem. I passed by your window and marked with one eye How the owl and the panther were sharing a pie. The little window where the sun Came peeping in at morn. Henry John once mentioned Barrie's book *A Window in Thrums* and he thought that this was an improbable title and he must have misheard. Surely it was really *A Widow in Thrums*?

> Said the desolate widow of Thrums:
> 'I sit here and twiddle my thumbs.
> > From early till late
> > I just sit here and wait
> But nobody, nobody comes.'

He tried to work in the widow by the window, but he couldn't think of a rhyme for window, except the blowing of the wind O, which was feeble. In fact the -ind sound in wind and window was most unusual. The verb wind was pronounced like mind, kind, find. That was why poets were allowed to pronounce wind (the kind that blows) like find, for otherwise it would be impossible to rhyme it. O wind, If winter comes can spring be far behind? That was what was known as a rhetorical question. If the wind had answered no, the poem would have ended very oddly indeed.

> Dear sir, do you mind if I make a suggestion?
> Don't answer! 'Twas but a rhetorical question.

Demander à quelqu'un de faire quelque chose. But to ask someone to do something and to ask a question were really two quite different meanings. *Peto* was different from *rogo*. Peto was also one of Falstaff's pals in *Henry IV*. Because he was always asking for things? Or was it just a form of Peter? This matter of rhetorical questions, though, was interesting, for you could also have rhetorical instructions, which could if taken literally produce results just as ridiculous as anything that could happen to a rhetorical question. Mr Carew, would you please tell me where Jove bestows when June is past the fading rose? Mr Carew, Mr Carew, I'm asking you a question. Please Mr Carew, where does Jove bestow when June is past the fading rose? Mr Carew turns impatiently to his questioner:

> Ask me no more where Jove bestows,
> When June is past, the fading rose.

One, two, three, four, Mr Longfellow, life is but an empty dream. Five, o sadly five six seven eight, life is but an empty dream. Mr Longfellow is nettled:

> Tell me not in mournful numbers,
> Life is but an empty dream.

Mr Clough, it hurts me to say this, but the fact is that the struggle nought availeth and the labour and the wounds are vain. That's the simple truth, Mr Clough, sad though it is. The enemy faints not, nor faileth, and as things have been, things remain. No no, Mr Clough replies:

> Say not the struggle nought availeth,
> The labour and the wounds are vain,
> The enemy faints not, nor faileth,
> And as things have been things remain.

It is safer to begin a poem with a positive rather than a negative command. Arise! Awake! Avaunt! Come into the garden Maud. The poet is then not contradicting what nobody has said, and even if the reader wants to imagine somebody contradicting what the poet has said this doesn't spoil the poem. Though it once struck him that the words 'I won't' spoken in a Yiddish accent sounded very like avaunt. Vill you come into ze garden Maud? Avaunt! Vell, if you vaunt you vaunt. I vos only esking. Will ye no come back again? Well friends, I'll make every effort but on the whole it seems unlikely. Is this the face that launched a thousand ships? Was it a vision or a waking dream? And is this Yarrow? And shall Trelawny die? Ask me no questions and I'll tell you no lies. Sticks and stones will break my bones but words can never hurt me. Ah but they can though, words can hurt very much. There were masters at school who caused more suffering with their sarcastic tongues than others did with the tawse. The word is mightier than the tawse. What power these schoolmasters had to sneer and buffet, what a strange thing that for so much of the year all children should be wholly at their mercy. Yet they could also be friendly and helpful. Billy Williams the maths master once told them a rhyme for finding π to dozens and dozens of decimal places. It began

> Sir, I send a rhyme excelling
> In purest truth and noble spelling,

and the idea was, you counted the letters of the words: 3.14159265358. He couldn't remember the rest of the verse, but the last line was

> Though Doctor Johnson fulminate.

Billy Williams also told them that algebra was from two Arabic words ALJEBR WALMUKABALA, which he wrote up in capitals on the blackboard. And Johnny Horne in chemistry told them that Beecham's pills were made from breadcrumbs and Mexican aloes and that soap was largely sodium stearate and that stearic acid was $C_{17}H_{35}COOH$. And Nunky Shaw in Latin couldn't help sending out small showers of moisture when he talked which fell on the boys in the front seat, but he was considerate about it and regularly took out his handkerchief and wiped the faces of the affected boys saying, Did I wet you my boy? I'm sorry my boy. And Boozy Pearson (so called because it was alleged that he had once been observed entering a pub) used to send a boy out at the lunch inty to buy him a mutton pie at Chirnside's. Our hero found the humanness of this very touching. The boys made up a fanciful compassionate legend about Boozy Pearson, that he was a lonely widower who had taken to drink after his wife died. The boys rarely bore malice against their teachers, and liked to imagine them in private life acting like ordinary people. But was there such a thing as an ordinary person? Sometimes he thought of everybody except himself as somehow banded together as ordinary while he himself was odd, and at other times he was overcome with a sense of the mystery of people, the impenetrability of their real selves. What was this or that person REALLY? It was the same with history: what REALLY happened when Harold was killed at Hastings, what was Robert the Bruce REALLY like, how did Charles I REALLY think and feel? One could never know the answers. Perhaps there were no answers, no single answers anyway, and everything was a matter of how you looked at it. For that matter what was he himself REALLY like? He was dozens of different people at different times, and as for the different reflections he had in the eyes of other people – they were innumerable, and impossible to assess. He read a story once about a scientist who after years of research at last succeeded in inventing a special kind of time machine, which could pick up the speech of men who lived in the distant past. By setting it in a special way, for time and place, he could even pick up the words of a particular historical character. People urged him to pick up the actual words of Jesus, and after much endeavour he announced that he was able to do it and that he would transmit the words over a kind of wireless set. People assembled in enormous excitement when the time came for the words of Jesus to be recovered and transmitted. When they came they were a far away sound of wholly unintelligible words in Aramaic.

He was at the same time obsessed by history and sceptical of it. He remembered reading in a Latin reader a sentence attributed to Cicero: *nescire autem ea quae antequam natus sis acciderent semper esse puerum*, not to know what happened before you were born is to remain always a child (but why *puerum*? shouldn't it be nominative after the verb to be? it must be because of the impersonal nature of the construction). He thought that a very impressive statement. He saw himself and his own age as the surface of a huge iceberg floating in the sea of time. But you could never really examine the submerged part, only guess what it was like from certain signs and sounds. And ice mast-high came floating by, as green as emerald. If the visible part was mast-high and the invisible part, he was told in geography, was much much larger than the visible, what an enormous area of iceberg must be under water. Iceland and Greenland. Greenberg was a common Jewish name, as were other names ending in berg. A Scotsman and a Jew were once arguing about which nation had done more for civilization, and the Jew seemed to be winning until the Scotsman said: Ah, but Jews have contributed nothing to Polar exploration. The Jew, however, had the last word. What, he said, is Iceberg a Presbyterian name? By Greenland's icy mountains, the hymn which Spooner had quoted as By Iceland's greasy mountains. Spooner was a real person, Henry John had told them, and still alive, though an old man. The Reverend William Archibald Spooner, warden of New College, Oxford, was addicted to the accidental transposition of initial sounds or syllables of words in a context, which thus came to be known as spoonerisms. He suffered from weak eyesight due to albinoism. Did he eat with a runcible spoon? Our hero was astonished to find that runcible was a real word, not just a nonsense word invented by Edward Lear. It was more like a curved fork with three prongs, for taking pickles out of a jar. Was it really a form of rounceval, coming originally from Roncesvalles where Charlemain with all his peerage fell by Fontarabbia? What then was a runcible hat? The kind of hat that Roland wore? And a runcible cat? No no, he rejected the pickle-fork and Roncesvalles. Runcible had its own mysterious meaning, impossible to suggest by any other word. Lear had known nothing of pickle-forks, he was just using a Leary word.

> One two three O'Leary,
> Four five six O'Leary,
> Seven eight nine O'Leary,
> Ten O'Leary postman.

Or was it a-Leary, not O'Leary, that the girls sang in the Meadows as they skipped? Who was that Leary or O'Leary anyway? Not

Edward Leary. Not King Leary. Not Stevenson's Leerie. And what was the postman doing? The chant went on:

> Open the gate and let us through sir,
> We are children home from school sir.

He always associated these lines with the level crossing at Leven, where they had twice spent a summer holiday, once in a house on Wagon Road right beside the level crossing. He used to watch the Fife Coast Express go by, not very fast because it had just left the station, and it was wonderful to see it crossing over on the points as it came off the loop line that ran by the platform to go on to the single line that ran between Leven and Lundin Links. On Mondays, though, there was a non-stop train from London that roared through on its way to St Andrews. CRAIL VIA COAST the daily trains had on a curved sign stuck in front of the engine, white letters on a red background. Via was an ablative, his father was careful to point out, because it meant by way of. Via media was the middle way that Queen Elizabeth thought up to avoid extremes in religious affairs, pleasing Catholics by calling herself supreme governor not supreme head of the Church and pleasing Protestants by having only 39 instead of 42 articles. They had to make a list in parallel columns: Pleased Catholics by and Pleased Protestants by, and then write at the bottom, Result: no civil war. The Hebrew for way was *derech*, and *derech eretz*, the way of the country, meant the ordinary customs and habits of the secular British society in which they lived. The rabbi was one of those Jewish leaders who advocated *torah im derech eretz*, the Law together with the secular customs of normal gentile life, a via media too in its way, or a *baba metzia*, middle gate, but that was really Aramaic not Hebrew. The Hebrew for via media would be *derech memutsa*, a course steered between extremes. This middle wisdom accosted him from all directions. *Meden agan*, nothing too much, they were told in Greek: that was one of the two slogans written above the entrance to the Delphic oracle. The other was *gnothi seauton*, know thyself. And they had it again in Latin, Horace's *aurea mediocritas*. *Auream quisquis mediocritatem diligit*, whoever loves the golden mean, and the boys were left in no doubt that the advice was meant for them too. Golden mean was a bit odd, though, because he thought of silver as the mean between lead and gold. Gold was an extreme. If he had been choosing the casket in Portia's house in Belmont he would have chosen the silver one, showing a decent respect for the middle way, *argentea mediocritas*, the silver mean. Tell me where is fancy bread. Tell me what doth silver mean. His mother told him that when she was a girl at school they used to say, Tell me where is fancy bread? In the baker's shop. Probably in an Edinburgh baker's shop at that, for Edinburgh was marvellously rich in all kinds of fancy tea-bread and had long been so. Looking back in 1825 the eighty-year-old Henry Mackenzie remembered the tea-breads of his boyhood. 'When I was a boy', he wrote, 'tea was the meal of ceremony and we had fifty-odd kinds of tea-bread. One Scott made a little fortune by his milk-bakes. His shop in Forrester's Wynd (where my father also had a house) was surrounded at five o'clock by a great concourse of servant maids, – at that time there was scarce a footman except in families of the first distinction. A similar reputation was enjoyed by the rolls of one Symington, a baker of Leith.'

One Scott, one Symington, a minimal kind of fame but fame nevertheless. A Mr Wilkinson, a clergyman. Border fighters used to rush into battle shouting their names prefixed by the indefinite article. A Scott! A Scott! A Wilkinson! A primrose by a river's brim! A brimrose by a river's prim! Prunes and prisms! An onward rush of charging men shouting slogans. Here we come gadarene swine in May. Are you the swineherd? No, I'm the swine gaderer. Gadzooks! And of Gad he said: Blessed be he that enlargeth Gad. He dwelleth as a lioness, and teareth the arm, yea, the crown of the head. Gad like his brother Asher was the son of Jacob and of Zilpah, Leah's handmaid. Hath not a Jew hands, hath not a patriarch handmaids? Very puzzling behaviour. Be good sweet maid and let who will be clever. Let Hugh Will be clever. Hugh Wilby. High Hereford. What thou wouldst highly, that wouldst thou holily. Holily? Ho lily of the valley! How do you grow lily? Slowlily slowlily. With silver bells and cockle shells and pretty maids all in a row. He was never able to visualize that line, it always remained just a jingle. Like she sells sea-shells on the sea shore. But in fact he saw her selling her sea-shells much more clearly than he saw bells and cockle shells and pretty maids in the garden. She had a tray strapped to her, like the uniformed boys who sold chocolates and cigarettes at Waverley Station, and on it were empty mussel shells with their blue-and-white glinting linings, and buckies and limpets. The tongues of large mussels were best for bait if you were fishing from the harbour wall, but limpets would do at a pinch: you had to squeeze the soft bit out and it was hard to get it to stick on the hook. In the rock pools were grannies and peoches hiding under stones and behind curtains of seaweed. If you kept quite still by a pool you could see them coming out; and crabs walked, slowly and clumsily, and soldier crabs came half out of their shells and moved about with their houses. Even limpets would loosen their hold on the rock, only to tighten it again at once if you touched them. It was his ambition to find a large hairy-legged edible crab, a partan, and sell it to a fishmonger for extra pocket-money. He never found one though: it was always the ordinary green variety, useless enough creatures though he had an affection for them. He would let the very small ones run up his hand and arm. They were too small to nip with their nippers and only gave a not unpleasant tickling sensation. The tiniest baby ones were like insects as they scurried about. The sea anemones were rather frightening with their sticky tentacles that waved in the water and then closed in over living things: when they were left high and dry by the receding tide their tentacles disappeared and they stayed round and smooth like brown lumps of jelly until the tide came in again. I must down to the seas again, to the lonely sea and the sky. They sang that in the school choir to a beautifully sad melody which slowed down to a lingering interval at the end of each verse. And a grey mist on the sea's face and a grey dawn breaking. At night he would listen to the hush-hush of the breaking waves, more continuous and more melancholy than the sound you heard when you were actually on the beach and heard each splashing wave-break separately, followed by its spreading seething sound. He would build whole canal systems with bridges and basins and wait for the tide to come up and fill them:

> My holes were empty like a cup,
> In every hole the sea came up,
> Till it could come no more.

He would build railway systems too, that would cross the canals on bridges or go underneath in tunnels. There were stations as well, some with platforms on each side and the two lines running between and others with the platform in the middle and the two lines going round different sides. There was always a bridge at a station: cross the railway by the bridge only: and a little booking office of hard-packed damp sand. But best of all were junctions and points. You could shift the points with a small piece of drift-wood. If you built the railway sloping downwards towards the sea you could use a golf ball as a train and send it to the right or the left or straight on according to the way you placed the piece of wood. If you were lucky enough to find a long straight narrow piece of wood you could build a wide bridge supported at intervals by sand pillars, and you could make your railway cross the Firth of Forth. But the call of the rock pools was stronger even than that. Water was best. *Ariston men hudor*, as Pindar said in the only phrase from him that he knew for they never read Pindar at school but the Greek master would quote that phrase continually. The Hebrew word for water was always plural and he could understand why. *Al mei menuchot yenahaleni*, he leadeth me by the waters of restfulness.

Yes, he found water restful, even rain, if it dropped gently from heaven and didn't pour down tumultuously. I hear lake water lapping with low sounds by the shore. They had to learn Innisfree by heart, and he liked especially to recite the concluding lines with the three heavy slow words, deep heart's core, falling like three stones dropped into a pool. How different from the noisy poem by Mrs Hemans which they had learned in the junior school and which he used to recite with enormous energy: The breaking waves dashed HIGH On a stern and rock bound coast. It was about the landing of the Pilgrim Fathers in America, where they sought, as the loud final line proclaimed, FREEDOM TO WORSHIP GOD. He liked that kind of shouting poetry then, but soon came to prefer poems like Break, break, break, on thy cold grey stones, O Sea. He knew that shore, he knew those cold grey stones, they were on a deserted beach between Granton and Portobello glimpsed one winter afternoon from the top of a tramcar. He associated it with that marvellous line in the twenty-third book of the Iliad where Achilles after the death of Patroclus walked by the loud-sounding sea

> *en katharo hothi kumat' ep' eïonos kluzeskon*
> in an open place where the waves plashed upon the shore.

Once late at night when they were on holiday in Crail he went by himself to the beach so that he could walk alone by the sounding waters reciting that line. One of his earliest memories was of his father reading to him, Far and few, far and few, Are the lands where the Jumblies live, and those lines haunted him in the same way, infinitely melancholy, yet pleasing. Ultima Thule. That was supposed to be the Orkneys – or was it the Shetlands? Far and few islands. He knew them only on the map on the classroom wall, which showed the Shetlands so far north that they had to be put in a separate inset. He liked maps, he liked to trace rivers from their source to the sea, and whenever he saw a real river or stream he wanted desperately to follow it all the way up to its source and then back and all the way down to its mouth. Even the weariest river winds somewhere safe to sea. He wished he could float down a river on a raft like Tom Sawyer and Huckleberry Finn. They had Mark Twain's book for home reading in English. He never quite understood what these home reading books were for. They were down on the list of books they had to buy and he always read them, but they were never mentioned in school and nobody ever asked questions about them. Another of the home reading books was *Penny Plain* by O. Douglas, who was John Buchan's sister. He liked its picture of tea-time fireside cosiness in a Scottish country town in winter, and that was the only impression of the book that stayed with him for any length of time. He was told that the town in the book was really Peebles, which he visited the year of his Barmitzvah, when they spent their summer holiday not far away at Romanno Bridge, the only time it was not spent beside the sea. Their house was right beside a river though, the Lyne Water, a tributary of the Tweed, and there he caught his first trout, racing proudly home to give it to his mother to cook for his supper. But he had not counted on what it would actually look like on the plate, with its dead cooked eye dully reproachful: he did not enjoy eating it at all. Ever after that if he was given a whole trout to eat he at once cut off the head and put it out of sight. He could not bear to see a fish flapping in agony either and always hastened to put it out of its misery with a swift bang on the head. Yet he loved catching them, and the feel of one at the end of his line was a uniquely thrilling experience. There was no interest in any stretch of water that did not have fish in it. It was the fish within that made water a living part of the countryside. Minnows and sticklebacks were better than nothing, but trout were best of all. He once saw a man catch a pike in Duddingston Loch, a long fierce-looking fish, but he had no ambition to pursue a monster of that kind. One morning at Romanno Bridge he found a young man fishing with a laughing and chattering girl clinging to his arm. They struck him as an inordinately silly couple, and he hoped the girl would frighten away the fish so that the young man would catch nothing. But he did catch a rather small trout, and to our hero's horror calmly took it off the hook and put it live into his jacket pocket before casting again. The girl made no protest. He would have liked to see them both fall into the water, but eventually they made off upstream without mishap, the girl still laughing and chattering. Two weeks later he was in the synagogue chanting the day's portion of the law and of the prophets to prove to the assembled company that, having celebrated his thirteenth birthday, he was in the eyes of Jewish law a man, responsible for fulfilling all his religious obligations.

IO

IT WAS EASY to rise early in the summer time, when light came and the birds began to sing many hours before the normal time for rising. Walter Scott, however, got up early all the year round, and had finished most of his day's writing by breakfast time. Our hero knew well the Scott house in George Square, where Walter had lived with his parents until his marriage. After that his Edinburgh house was at 39 North Castle Street, and he lived there when the court was in session. Our hero knew all about his routine in Castle Street, for the boys at school who wanted to compete for the annual Scott essay prize had to read John Buchan's little biography, *The Man and the Book*, an abbreviation for young people of his substantial biography of Scott, as well as a set novel. But he went further, and got Lockhart's *Life* out of the Carnegie library volume by volume, sinking himself with relaxed pleasure in that discursive account of Scott's life and habits. The first question in the exam for the Scott essay prize was to describe a typical day at either Abbotsford or Castle Street during Scott's most flourishing period. He chose Castle Street. Breakfast was his chief meal. Before that came he had gone through the severest part of his day's work, and he then set to with the zeal of Crabbe's Squire Tovell –

And laid at once a pound upon his plate.

(He had no idea who Crabbe's Squire Tovell was.) No foxhunter ever prepared himself for the field by more substantial appliances. His table was always provided, in addition to the usual plentiful delicacies of a Scotch breakfast, with some solid article, on which he did most lusty execution – a round of beef – a pasty, such as made Gil Blas's eyes water – or, most welcome of all, a cold sheep's head, the charms of which primitive dainty he so gallantly defended against the disparaging sneers of Dr Johnson and his bear-leader. A huge brown loaf flanked his elbow, and it was placed upon a wooden trencher, that he might cut and come again with the bolder knife. What a picture! A cold sheep's head was an unthinkable article of diet at any time, let alone for breakfast. What had Dr Johnson said about it? He knew about the bear-leader, Boswell, for Henry John frequently strayed into anecdotes about Boswell and Johnson when they were supposed to be reading something else. He knew Johnson's more unjustifiable insult to Scottish food, his definition of oats as a grain which in England is generally given to horses but in Scotland supports the people, and Lord Elibank's reply, Ah, but where will you find such horses and such people? No round of beef still less the unthinkable sheep's head on the rabbi's breakfast table. Porridge was the main breakfast course in his household, first Quaker Oats, then, as a result of the persuasions of a Fife grocer when they were on holiday, Scott's Porage Oats, which seemed more genuinely Scottish, so that ever afterwards he thought of porridge as English and porage as Scots. Porage oats and forage oats. Hot porage with very cold milk (or cream on special occasions): the job was to keep the milk separate so that it wouldn't be warmed by the porage and the porage wouldn't be cooled, for the contrast in temperatures was of the essence. It had to be stirred properly when being cooked, for lumps in porage were intolerable, absolutely sick-making. Not too thick, not too thin, the proper kind of porage required great art in preparation. The benighted English, he was told, put sugar on their porridge, a revolting habit, for sweet oatmeal was a vomitable thought, like putting jam on oatcakes, which clearly demanded cheese. Sugar was all right on dry cereal, which they had on shabbos mornings when it would have been improper to cook anything for breakfast: post toasties or grape nuts or force (high o'er the fence leapt Sunny Jim, Force was the food that somethinged him). But all other days began with Scott's porage oats. Titus Oates seemed to him a very odd name. No wonder the man was an impostor. Tight as oats.

> Alone she cuts and binds the grain
> So tightly, there's a local sayin',
> 'As tight as oats'.

Then there was Captain Oates, who walked out into the snow and died. And ancient shepherds piped on oaten reeds:

> *Tityre, tu patulae recubans sub tegmine fagi*
> *silvestrem tenui Musam meditaris avena.*

Tityrus, you lying under the shade of a spreading beech tree cultivate the rustic Muse on a thin oaten straw. But the note in the school edition of Virgil's *Bucolics* explained that as an oat-straw could not be made into a musical instrument *avena* must be used for a reed or something of the sort. What Scottish wag was it who applied that second line to the Scots, rendering it as: You cultivate the muses on a little oatmeal? Porage makes poets. Not Juvenal's *indignatio* but *avenae puls facit versum*. Wee Paulin told them that *fagus* didn't mean a beech tree, as all the dictionaries said, but a Spanish chestnut, and this had been conclusively proved by Professor Richmond of Edinburgh University. He carefully wrote Spanish chestnut not beech in the margin of his little blue text (edited with notes and vocabulary for the use of schools by T. E. Page, M.A., LITT.D.), and added, as proved by Professor Richmond. But one day Wee Paulin came into the classroom saying, Boys, Professor Richmond has re-canted. I have just heard that the other week he addressed his students in Second Ordinary Latin on the subject, saying that he had been persuaded by a South American botanist that the Spanish chestnut was not domiciled in Italy until long after Virgil's time and that *fagus* meant a beech tree after all. It was a grave disappointment to have to return to the conventional view after more than a year of secret superior knowledge. Fagus. He knew from school stories that in English schools the big boys made servants of the little boys, whom they called fags. A revolting practice. He would never have stayed in such a school. A fag was also a cigarette, for some reason. No one in his family smoked cigarettes but like most of the other boys at school he collected cigarette cards. He acquired them by all sorts of barter and exchange, sometimes by begging in the streets from any-one he saw opening a new packet of cigarettes, sometimes by the sheer luck of finding on the pavement an empty packet with a card in. And of course you could win them in the special cigarette card game you played by dropping your card down from a fixed place on the wall and winning the other cards it covered when it fell. There were all kinds of series, the largest being Do You Knows, which were educational as well, for they imparted a great variety of information. General knowledge it was called, and they had had occasional periods set aside for this subject in the junior school. They had also had weekly periods on currenty vents. Currenty vents meant recent news, and on Fridays when this period occurred he would try and glean something from *The Scotsman* before going to school. He re-membered his father once talking animatedly about the resignation of Loy George, a name that figured frequently in his conversation. This was when he was away down in the junior school and they had a lady teacher. Does anybody know why Loy George resigned as prime minister? she asked. He had heard his father say that morning that Loy George had resigned because he had no alternative, so he put up his hand and said, Because he had no alternative. Very good said Miss Douglas, but he still had no idea why Loy George resigned. He was presumably resigned to resigning. Resigned? Signed again, re-signed. I've already signed that. Never mind, re-sign it. I'll sign it too, there'll be signer and co-signer. Seigneur. He once looked at a French Bible and was surprised to find that God was le Seigneur. Not the signer but the sir, the sire, the lord. Signer and co-signer, sine and cosine. Sine and cosine are as it were cousins. Fair cousin, you debase your princely knee to make the base earth proud with kissing it. Fair cosine and his tall scraggy father auld lang sine. Do not cozen me, cousin. I cozen you not, coz, 'cos I am an honourable man. A man of the world, a cosmopolitan. The Greeks were the first cosmographers as they were the first geometers and physicists. Of the Greek scientists he knew about Archimedes principally. Heureka, he said in his bath, though it was generally printed Eureka without the rough breathing. Heurisko heureso heureka heuron, 2nd aorist heuromen, to find. There was still a lot of Greek in mathematics and the sciences, not only alphas and betas and so on but surprising letters like mu, the coefficient of friction. They did inclined planes in dynamics, but he was not very good at calculations involving balls rolling down them. When faced with such problems unlike the planes he didn't feel inclined. The Greeks however didn't know about logarithms which were invented by John Napier who lived at Merchiston Castle. In 1614 Napier dedicated his book of logarithms to Prince Charles. Log tables were the only books they were allowed to bring to exams. It was funny to talk about logs in maths: he thought of Mrs Leo Hunter's delightful piece, the Ode to an Expiring Frog:

> Can I view thee panting, lying
> On thy stomach, without sighing;
> Can I unmoved see thee dying
> On a log,
> Expiring frog!

They used to collect tadpoles in jars in Dunsapie Loch and keep them in a sunken basin in the back garden until they turned into frogs. At first the tiny frogs still had their tadpoles' tails but they gradually lost them. That was nature at work, but nature was best of all in the early morning by the seaside or in the country. The first day of their holiday in Kilrenny he and his brother crept out of the house very early before anybody else was up and explored the common behind the house. Everything was quiet, and they could hear the burn rippling along to join the sea a few miles further down. There were no trout in that burn as far as they could discover yet he was reminded vividly of it and of the early morning frolic on Kilrenny common when he read later at school in *A Book of Verse for Boys and Girls* edited by J. C. Smith that poem by James Hogg:

> Where the pools are bright and deep,
> Where the grey trout lies asleep,
> Up the river and over the lea,
> That's the way for Billy and me.

Morning adventure. O it's nice to get up in the morning when the sun begins to shine, at four or five or six o'clock in the guid auld summer time. Ah, but there was another side to it as well:

> But when the snaw is snawin and it's murky overhead,
> O it's nice to get up in the morning – but it's nicer to lie in
> your bed.

Sometimes on winter mornings his bed was so warm and the thought of encountering the cold room outside it so intolerable that he dressed under the bedclothes, with many contortions. Summer was the time for mornings. He would wake early though it had long been already light and listen as the milk carts came trot trot trotting by, the brisk step of the horses suggesting efficiency and eagerness. One after another they trotted in from country farms, milk traps they really were, with two churns mounted at the back. The sound would emerge from the distance, grow nearer and louder, then die away: trot trot trot trot TROT TROT TROT TROT TROT trot trot trot trot, and always before it had completely disappeared another one was heard arriving. It was a beautifully cheering sound, the day beginning again with happy routine, and he knew what Robert Louis Stevenson meant when he talked of listening to the comforting noise of the carts coming in in the early morning. But when he discovered Tennyson's cheerless and drizzly morning he knew that too:

> far away
> The noise of life begins again,
> And ghastly through the drizzling rain
> On the bald street breaks the blank day.

Yes, there were days like that. On certain cold wet winter mornings his street did indeed look bald and the day blank. Once waking in winter darkness thinking it was the middle of the night he heard the sound of voices shouting in the street. Terror seized him at these inexplicable midnight sounds, and then he heard the rattle of dishes downstairs and realized that although still quite dark it was morning and what he had heard was the shouting of rival paper boys and boys from the dairy delivering milk and morning rolls. He felt foolish for having been so scared. To every thing there is a season, said Koheleth the preacher, and a time to every purpose under the heaven. Right, right. Shouting voices in the street were terrifying in the middle of the night, but positively cheerful if you knew that it was morning. Top of the morning to you. The school morning was divided by a break of ten minutes, officially known as the ten minutes interval but always called by the boys the ten-minute inty, and everyone swarmed out on to the gravel playground in violent and aimless movement. Then there was the half-hour lunch inty, which divided the school day as a whole. And there were two wee five-minute inties in the course of the afternoon. You always went outside during an inty, even on the coldest day, and whatever the weather you never took your coat, for somehow being outside in an inty was not the same as being outside for any other purpose. The school playground abutted on to the Meadows, and the boys were not prevented from playing there in the lunch inty. If found indoors they were ejected, and if they were found in cold weather sitting on top of one of the large rectangular flat-topped radiators to warm their bottoms they were briskly whisked off with the horrid warning that if they continued to sit on radiators the base of their spine would become soft and they would have to spend the rest of their lives bent over like a hoop. Too much warmth was always suspect. Sitting over the fire with a book was a guilty joy, a wrong way to endure cold weather. One ought to be outside briskly walking, with a healthy glow not a fireside flush in one's cheeks. The cure for this ill is not to sit still or frowst with a book by the fire, but to take a large hoe and a shovel also and dig till you gently perspire. His mother recited Kipling's poem to him with conviction, and often during the Christmas holidays when he was huddled by the fire reading he was encouraged to go with his brother and sister on a sharp walk to Blackford Hill. It was a struggle to leave the fireside warmth, but once he was out and moving he became possessed by a wholly different mood and the kind of warmth achieved by scrambling up Blackford Hill and running running down

filled his whole body with a tingling pleasure. Then on return a solid
winter tea by the fire, a proper reward for having taken outside
exercise. These teas were a splendid mixture of the Scottish and the
Jewish. There were pancakes and scones, to be eaten with jam, and
cookies and even on occasion cream cookies, which were buns split
on one side with cream inside the split, and those delicious dome-
shaped little biscuits made by Kleinberg the Jewish baker, which our
hero could eat in infinite numbers without ever feeling full. Kleinberg also made almond macaroons, regarded as great luxuries and
normally served for tea only on Passover, for biscuits made of almond
paste contained no leaven and were fully pesachdick. Throughout
the rest of the year coconut macaroons, which were less expensive and
less luxurious, would sometimes find their way to the tea-table: these
were pretty fine, but inferior to their almond brethren. The relation
between macaroons and macaroni puzzled him, and he came across
the word macaronic in some collection of poetry once and thought at
first it was the adjective from macaroon. But it was macaronic poetry
not macaronic biscuits that was being discussed and he had to look
the word up in the multi-volumed Century dictionary that stood in
its own special bookcase in the rabbi's study. Characterized by a mixture of Latin words with words from another language or with non-
Latin words provided with Latin terminations, as a kind of burlesque
verse. But he'd been doing this for years.

> He asked the classical magister
> 'What is the Latin for assist, sir?'
> 'Why boy, the answer's easy, very:
> The Latin is auxilium ferre.'

In the busy summer season they ran an extra ferry across the Forth,
known surely as the auxilium ferry. Macaronic then had nothing to
do with macaroons. What about cameroons? He found them or it on
the map of Africa, so it wasn't just a spoonerism for macaroons. The
March of the Cameroon Men. He envisaged them as black highlanders. March, march, Ettrick and Teviotdale, Why the deil dinna
ye march forward in order? They sang that to a tramping tune conducted by Mr De la Haye in his flowing tie. That was Scott, and the
other song they sang which he always associated with it was not, as
he long thought, by Scott but, as he discovered quite by accident
when looking through an anthology, by Hogg:

> Lock the door, Lariston, lion of Liddisdale,
> Lock the door, Lariston, Lowther comes on,

The Armstrongs are flying,
Their widows are crying,
The Castletown's burning, and Oliver's gone.

Ah those savage Border fighters, cattle lifting, house burning, reiving and plundering. Thou bold Border ranger, beware of thy danger, thy foes are relentless, determined and nigh. Henry John waxed eloquent about the Border Ballads and told the boys how Scott had been fascinated by them. The Minstrelsy of the Scottish Border. Jimmy Allen, who taught Latin and Greek, kept schoolboy boarders in his house, and once he heard someone practising the piano as he passed it and said to himself: Minstrelsy of the Scottish Boarder. But our hero was moved by the ballads all the same. His own ancestral history was also full of suffering and violence, but endured not inflicted – at least not unless you went right back to Bible times and thought of the campaigns of Joshua and David. What different worlds though, what different different worlds, blue bonnets over the Border and the border that was drawn from the top of the hill unto the fountain of the water of Nephtoah and went out to the cities of Mount Ephron. And yet perhaps not so different after all, perhaps the reiving blue bonnets of the Scottish Border were not really so unlike Joshua's rampaging host. For the Jews too had been a warlike people in ancient times, and wasn't it because he had been a man of war and not of peace that King David had not been allowed to build the Temple, a task that was left for his son Solomon whose very name meant shalom, peace? And then there were the Covenanters, who identified themselves with the biblical people of Israel and continually had the words of the Hebrew Bible on their lips. They were fighters too, persecuted and warred against, holding their secret conventicles in the hills while their fighting men kept watch for the enemy. He could not think that theirs had been a Jewish spirit though, at least not any Jewish spirit that he had experienced, for they were narrow and fanatical and spoke in scriptural words that they had borrowed mechanically from another nation's history. After he had read *Old Mortality* he lost the admiration for the Covenanters that had been inculcated in him in the junior school, though he thought Scott was very fair to them and could see their good qualities as well as their intolerance and pig-headedness. But perhaps to the Greeks and the Romans the Jews had been merely intolerant and pig-headed? When Judas Maccabeus and his followers refused to follow the religious customs demanded by Antiochus as a mere matter of secular conformity, were they not behaving fanatically?

Didn't medieval Christians regard Jews as wilfully obstinate un-believers? Indeed, could the Jews have survived as a people through-out two thousand years of exile if they hadn't been in some degree pig-headed and obstinate? But the Covenanters were in their own country and there was no question of their surviving as a people. Besides, the Jews were *right*, and you can't call people pig-headed and obstinate if they are simply adamant in refusing to bow to erroneous opinions. Still, these were disturbing reflections. The cold huddle of grey hills where the Scottish Borderers lived and below which fate had at last cast his own family was very different from Mount Zion and Mount Hermon and Mount Moriah and Border sheep were different from those kept by David when he was still a shepherd boy just as Border landscape was different from the olive groves and fig trees of ancient Palestine, yet – yet – what was it that nagged at him, modifying and qualifying his first feeling that the folk of Ettrick and Teviotdale in the old days were so unlike his ancestors and suggested that in their primitive violence they were perhaps not unlike the fighting tribes that broke into Palestine from Egypt and conquered in a far from gentle manner the land that had been promised to them? Still, that was more than three thousand years ago and if you went back as far as that in considering the Scots or the English you'd get beyond woad-painted ancient Britons to something pretty savage indeed.

There were reminders of the past all round him in Edinburgh. On rocks at the back of Blackford Hill they had railed in a section which showed the marks of ancient glaciers. And Arthur's Seat, an extinct volcano, what had been its connection with Arthur and how had it come by its name? The historical layers of the city lay open to the eye: the old town lying between the Castle and Holyrood, the early and mid eighteenth-century town between George Square and Arthur's Seat, the eighteenth- and early nineteenth-century new town north of Princes Street Gardens, and south of the Meadows the genteel Victorian streets that linked Marchmont to Blackford Hill. Each part had its atmosphere, each its degree of gentility or rough-ness. The next street parallel to his, for example, consisted of flats and not of terraced houses as his did, and was therefore visibly further down the social scale. Their back greens backed on to the back gardens of his street, but they were communal greens where people beat carpets and hung washing, not private gardens where householders sat. Those back greens, unlike the gardens, were accessible to anybody from the street, and singing or accordion-playing beggars would come there and perform, looking up to the many storeys of windows whence pennies were tossed down to the grass below. One summer day he was playing an elaborate game in the kitchen with his brother; it involved lining up the kitchen chairs and sitting in carefully allocated positions. In the middle of the game he heard through the open window an accordion playing in the back green opposite, and he couldn't concentrate on the game because the tune moved him and he wanted to listen to it and remember it. He left his allotted place and went to the window and stood listening. His brother was angry. But nothing mattered except that he should possess that tune and never forget it. It was a summer tune, floating into the house through a summer-time open window. There were summer tunes and winter tunes, like summer streets and winter streets. Causewayside, now, was a winter street and Nicolson Street was a winter street, but Marchmont Road and Warrender Park Road and Spottiswoode Road and Thirlstane Road were summer streets, while Oswald Road and Grange Loan were streets of high summer. Some streets and districts he considered ambiseasonal, like the Meadows, which reflected with clockwork precision the seasonal changes in playing habits: the first day of football in the Meadows was a clear message that summer had ended. There were also morning streets and afternoon streets and evening streets; he knew Tennyson's

land
In which it seemèd always afternoon.

It stretched south from Grange Loan and Blackford Avenue. There were certain kinds of flats, respectable, even prim, built of that grey-yellowy sandstone so characteristic of Edinburgh houses, mildly genteel flats, not very rich, not very poor, where people were always having tea and the very small front gardens were filled with wall-flowers in the spring; yes, certain kinds of flats which as he walked past seemed to move him with a quiet sad message about the ordinariness of ordinary existence, the sameness of things, the ticking away of unadventurous lives in decency and respectability. He felt a surge of pitying affection for their inhabitants, but could not explain why. It was quite different with working-class flats, dark grey in colour, with no bay windows, where women shouted down from high plain windows to call their children in for their tea. There was no-thing sad about them. All was vigour and movement. They were the people who hung up their carpets in springtime and beat beat beat them with rhythmic thuds for hours at a time: strong-armed women who seemed to take a fierce pleasure in such outsize domestic duties. Amazons. There were Jewish amazons too, in Buccleuch Street and West Richmond Street and Rankeillor Street and Montague Street (always pronounced MonTAYgue) who called in their children in strong Yiddish accents, though the children replied, when they did, in the true Edinburgh keelie tongue. They stuffed their children with food, terrified of under-nourishment, seeking in a plentiful diet security against memories of penury and persecution. Ess mein kind, ess; eat my child, eat, the mothers would chant, obsessed victuallers standing over their offspring in moods of alternating affection and belligerence.

When he went for his violin lessons (his female piano teacher came to give him lessons at his own house, but for lessons from his male violin teacher he had to go to the teacher's house: he thought this had something to do with the difference in sex) he discovered what for him was a new part of Edinburgh, Comely Bank, but the flats of Learmonth Gardens were not unlike the genteel flats of the south side, and he recognized their sadness. He had trouble when playing with the heel of the bow, and his teacher tried to show him exactly how he should move his wrist by having him put his hand on top of his own when he showed how it was done, so that he could feel the movement. His hand lay lightly on the long hairy fingers of his teacher, moving to and fro with the teacher's hand. Eftsoons his hand dropt he. He read about efts in *The Water Babies*, a book which bothered him, and wasn't quite sure what they were, though he suspected they were rather like newts. He and his brother kept newts in a large bowl in the drawing-room, but they escaped one day, trailing their way across the floor to freedom, and were never seen again. Well, they were never meant for a drawing-room and he hoped they were happy. One of them was called Sir Isaac, after Newton: Sir Isaac Newt. He discovered gravity out of his bed at midnight by means of a falling apple. 32 feet per second per second. A sort of small centipede, a trigintapede, moving 32 feet per second. His father enjoyed the story of the Yiddish-speaking defendant in a court of law who when asked his age replied I am dirty and my vife is dirty too. The rabbi had a primitive sense of humour, as all scholars and idealists probably had. His favourite story was Who wrote Hamlet? Please sir, I didn't. Then the inspector told the headmaster of the boy's incredible reply and the headmaster roared with laughter, and then said, I bet the little blighter did it after all. When the inspector dined with the local vicar that evening and told the richly comic story of the boy's answer and the headmaster's comment, the vicar screamed with laughter for many minutes before calming down and asking, And did it eventually transpire who was the culprit? The rabbi would laugh until the tears ran down his cheeks as he came to the end of the story. His own preference was for the pungent short riposte. Spring in the air. Why should I? His family is in the iron and steel business: his mother irons and his father steals. He stored these in his memory from seaside entertainers and occasional comedians heard through headphones on the wireless. Henry John told the boys about an American (why American?) who after attending a lecture on Keats went up to the lecturer and said, I enjoyed the lecture very much, but tell me, what *are* keats? He thought that far-fetched. You could do it with any name that ended in an s. An excellent lecture on Moses, but tell me, what *is* a mose? Or even, A splendid talk on Dickens, but what *is* a dicken? What the Dickens. How did the novelist become an exclamation? A euphemism for what the devil? Thickens was the only word he could think of to rhyme with Dickens (unless you cheated with things like pickin's, good pickin's for pickaninnies after the picnic), and that was appropriate enough: in Dickens the plot thickens. Ah but there was sickens. The plot thickens; the hero sickens; well done Dickens. (Martin Chuzzlewit.) As well as what the Dickens there was Great Scott. There's glory for you, to have become so famous a writer that your name is used as an exclamation. But why just these two? Good Shakespeare! By Wordsworth! Great Scott, I'd rather be a pagan suckled in a creed outworn. Would you, great Wordsworth? I would, by Hogg! By George, Gordon Lord Byron! The same. You have read the poems by George Gordon Lord Byron? No by George! Good Lord! Dr Livingstone I presume? What presumption! On Stanley on! From the older members of the rabbi's congregation he occasionally heard Yiddish exclamations, mostly of sorrow or distress, like *oi vai* and *oi gevalt*, but the exclamatory vocabulary in that language seemed limited. Hebrew too had few words of exclamation, *hoi goi chotei*, ah sinful nation, exclaimed Isaiah in that opening chapter that was read in a specially mournful chant on the sabbath before the fast of the ninth of Ab. *Echah yashvah vadad*, how doth the city sit solitary, begins the author of the book of Lamentations. Greek had a greater variety of exclamations of distress, *o popoi, omoi, pheu pheu*, and he liked the Latin *eheu*. There was also *hei mihi* and *vae mihi*. The French *hélas*, however, seemed altogether too literary and he couldn't imagine anyone exclaiming it spontaneously in a moment of sudden grief. But then he didn't suppose anyone spontaneously exclaimed *eheu fugaces* either. Exclamations in general were fascinating words. There were strange nautical ones like Avast! and Belay! One might almost meet them in a folksong, beginning

As I was walking down the street I met a vast belay.

The potentialities of that adventure were immense. *Atque omne immensum peragravit*. When they read Lucretius at school and came to the line

tantum religio potuit suadere malorum

they were told firmly that *religio* in this context meant superstition, not religion. Otherwise it would have been a shocking line for schoolboys to learn.

Oh all those equivocations and qualifications and explanations and palliations and obfuscations, how they wove in and out of everything, how muddied ordinary language was, how impossible to say what you really meant, how unattainable – or perhaps just how meaningless – was true honesty in relations with people. The natural world was more honest, the weather, the light and the dark, evening and morning, ducks on Blackford pond, they asked no questions and were told no lies. Morning's at seven, the hillside's dew pearled. Look the morn in russet mantle clad walks o'er the dew of yon high eastern hill. *Rhododactylos heos*, rosy-fingered dawn. A birdie with a yellow bill hopped upon my window sill. Birds hopped and chirped, flowers bloomed and faded and bloomed again, the sun rose and set and rose again, but people were unpredictable, he himself, his feelings, his moods, no clarity anywhere, no possibility of really explaining or of being explained to, irredeemably muddied. Yet would he want it otherwise? Totally predictable persons, a totally predictable self? Didn't he enjoy the mystery, the doubt, the confusion, the sense of never fully knowing what it was all about so that in a way anything really anything could happen? One could wake up in the morning and think, today everything may turn out to be ABSOLUTELY DIFFERENT. The laws of nature might be suspended and he could find himself able to fly, or could make himself invisible and wander anywhere without anybody knowing. How could anyone be sure that this would not happen? Everything was really quite mysterious. He would not have it otherwise. Nonsense came in too, akin to mystery, so that the 'Hunting of the Snark' held a message of inscrutable profundity. And words in patterns could distil their own strange meaning. He tried to compose a wholly alliterative line and it came out with meanings he didn't expect. He much admired that set of verses that ran unerringly through the alphabet alliteratively and began

> An Austrian army awfully arrayed
> Boldly by batteries besieged Belgrade

and as it moved it clearly took the author where he had originally no intention of going. He tried to construct similar verses – and with a longer line, so that the challenge was greater – but though they led him to the strangest places he always had to give up before he reached Z. One of them began

> After an anxious afternoon awaiting Annabel
> Bertie began belatedly Bermudan bagatelle

but he got stuck not so much with the letters as with the story they demanded. He convinced himself that Bermudan bagatelle was a West Indian version of the game of Corinthian bagatelle, which was played with balls on a special board, and he considered that Bertie would be likely to embark on such a game late in the day to take his mind off his long and fruitless afternoon wait for Annabel. But what then? Curious caves and dire distemper reared their heads in the next two lines and Bertie's fate became preposterous. Apt alliteration's artful aid, avaunt! But it wasn't only trying to follow an alliterative scheme that might lead to strange places. He would sit down to write a poem for the school magazine about a scene he remembered or an incident that had impressed him and more often than not it would emerge as about something quite different. Even a mood could suffer a sea-change in the process of writing and what began as sad or broody could modulate as easily in the reverse direction. Words took control. Sometimes he thought of a fine last line without any idea of what was to come before it, and when he finally wrote something that led up to it it would bear no relation at all to any idea or feeling he had when he first thought of the line. But what emerged was often pleasing and, what was more, revealing. It existed outside himself as a shape and a meaning that revealed something he had not known when he sat down to write. This was his lack of method, he thought, his impulsive way of doing things without a completely worked out plan beforehand; real writers surely didn't work that way, surely they had every sequence of meaning planned before they started their proper writing. Yet he wondered. What about Kubla Khan and the Person from Porlock? Clearly different poets had different methods. Sometimes in bed at night he would string together words without thought, just as they popped into his mind, to see what would happen. Sometimes strangely impressive lines emerged, which he was determined to write down the next morning, but by the next morning he had forgotten them. Only once he remembered, and wrote the line down:

After the mandrakes, would there beauties be?

He wasn't happy about the inversion, but the rhythm needed it, for Would there be beauties? (like Can ye sew cushions?) was rhythmically impossible in this context. Wasn't an archmandrake an official in the Greek orthodox church? It sounded impossible, and he had to look it up, disappointed to find that it was archimandrite. Archie Mandrite. Once walking past the Jewish butcher's shop he heard the female voice of a familiar Edinburgh Jewish character who always had trouble with the 'tch' sound shouting: Artsie! Put the tsicken on the tsair! Who Archie was (hardly a common Jewish name) and why he should have been adjured to put the chicken on the chair were mysteries that delighted him for months, during which time he used the sentence Artsie! Put the tsicken on the tsair! as a kind of talisman against ennui or sorrow.

But a summer morning was no time for vacancy or pensiveness. No vacancies. O that first warm day which called for a summer shirt and a blazer, walking across the Meadows light, unencumbered, blithesome and cumberless (skylarking with Hogg), ready for anything. Those heatwaves when his mother made special salads and a large glass jug of home-made lemon squash stood on the sideboard, constantly replenished. Time stopped when real warm weather came and the smell of warm cut grass from the streets' front gardens graced his nostrils, proclaiming summer, summer, the apple-tree the singing and the gold. Dr Matheson called one such day and took them a ride in his open Ford, the leather upholstery of the back seat burning in the sunshine, and once coming home, alas, from a seaside holiday in Fife on a hot sunny day at the beginning of September, with the window of the compartment all the way down so that sun and air could come in, the train passed little coves with the waves plashing warmly gently, *kumat' ep' eīonos kluzeskon*, and he longed to get out at each one and disport himself in the water. At St Andrews once there was a run of days like that with the sea like glass and the little lines of ripples so unlike the nobly tall curving waves that broke loudly on the shore at other times. He once lay slumbering on the sand at Crail as the tide crept steadily forward, and was awakened by a change in the sound of the sea: the tide was now almost full in and the waves had changed from little spreading ones to large pounding ones, coming down in heavy sequence, thud, thud, thud, with seethings in between. A cloud obscured the sun and a wind had sprung up: when he had dozed off the atmosphere was lotos-eating but now there was something stark in the look of the beach and the sea and he remembered the trawler that had gone on the rocks in a storm near Fife Ness and seeing it next morning pounded helplessly by unremitting waves. Yet some storms were splendid too, and to walk along the harbour wall when there was a real sea running and you were liable to get drenched with spray had its own exhilaration. Welcome wild north-easter, they sang in the school choir with Mr De la Haye, and he knew what Kingsley meant. He used to want to say, Welcome wild north-easter, Bird thou never wert, which was in fact truer of the north-east wind than of the skylark. (This doubt about birds being birds. Bird thou never wert, skylark, and O cuckoo shall I call thee bird or but a wandering voice? The Scots however faced the facts; Hogg's skylark was a bird of the wilderness and the cuckoo of J. Logan or M. Bruce, though addressed some-what extravagantly as a beauteous stranger of the wood and a delightful visitant, was emphatically a bird, a sweet bird.) Everybody talked of Edinburgh's east winds and linked them with the city's snobberies – east windy and west endy – but at geography they learned that the prevailing winds in Edinburgh were south-west, and east winds were uncommon. East is east and west is west etcetera, but Kipling was wrong, the twain were always meeting and how meet that was. Were the Jews originally an eastern people? Not as Eastern as the Chinese or the Indians, obviously, but Near Eastern. Was that enough to be oriental? It depended where you stood. Indeed from one point of view China was the very far west: you could get there by keeping going westward past America, the way the first explorers hoped to reach the Indies. It was all so ridiculously relative, like north on the map always being at the top when it might just as logically be at the bottom. But when the train crossed the Forth Bridge he saw the directions clearly enough, eastward to the widen-ing Forth estuary and the North Sea and from the other side of the train westward up the Forth towards Stirling. Below on your right as the train puffed slowly north was Dalmeny and Cramond, then there were Granton and Leith, and, though he couldn't see them, he thought of the towns along the south shore of the firth, Portobello, Musselburgh, Prestonpans, Cockenzie, Port Seton, Aberlady, Gullane, North Berwick. There they were, stretched out along the coast, and they were always there even when you didn't see them or think about them. Opposite was Fife, the holiday county, and the little coastal towns there from Aberdour and Burntisland to Anstruther and Crail facing their Midlothian and East Lothian opposites, seeing on a clear day the smoke from Auld Reekie and the guardian shape of Arthur's Seat as something distant, belonging to a far-off workaday world. Coming back from holiday after crossing the Forth Bridge, approaching Edinburgh from the west, he saw from the train the first tramcar and yes, yes, the holiday was over, this was a city scene, with streets that had houses on both sides and when he looked out of the window no sea or harbour but no. 18 opposite and the red-headed girl shining the brass plate on the gate. The term had already started at Sciennes School and when he woke in the morning, lying late because his school was still on holiday, he could hear the children shouting in the playground, and then at ten to nine the bell rang, the children rushed in, the noise stopped, the sounds of an ordinary Edinburgh weekday took over. When his own school started at the end of September or sometimes even at the beginning of October seagulls would fly in from the Forth to consume the crumbs scattered by sandwich-eaters at the lunch inty and the sound of their crying comforted him, a holiday sea noise, blithe spirits. Yes, melancholy and raucous though their cries sounded, to him the birds spelt sea and harbour wall and the fishing boats setting out at high tide, happy happy.

Happiness was anticipation, awareness of happiness was always retrospective. Now, the long summer holidays beginning, going away next week, packing the night before, getting the trunks and suitcases out – what relish, what joy. Then in the morning, waking up with today, today, the trunks packed, the taxi at the door, the station, the train pulling out, the magic journey beginning. Happiness was beginnings, long weeks waiting unspoiled, unbroken into. Bliss was it in that dawn to be alive. Once on the West Braes at Crail he had rolled all the way down in the long grass, conscious of irrational exultation in that moment. And dark as winter was the flow of Iser rolling rapidly. 'Tis I sir, rolling rapidly. Dr Johnson, Henry John had told them, had once gone to the top of a hill near London and, saying to his companions that it was a long time since he had enjoyed a good roll, had calmly lain down and rolled to the bottom. Sir, sir, I am very much obliged to you sir. Please sir, please sir: the schoolboy's cry from class to class sounds as the years of boyhood pass. *Labuntur anni*, from Class D to Class H, from 3 lower junior to 6 upper junior, from IA to the VIth, a lifetime. *Labuntur anni*, Laurie, I'll lay me doon and dee. And become posthumous, posthumous. Everything tends to the future perfect, it will have been. Was that why in Hebrew a future tense could be turned into a past tense by the addition of the prefix meaning 'and'? By the time you read this the Lord will have said unto Moses. A tense situation. Try clutching on to the present, it's now, it's now, it's now, but something distracts your attention and lo! it was then. And Moses was sick and the lot fell upon Aaron. The boys at school assured each other that that is what the minister read when he turned over two pages of the Bible together, without realizing it. And Eli was sick and brought up Samuel. But it couldn't be done, as he found out after checking the biblical text. You might just as well say that Eli was sick and brought up first Samuel, then second Samuel. First kings and second kings. Like Henry IV Part I and Henry IV Part II. First kings first. My first is in winter but not in spring. He used to make up dozens of those simple rhymed puzzles, with the last line summing up: my whole is a somethingy somethingy some. Once they had to invent a Latin crossword puzzle as an exercise. He started one so elaborate that he was unable to finish it, and later crossed words with the Latin master about it. Verb sap. Knowledge cannot increase without language and what rises in the Tree of Knowledge is verb sap. A sap was also a silly ass, a fatuous fool, don't be a sap. I know you can't help being a fool, one of the masters used to say to any boy who had done something stupid, but don't be a SILLY fool. When he was quite little he imagined that a fool was a kind of animal like an ass, since silly fool and silly ass meant the same thing. He saw the fool clearly, it was something between an ass and a wolf, with very pointed ears and a most ridiculous grin on its face. Though it was black in colour it seemed to wear a red and white band round the middle of its body. Then there was gooseberry fool. And April fool. They used to pin a piece of paper on to other boys' backs, reading KICK ME. When you caught someone out in an April fool bluff you would call Huntygouk. Hunt the gouk, hunt the cuckoo. O cuckoo, shall I call thee bird, Or but a wandering voice? Call me gouk when you are in Scotland, friend. You really wouldn't want to call a bird

Butter Wandering Voice. Margarine on the other hand sounded like a girl's name.

> Dear Margarine, you set my heart a-flutter,
> I love you better than fresh dairy butter.
> You are more lovely than the Fairy Queen,
> O will you marry me, sweet Margarine?

Tangerine was like a girl's name too. Daughter of William of Orange? A sour man with a lemon soul. I'm sorry madam but we're out of plaice. Buy my halibut? By my halibut! By cod! Holy mackerel! Fish fiddle de-dee! He has gone to fish for his Aunt Jobisca's Runcible Cat with crimson whiskers. But I was thinking of a plan to dye one's whiskers green. Or to dye one whisker green? On a dyeing green. Well, there were bleaching greens. And Juniper Green. His eyes were green as leeks. But one eye itched, and he rubbed it, making the green one red. As with the first traffic lights they unveiled in Lothian Road and all Edinburgh came to watch and marvel.

How much traffic there was with lights. Chanukah lights, Christmas lights, sabbath lights. How does the little liver pill find its way to the liver? It's guided by the lights. When they change to green the carter drives on. Sunlight soap (Why does a woman grow old sooner than a man? the soap's printed wrapper asked. But sunlight soap would prevent that.) And Lo! the Hunter of the East has caught The Sultan's turret in a Noose of Light. The light of dawn: How art thou fallen from heaven, O day-star, son of the morning. *Helel ben shachar*, from *halal*, to be bright, to shine, so that they translated it Lucifer, light-bearer, son of the morning. Isaiah was referring to Nebuchadnezzar, whose brightness and glory contrasted so sharply with his subsequent fall, but early Christian interpreters having translated *helel* as Lucifer made him into Satan and hence derived the myth of his fall from heaven. *Lucem ferens*, bearing Lux for the week's washing. Lucifer, the message boy from Cameron's bearing Lux. If you haven't got a lucifer to light your pipe. Yes, light played an ubiquitous part ever since God created it with his fiat lux, *yehi or*, let there be light. There was yellow light and golden light and white light, according to the time of day and the season of the year. Best of all he liked the evening summer sunlight, warming the close of day with benedictory rays. They had gas-light until he was six and a half, with an open fish-tail flame hissing quietly in the lavatory and in all the other rooms a flame disciplined and brightened with a mantle, a thing so fragile that often when his father was fitting a new one his fingers would slip and he would destroy it. When they first put in electricity he would turn the switch in the kitchen half on and half off and enjoy the curious noise it made as light sparked across the gap inside. Once he put the blade of a kitchen knife across the open socket into which his mother would plug the electric iron, and was thoroughly frightened by the ensuing flash and the warping of the blade: fortunately the handle was ivory or something that looked like it and didn't conduct electricity. When they did electricity at school he realized retrospectively what he had done all those years before and trembled at his narrow escape. The chandelier in the dining-room was hung with a red silk shade and could be raised or lowered by a pulley-like device, but right up at the top, on the very ceiling, there were three naked bulbs each surrounded by a plaster leaf-cluster, and these high extra lights were only switched on on special festive occasions. In shul there was the *ner tamid*, the perpetual light, traditionally of oil but now of electricity, always switched on. His mother on the anniversary of her father's death lit a Price's night-light and kept it burning all night, in remembrance, as Jews always did on the anniversary of a near relation's death. He didn't remember his maternal grandfather, who had died soon after he was born, but his father's parents were for long part of the family pattern. He came across the night-light once unexpectedly, burning strangely on the chimneypiece of his father's study, and it scared him slightly, not at first realizing what it was and why it had been lit. Then there was the havdalah light, made of tapers plaited together into a thick twist, which he or his brother would hold while his father formally proclaimed the end of the sabbath, the havdalah, the separation, between that special day and ordinary week-days. Blessed art thou O Lord our God, King of the universe, who createst the light of the fire, *borei morei ha-esh*, his father would chant, spreading his hands towards the light, and then go on to bless God for making a distinction *bein kodesh le-chol*, between holy and profane, between light and darkness, between Israel and other nations, between the seventh day and the six working days. But even the six working days were not wholly secular, for he had to recite privately the long Hebrew morning service, *shacharit*, suitably adorned (after his Barmitzvah) with the ritual *tefilin*. Pages and pages and pages, though scarcely needing to be looked at for soon memorized by constant repetition, recited mutteringly at high speed in his father's study while the maid prepared breakfast. *Minchah* and *ma'ariv*, the afternoon and evening prayers, he was not expected to recite on week-days, and he doubted if the rabbi recited them either, though pious Jews were supposed to. The formulas of Hebrew liturgy were built into his memory and slipped off his tongue effortlessly; only occasionally did he reflect on what he was actually saying and wonder sometimes at what ancient liturgists had put into his mouth. Men thanked God for not having made them women, and women for having made them according to his will. If he had been a girl he would have deeply resented that.

How little they suspected, as he turned up at school in the morning, how little the other boys suspected of his daily pre-breakfast encounter with ancient Hebrew liturgy. Into the pedagogic world of chalk and ink and long corridors he moved naturally, rushing from classroom to classroom between periods as others rushed, storming into the playground at the inty as others stormed, awaiting the release at the end of the school day as others waited. He carried his books wrapped round in a strap, a sign of maturity, for when he was smaller he had brought them in a school bag, now regarded as something for little boys. Each evening he would put out on the little side table in the dining-room the books that he would need in school next day. The dining-room was the hub of the house. Here all homework was done, the children sitting round the big dining-room table with their separate studies, to be interrupted at meal times when their mother or the maid had to set the table. The dining-room was also the family sitting-room with armchairs at either side of the fireplace and two others opposite each other by the bay window. The drawing-room upstairs was used only for practising music and for piano lessons, for formal tea parties, and on Sunday evenings for family gatherings sometimes with song and music. Up above that, up a narrow staircase which was covered with yellow linoleum not with a proper carpet like the main staircase, was the cluster of top-floor rooms where the children slept, two bedrooms and an attic box-room. The box-room had a skylight which led on to the roof, and on warm days in summer he would sometimes climb out and sit and read poetry on the slates. There they erected their first wireless aerial in 1923, stringing copper wire between two opposite chimney-pots, careful to use insulators at each end, but this did not prove satisfactory as the wire ran parallel to the lead strip along the roof line, so they got a man to erect a more elaborate aerial, running obliquely across the roof line from a specially erected wooden gallows (as it seemed) to a chimney diagonally opposite. He first read book I of *The Faerie Queene* on the roof one July evening, and thought it a most appropriate setting for such an activity. Places demanded appropriate activities. The Cat walked by himself and all places were alike to him, but humans were prisoners of local atmosphere. When he read in one of Stevenson's essays that RLS had held that some places speak distinctly, demanding an appropriate story, he exclaimed aloud in agreement. Stories should be tailored to the suggestions of particular places. How different for example was Arthur's Seat from Blackford Hill, Leith from Portobello, even Bruntsfield Links from the Meadows. As for the Castle, brooding over the city, it was too much always there, too permanent and accepted and matter-of-course a feature of the skyline to arouse romantic suggestions. Did Morningside suggest Lucifer son of the morning? By no means. It was genteel and intimate and pleasantly ordinary, decent and friendly and unadventurously urban, with flats and houses from which issued every morning solicitors and schoolmasters and branch managers of banks. But somewhere in Morningside there was a lunatic asylum – he had never seen it – and the name was used familiarly to suggest the place where mad people were sent. Quite daft, he ought to be sent to Morningside, they would say at school. Yet the word had no connection with the visible and agreeable ordinariness of Morningside Road and the respectable streets that went off it at right angles. Tollcross was the sentinel guarding the divisions; from there you went east by Lauriston past the back of his school and of the Royal Infirmary and near the Graham Street synagogue and past Heriot's to where the Middle Meadow Walk came in opposite Forrest Road; or south-east by Brougham Place to Melville Drive and the south side of the Meadows, his own much frequented territory; or south through Bruntsfield and Morningside to the Braid Hills; or south-west by Craiglockhart and Colinton to the Pentlands; or north down Lothian Road to the West End. What diversity, what richness, innumerable cities in one, country places and metropolitan streets flowing into each other. From the West End you could get a tramcar to Murrayfield, and from the car terminus a tiny little bus ran to the zoo at Corstorphine. He would lie in bed and make journeys in his head, changing the feeling with each district, imagining suitable characters and adventures. There was a little tailor's shop in Polwarth Terrace, on the way to Craiglockhart, where he got his first suit with long trousers, fitted by a sad man with a thick moustache, a little shop, a little sad tailor, with no other customers that he could see and an air of desperately trying to make good as something more than a little sad tailor's shop. What was such a man doing trapped between Craiglockhart and Tollcross, a doomed tailor surely, with crossed ambitions and strange inner thoughts? The suit with the long trousers was greeny-grey, reminiscent of the tailor, the shop, the sadness.

'Southward of Morningside lie the Plewlands, ascending the slope towards beautiful Craiglockhart Hill, now being fast covered with semi-detached villas, feued by the Scottish Heritages Company, surrounding a new cemetery, and intersected by the suburban line of railway.' That was the voice of the Edinburgh historian of the 1870s, and those semi-detached villas were now solidly entrenched as a quietly determined part of southern Edinburgh respectabilities. As for the suburban line of railway, he knew best the stretch between Newington and Blackford Hill and had often watched the trains from Blackford Hill or from where Oswald Road went over the railway line as they puffed in their suburban circle round the city. Goods trains went on the line at night, and often on a still night he could hear the puff puff puffing of an engine and sometimes from further distance borne the lonely whistle of a night express going east then south from Waverley. These sounds did not carry in the daytime; only when the rest of the city was still could he hear the puffs and the whistles and sometimes even the distant clanking of trucks knocking against each other. Mysterious and beautiful noises they were, indicating adventurous nocturnal activity. Passenger trains at night, their moving windows lit up, had a special fascination, and when he heard the whistle crying in the darkness he imagined the travellers sitting in their lighted boxes being carried through the surrounding black and the engine driver, his face lit up by the fire, watching for the lights at the corner of the signals as he drove his train through the deserted nightscape. But the suburban passenger trains went only during the day, and chugged unadventurously along on their douce daily rounds. He was startled to find, on reading Goldsmith's 'Deserted Village' at school, how different Goldsmith's trains were.

> And all the village train from labour free
> Led up their sports beneath the spreading tree.

Neither LNER nor LMS, that train. And when Goldsmith talked about trade's unfeeling train he was not discussing the insensitivity of goods trains. Nor when he wrote

> She only left of all the harmless train

185

was he describing the last, innocuous survivor of the Waverley–King's Cross service. And then there was

> His house was known to all the vagrant train.

Not the signalman's house by the level crossing. Perhaps the joys of the suburban puffer were indicated in

> These simple blessings of the lowly train.

Was it the royal train, going up to Aberdeen en route for Ballater, that was indicated in

> The dome where pleasure holds her midnight reign,
> Here richly deckt admits the gorgeous train?

(Perhaps in Edward VII's time.) And what was the loveliest train which was thine, sweet Auburn? A splendid toy train? He responded to Goldsmith's charm, but thought his indiscriminate use of the word train sloppy. He used it simply to mean a number of people, often because he needed the rhyme. But for our hero a train was essentially a steam train running on a railway line and was associated with adventure, freedom, holidays, and mystery. Such trains did not figure much in poetry, but RLS wrote about them and how absolutely right he was in describing how it felt to be carried through a landscape past things and people without being able to stop and connect with them:

> All of the sights of the hill and the plain
> Fly as thick as driving rain;
> And ever again, in the wink of an eye,
> Painted stations whistle by.
> Here is a child who clambers and scrambles,
> All by himself and gathering brambles;
> Here is a tramp who stands and gazes,
> And there is the green for stringing the daisies!
> Here is a cart run away in the road
> Lumping along with man and load;
> And here is a mill and there is a river:
> Each a glimpse and gone for ever!

He knew Waverley Station before he knew any of the Waverley Novels and though the nearby Scott monument was a wholly familiar feature of the Edinburgh scene he never connected the station with Scott until the origin of its name was pointed out to him. He would stand on a footbridge in Princes Street Gardens and watch the trains pulling out from Waverley towards Haymarket. The novel *Waverley* he read one August in Crail. He had been in the Carnegie library to take out books for holiday reading and had seen a beautiful new clean copy of *Waverley* bound in bright red; nobody had yet taken it out. So he took it among his holiday books – they were allowed extra books and an extended six weeks borrowing period for going on holiday – and read most of it by the rocks at the foot of the Castle Walk. Once or twice he took it to the beach and got sand in the binding which he tried hard to dislodge by banging and shaking but he never got it all out. Fortunately nobody noticed anything wrong when he returned the book. He went through most of the Waverley Novels after that, in leisurely fashion for they were not books to be gulped but to live in for long periods at a time, unlike novels like *King Solomon's Mines* which he would gallop through in a couple of sittings and still less like *The Scarlet Pimpernel* which he read right through without any pause at all. He began to have a sense of difference between a novel you read through quickly in order to find out what happened next and a novel that created a world you lived in so that when you came to an end you were aware of a sense of loss. He found the *Pilgrim's Progress* in a house they took for the summer at Port Seton and thought its action curiously unreal in spite of the homely vividness of the style. He was disturbed by the mixture of realism and allegory, quite a new mode of literature for him; he couldn't understand on what level of probability the story was supposed to move. And its religious and ethical notions were far more alien to his Jewish soul than anything in nineteenth-century fiction. What shall I do to be saved, indeed! Stop worrying about the future of your soul and give your wife a hand with the dishes. (Sometimes, in the quite long periods when they had no maid and his mother was ill, the rabbi would make the porage in the morning and help with the washing-up. At those times his own task was to light the fires – he loved lighting fires – and clean the boots and shoes.) The personal and social problems of Elizabeth Bennet, the adventures and frustrations of Pip, the sorrows of Maggie Tulliver, the fortunes of the Newcomes, these he could understand and associate himself with, their moral situations were real for him. So were those of the innumerable school stories he read about new boys at English public schools surviving bullying and misunderstanding to emerge at the end triumphant and exemplary. But Christian's adventures remained puzzling. How much better he understood Edward Waverley, torn between the picturesque glamour of Highland Jacobitism and the practical demands of life, wavering just as he himself wavered between the alternating appeals of the pipe band and the brass band in the summer concerts in the Meadows. Oh he understood Edward Waverley all right, with his head stuffed with romantic literature and his entrapment by Scotland. He wondered how Scott could ever extricate him after the collapse of the Forty-five and save him from exile or death. And when he was saved, and married Rose instead of Flora, our hero was not entirely convinced, any more than he was convinced by the hasty and perfunctory contriving of Frank Osbaldistone's marriage to Diana Vernon after their apparently final parting. Yet he wanted novels to end happily and was angry with Charlotte Brontë for leaving it up to the reader to imagine for himself, if he wished, a happy ending for Villette. A happy ending had to be real and persuasive or it couldn't count: he did not need Henry John to tell him (as he did) that the end of Barrie's Little Minister was all wrong. In fact he thought that book dishonest all through, though he couldn't precisely explain why. Barrie always made him uncomfortable. He squirmed through Peter Pan, and Mary Rose left him simply angry. Light-hearted refreshment he found in the two dark green volumes of the *Pickwick Papers* which he read again and again, rejoicing in the lively language of Sam Weller, in Mr Jingle's staccato anecdotes, in the election at Eatanswill and the behaviour of Mrs Leo Hunter, in the hypocrisies of the Reverend Mr Stiggins, and much more. Dodson and Fogg, though, and the trial of Bardell versus Pickwick, were disturbing as well as funny: he did not like to see innocence taken advantage of. As for Mr Pickwick in prison and the reformation of Mr Jingle – he rarely re-read that part of the book. Oddly enough, he missed the humour of many of Dickens's names until Henry John pointed them out in the classroom. He had called the town EatANSwill until Henry John, choking with pedagogical laughter, had said Eat-an'-swill, just as he had pronounced Dotheboy's Hall to rhyme with Sotheby's Hall until the same master repeated with lingering chortles DO-THE-BOYS.

Substitute worlds? Well, why not, when reality itself was so problematical and the meaning of things shifted according to time and place and mood? Sometimes, harassed by a difficult batch of homework and the thought of a dreary day at school on the morrow, he would will himself into a mood of imaginative excitement or pleasingly sad reflectiveness in which these practical problems dwindled into total insignificance. It was not that he could say I am the captain of my soul, for he was in fact very much at the mercy of mood, but there were occasions when he could deliberately enhance and exploit an incipient or potential mood to escape the pressures of everyday life. He knew too exactly what Browning meant about the sunset-touch and the chorus-ending from Euripides, how they could constitute revelation, changing everything. He was an unstable person, he felt, he had no real character, he was a flux of shifting patterns of thought and feeling. But perhaps the faces other people wore were less fixed and definite than he imagined. Perhaps there were no stable characters? Or perhaps at least literary people were less stable, more subject to shifts in mood, more able to enter into others' feelings and speak from within others' characters? Didn't he have then the literary attitude, wasn't he proud of it, wasn't his difference from others a superiority? It was the old story of both triumphing in being different and wanting to be like everybody else. Never mind, never mind, life is all a variorum, prospects are immense, unpredictable, extraordinary, possibilities are endless, every succeeding moment in time is freshly minted, absolutely new, carrying us forward into an unknown world. Yet he was linked irrevocably to the past, bound by warm ties and continuing traditions; he would like, when he was middle-aged and his parents gone, to come back to the same old family house and dwell there in the same rhythms of life, perpetuating, re-enacting, saying to the dead with tears, It's all right, I am still here, we still go on as in your time, the pieties are preserved, the generations joined, the same songs are chanted in the synagogue, the same shouts come up from the Meadows, the same leafy summer evenings bring peace to the heart, the same sea washes the shores of the Forth, we are not strangers, not strangers. Ah, but it was not true. It would only be his own life he would re-create, not his father's, whose early years were spent in remote and unknown places, still less his grandfather's, a stranger in Edinburgh, and still less again the life of his great-grandfather who never set foot in Britain. Was his own generation then the model, the final adjustment, the perfect balance between Jewish background and Scottish foreground? Absurdly, the answer was yes. He was sure it was yes. This assurance had to be set beside his sense of flux, of the unexpected continually round the corner, of relentless time, the 'already' perpetually turning into the 'not yet'. If he could solve this paradox, of continuity and change, of yearning to keep the present still present when it had long turned into the past and at the same time welcoming every prospect of the new, the different, the unexpected, of holding on to the moment saying it's here it's here, I'm savouring it,

I won't let it go, and yet opening one's arms to the future with adventurous joy – if he could reconcile these opposites he would have solved – what, the riddle of life? Ridiculous. He would at least have seen into something central in human experience. But was not the contradiction itself the centrally human thing? Did such contradictions exist to be resolved, were they like problems in geometry? Henry John quoted to them Keats on negative capability and he felt, that's it, to be satisfied without resolutions, to accept the contradictions, wasn't this to be most truly and sensitively human? If we had everything neatly worked out, what barrenness, what lack of imaginative variation, what loss. So in his mid teens he had already decided that all solutions were suspect, all philosophical systems violations of the experienced mysteries of living. So long live the insoluble problems, the paradoxes, the mysteries. This had nothing to do with *credo quia absurdum*, with trusting to faith rather than to reason. It was not that you believed what you could not prove; you only believed as much as you could prove; for the rest, you accepted the contradictions, seeing them as a reflection of complexities too subtle for the human intellect and at the same time nourishing to the human imagination. Acceptance was not the same as belief. You believed a minimum but accepted a maximum. That way you could enjoy other people's beliefs without sharing them, you could understand, sympathize, participate, and at the same time know and relish your difference, your awareness of the unanswerable, your battening on the mystery. Some day he would work this out into a coherent view. Now he only glimpsed it, and then only at times, but it comforted and strengthened him.

Philosophy was but a word to him. The rabbi had studied it in Berlin and Leipzig and had written about David Hume and on Kant and Judaism, but our hero was content to regard all this as playing with long abstract words and debating such unreal questions as the relation between mind and matter. What's matter? Never mind. What's mind? No matter. At school they read the Apology of Socrates in Greek, edited by Adela Marion Adam, M.A., and though he enjoyed its eloquence and its irony he paid no serious attention to its philosophical position. Bob Merry used to sing in his seaside show at Leven

> I'm a man o' learnin',
> As you can plainly see,
> Philosophy, theology,
> As easy as can be.

> Geography, zoology,
> Literature an' law,
> I hae them at my fingertips
> In fact I ken them a',

and the chorus began, Zinty tinty halligo lum, Mebbe you think I'm just in fun. He tended to put philosophy in that comic context and amused himself with inventing mock titles of philosophical articles. Are the abstrusions of paradeigmata quintessential or merely notional? Some cognitive aspects of hypothetical noumena. It was all a kind of jabberwocky, an excuse for verbal indulgence. One summer afternoon when he was walking to Blackford Hill with a volume of Keats in his pocket he met an older boy who had left school and acquired some notoriety as a rebel, and this boy declared that he was a dialectical materialist. What, you discuss materials in dialect? our hero inquired facetiously, but the dialectical materialist was not amused and launched into a somewhat incoherent explanation of his views, concluding with the bizarre remark that for all anybody knew the birds in the trees had exactly the same intellectual faculties within their little minds as human beings did. This seemed neither dialectical nor materialist, nor in any way plausible, but it stuck in his mind and for a long time after that encounter he associated dialectical materialism with a belief in the intellectual prowess of birds. Did not ancient diviners see omens in the flight of birds? They preferred however to examine the liver of animals, hepatoscopy, liver-watching. This was carried out in Rome by a haruspex. Hello, haruspex, how's the hepatoscopy? Can't see, I've lost my specs. And who expects hepatoscopy from a haruspex without specs? But isn't a haruspex expected to be speckless? Morally anyway.

> O do not vex
> The haruspex
> If loss of specs
> Doth him perplex.

Did the ancient Romans ever wear glasses? He thought not. Friends, Romans, countrymen, lend me your eyes. That made as much sense as lend me your ears but somehow it sounded absurd. Was that synecdoche or metonymy? They had to learn all those figures of speech, with examples. Synecdoche was using the part for the whole, then what was metonymy? A looser kind of substitution, perhaps, a name change, meta plus onoma. Then shouldn't it be metonomy?

Onyma must be a variant of onoma (there was anonymous too). Greek upsilon English y, Jimmy Allen used to intone to the class, so you had all those hypo and hyper words instead of hupo and huper. Yet you wrote hubris and not hybris. Now look: you said metonymy and anonymous, but onomatopoeia, so obviously sometimes the word came from onyma and sometimes from onoma. Well, what's in a name? Absit nomen. May I put your name down? I didn't know you had taken it up. Let go sir, down sir, put it down! What exactly did it mean, to take somebody's name in vain? The policeman took his name, but later discovered that he had nothing to do with the crime. So he had taken his name in vain. Could you take someone's address in vain?

> O Mr Smith of Argyle Place
> I recognize your form and face.
> Sir, your announcement gives me pain:
> You've taken my address in vain.

It would be nice to have an address like Sir Walter Scott's, simply Abbotsford. A consummate address.

I I

POTTERROW lay between George Square and Nicolson Square; he had a special affection for the grey old street. In Edgar's map the main street of the Potterrow is represented as running, as it still does, straight south from Potterrow Port in the city wall, adjacent to the building of the old college, its houses on the east side overlooking the wide space of Lady Nicolson's Park, between which and the west side of the Pleasance lay only a riding-school and some six or seven houses, surrounded by gardens and hedgerows. It has always been a quaint and narrow street, and the memorabilia thereof are full of interest. A great doorway on its western side, only recently removed, in 1870, measured six feet six inches wide, and was designed in heavy Italian rustic-work, with the date 1688, and must have given access to an edifice of considerable importance. It accommodated no important edifices in our hero's time, but somehow it was quintessentially Edinburgh. He wrote a poem about it beginning

> As I came up through Potterrow
> The sun rose red above the roofs.
> 'How strange,' I thought, 'I didn't know
> The sun could rise in Potterrow.'

That was on a cold morning in the Christmas holidays. In Potterrow, he was told, Burns's lady friend Clarinda had lived, but this association meant little to him. Burns was the author of 'To a Mouse', which they had to memorize in the junior school, the 'Epistle to Davie', the 'Cotter's Saturday Night', and lots of songs. Our hero was put off by the prevalence of sentimental rhetoric about Burns and felt no great urge to seek any full imaginative contact with the poet. So he did not often think of Burns as he walked down Potterrow. He thought once of potters and there ran through his head the slow strains of the Yom Kippur hymn, the moving *pizmon*, which began *ki henei ka-chomer b'yad hayotser*, For behold as clay is in the hand of the potter who extends it and contracts it at will, so are we in thy hand, merciful preserver. They sang that, with the chazan chanting the verse and the congregation coming in with the chorus, *ken anachnu be-yad'cha*, so are we in thy hand, on Yom Kippur Eve, before the long long day of fasting and praying, when he watched the windows of the synagogue for signs of growing darkness and the end of the ordeal. The afternoon went most slowly, and there were fewer good chants then, but as darkness gathered and the long day's praying drew to a close there was a surge of more passionate prayer, and when the chazan sang *P'tach lanu sha-ar, be-et neïlat sha-ar, ki fana yom*, Open unto us the gate, at the time of the closing of the gate, for the day is fading, he felt a tingling run through him and he forgot his physical discomfort. Locked away in another world in the Graham Street synagogue, in the shadow of the Castle and the old city wall. A man's a man for a' that. The moralizing humanitarian side of Burns appealed to the rabbi, who was in demand at Burns birthday celebrations and quoted with relish

> For a' that, and a' that,
>   It's comin yet for a' that,
> That Man to Man the warld o'er
>   Shall brothers be for a' that.

And had not Scott understood the fate of the Jew in the medieval world as shown in his creation of Isaac of York and the beautiful Rebecca? The rational pieties and rhetorical moralizing of eighteenth- and early nineteenth-century Edinburgh were highly congenial to the rabbi, who combined his rabbinical Judaism effortlessly with a special love of the Scottish Enlightenment. And was not the Cotter's Saturday night like the rabbi's Friday night?

> The priest-like father reads the sacred page,
>   How Abram was the friend of God on high,
> Or Moses bade eternal warfare wage
>   With Amalek's ungracious progeny . . .

Z'chor et asher asa le-cha Amalek ba-derech be-tsetchem mi-mitsrayim. Remember what Amalek did to you by the way when you were coming out of Egypt. The rabbi had no difficulty with his Burns speeches, quotations and Jewish parallels flew eloquently from his lips. And the Scots pronounced rabbi like rabbie. Rabbi Burns. (That was the proper Hebrew pronunciation too.) And did not the early Scottish historians trace the very name of their country back to Jewish history, to Scota, the daughter of the very Pharaoh who perished in the

Red Sea? She fled to Ireland, taking with her the identical stone that Jacob had used as a pillow when he had his famous dream in which he saw a ladder ascending to heaven, and that stone was eventually brought from Ireland to Scotland by Fergus, to become the Stone of Destiny on which Scottish kings were crowned and which the wicked Edward I stole and took to England, to place it under the coronation chair at Westminster Abbey. So the Stone of Destiny, Jacob's stone, was really Jewish and if justice were done it would one day be restored not to Scone in Scotland but to Jerusalem.

They turned east, to face Jerusalem, when they uttered the more solemn prayers, though strictly it should have been south-east. Or he could lift his eyes to the hills as the Psalmist did, to the Braids, the Pentlands, the Moorfoots, the Lammermuirs. Different worlds impinged, intersected. Coming out of school at the lunch inty he could go up Chalmers Street into Lauriston Place, the real workaday world, with tramcars clanging and shops open, and he could go right along to the furniture shop where they sold liquorice root at a halfpenny a stick, just as though it were not a normal schoolday at all. All done in half an hour. He had to be back before the bell rang and classes started again. But the stick of liquorice root in his pocket was there to remind him of the world beyond school to which he had penetrated in the very midst of school routine. And his own roots? Square roots, perhaps, or even cube roots. In the junior school they learned only Scottish history, in the senior school they learned first English and then European history. In some contexts This blessed plot, this earth, this realm, this England, was theirs, and in others This England was the enemy of This Scotland. At school they read Rupert Brooke's sonnet, there is some corner of a foreign field that is for ever England, and appropriated the emotion without trouble. And Wee Paulin loved to quote *eithe genoimen*, would I were in Grantchester, in Grantchester, not only for its illustrative use of the optative of the verb to be but for its local sentiment. They appropriated the Greeks too, Greek myths being presented as part of the English poetic imagination. Wee Paulin also loved to quote Matthew Arnold:

> 'Tis Apollo comes leading
> His choir the nine.
> The leader is fairest,
> But all are divine.

What's Hecuba to him or he to Hecuba? Philo of Alexandria long ago tried to reconcile Jewish religion and Greek philosophy, the Hebraic and the Hellenic. There were philosemites in Scotland who sought the reconciliation of the Hebrew, Greek and Scottish traditions. But at their most characteristic were they reconcilable? What was the high noon of Greek civilization? Fifth-century Athens he supposed. And of Hebrew civilization? There was no moment, really. King David's reign? King Solomon's? These kings ruled empires like other empires, and anyway they fell apart in the third generation, and it was during the centuries of confusion and backsliding, of dissolution and disillusion, of political struggle and external threat, that the prophets arose and the Hebrew biblical heritage was shaped and consecrated. At the end, exile and wandering. The Greeks were conquered too, but they stayed in Greece. What was the high noon of Scottish culture? James IV's reign, before Flodden? But that was a pretty brutal time. The golden age of the latter eighteenth century, his father's Scotland? That extended into the nineteenth, with Scott and Jeffrey and people with civilized imaginations. Had we declined since then? A Latin master had become fascinated by Spengler, and laid out on the blackboard the processes of the Decline of the West. But no, things were getting better and better. The rabbi's household believed firmly in progress. Was there not toleration, mutual respect, freedom, as there had not been throughout the long sad centuries of Jewish disabilities in the western world, and had it not all started with the Enlightenment and got steadily better? And with the League of Nations there would be no more wars. Knowledge increased steadily. New inventions and discoveries made life easier and would eventually eliminate poverty. Everything was evolutionary, ameliorating. Behind it all lay that genteel European classical culture in which – yes, it was true – in which even his Jewishness was subsumed. They admired the *kalos k'agathos*, talked of the *summum bonum*, which was not the same really as *chayim tovim*. Oh, no wonder those eighteenth-century Edinburgh chaps were congenial: this was their world still. Belief in enlightenment pervaded the rabbi's household. Though the rabbi criticized Matthew Arnold for not properly appreciating Hebraism, his sweetness and light were fully accepted: had not his own immediate ancestors come out of east European ghetto darkness into western sweetness and light? The rabbi taught his children to admire the Haskalah movement, and Haskalah was simply the Hebrew for Enlightenment. Jewish enlightenment began with Moses Mendelssohn and could and should, the rabbi insisted, be combined with

Jewish religious orthodoxy, but an orthodoxy purged of ghetto constrictions and ghetto superstitions. The version of Jewish history learned by our hero went like this: The Hebrew patriarchs discovered the one true God by their own disinterested virtue and thus founded a rudimentary Jewish religion; Moses, in leading the Israelites out of Egyptian slavery, led them to the revelation on Mount Sinai (the central fact in Jewish history) and the association of monotheism with ethical norms and a precise legal and ritual code; the Hebrew prophets emphasized the ethical and universalistic aspects of that code and in so doing revealed the true potential of the Jewish religion; the breakdown of the Jewish state, the return from Babylon, and the subsequent codification of Jewish records by Ezra were further stages in the emergence of Judaism as a religion in the modern sense of the word; the fight of the Maccabees against Hellenistic assimilation was a glorious moment in Jewish history and presented a worthy model for later Jewish nationalist and Zionist movements; the destruction of the Temple and the final ending of the Jewish state made it necessary for the Jewish people to preserve themselves in dispersion among the nations with the invaluable help of the elaborate codification and expansion of biblical law found in the Talmud; Christianity, originally a Jewish heresy, in maintaining the absurd belief in the divinity of Jesus and the doctrine of the Trinity, was inevitably led to malign and persecute the good, pious, scholarly Jews of the Middle Ages; with the eighteenth-century Enlightenment came release of the Jews from the ghetto and from many of the medieval restrictions and torments, which was a Good Thing and resulted in modern Jews being able to lead full lives as equal and respected members of the gentile society in which they found themselves while at the same time maintaining their religious separateness by the practice of their special rituals; nevertheless endemic antisemitism in Eastern Europe and elsewhere meant that the Jews were not wholly or finally safe, so that they needed Zionism as a protection, and they praised Theodor Herzl for having demonstrated that if Jews could settle as a nation in their ancient homeland they would then be respected like all other nations; at the same time a great new revival of the Jewish spirit would go forth out of Zion which would give new strength and religious illumination to those Jews who would (inevitably) remain in an increasingly enlightened diaspora. There was another point, and an important one. Christians were all right now. Nobody wanted to see them change their religion. The rabbi was not looking for proselytes – indeed he recoiled from the very idea. And by the same token he regarded Christian missionaries to the Jews as impertinent intruders up to no good. The Christian world remained and would remain the real world, and Jews and Christians could practise their different religions side by side under the umbrella of a common enlightenment.

And now? A shul in the shadow of Edinburgh Castle. For auld lang syne, my dear. We twa hae paidled in the burn from morning sun till dine. Oh they had indeed, he and his brother, in the Scoonie Burn and Braid Burn, burns galore (not Burns's burns, but still good for paidling in). His ancestors had remembered auld lang syne as they mourned by the waters of Babylon: it was Jerusalem they recalled. Jews had wandered mony a weary fit since then, but they still remembered Jerusalem. But did he? The picture of ancient Jerusalem that illustrated the Passover haggadah looked very strange, unlike anything in the least familiar to him, an artificial construct of a nostalgic medieval artist. Had he not been fitted somehow with a new past? It was the Lyne Water not the River Jordan, which he had never seen, that he recalled. He could sing Flow gently sweet Afton but knew no song about any Palestinian stream. One of the summer entertainers at Leven used to sing

> Will ye gae lassie gang
> And walk wi' me my honey?
> I'm no' Carnegie, but I've got a lot of money.
> I've got the brass my lass
> And it I mean tae scatter:
> It's in the Bank o' Scotland near the Banks o' Allan Watter.

He had never sat and mourned by the Water of Leith or any other Scottish water as his ancestors had done by the waters of Babylon. He had rejoiced by them. Was the Jordan good for paidling in? Did it have sticklebacks and minnows and frog spawn and, most of all, trout? And is there honey still for tea? Well, the land of Israel was supposed to flow with milk and honey. Could he see himself sitting under a palm tree eating bread and honey and drinking a glass of milk with the hot near-eastern sun overhead? More easily than he could imagine himself in a medieval ghetto certainly or even in the Jewish quarter of the eastern European town his great-grandfather had spent his life in. He would eat figs out of a wallet and gravely salute travellers who passed by on camels. But no, he was raised in a northern clime and could not do without the chill Scottish rain and the smell of bog myrtle on the Scottish hills in summer. Each year he acquired new memories of town and country, of sea and stream and hillside, of street and square and bridge, and they were steadily building up a past for him, a localized past in Scotland beside which his ancestral past was vague and remote. When he read Robert Chambers's essay on the Meadow Walks he recognized himself.

'Adjacent to the southern suburbs of Edinburgh there is a spacious meadow, which forms an agreeable place of recreation for the citizens in that quarter, being pervaded and surrounded by spacious and shady walks, somewhat in the style of the famous parks of London, or the still lovelier Christchurch Walk of Oxford. Happening, in my schoolboy days, to reside in that part of the city, I used to resort to the Meadow Walks, as they are called, both in the morning and the evening, for the purpose of conning my lessons – communing with Tytyrus, perhaps under that very species of tree [a beech after all, not a Spanish chestnut] which covered him with its branches while he piped the beauties of Amaryllis. These walks, I have since learned, were a favourite lounge, for the same purpose, with the illustrious Scott, who dwelt in boyhood in a house of which the rear windows look into the central alley. But, at the time I speak of, no such circumstance as this, even if I had been aware of it, was necessary to recommend to me a place so convenient for study, and so pleasant in itself. From this grassy and umbrageous domain the pinnacles and battlements of ancient Edinburgh could be seen immediately behind the broken screen of trees; but no sound from the crowded streets, near as they were, ever broke upon the ear.' He too knew that grassy and umbrageous domain and loved both the grassiness and the umbrageousness. It was hard to use those splendid long words in modern times. Some boundless contiguity of shade. People would take umbrage if you spoke to them like that. Henry John told them an old Punch joke. I hear the Americans have taken umbrage. Indeed? And where exactly is that? He thought of it more like taking snuff. Do you take umbrage? No thanks, filthy habit. Costly thy habit as thy purse can bear. Polonius. The old polony man.

> Hey the wee polony man
> Ho the wee polony man.
> Put a penny in the can
> For the wee polony man.

The rhyme remained, but there were no polony men in Edinburgh in his time. They were itinerant sausage vendors. Bologna sausage became polony sausage, then just polony. But in the *Heart of Midlothian* Scott used polonie to mean a dress for very young boys, including a sort of waistcoat, with loose sloping skirts, perhaps so-called because it was borrowed from Poland. Poland had attracted Scottish as well as Jewish merchants. Ane pedder is called ane merchand or cremar, quha bears ane pack or crame upon his back, quha are called bearars of the puddill be the Scottesmen in the realm of Polonia, qhuairof I saw ane great multitude in the town of Cracovia, anno Dom. 1569. Before the Union of 1707 there were Scottish merchants all over northern Europe. Among the Slavonians, who do not take to commerce, and have their merchandise done by other races, the Scots seem to have supplied all grades, from the merchant princes to the pedlars. The vacuum they left when the Union opened up the home market to Scots enterprise, seems to have been filled by Jews. So his ancestors may have rubbed shoulders with those of his schoolmates in Poland or in Hanseatic towns in the seventeenth century.

But it was the eighteenth century that saw the emergence in Britain of those stable and universal pieties which formed common ground between the rabbi and the Edinburgh philosophers. The rabbi became a freemason, as Burns had done, and at meetings of Lodge Solomon proclaimed the fundamental unity of all rituals under the fatherhood of God. This contented universalism existed side by side with his Jewish particularism in an odd way. Our hero was exposed equally powerfully to both doctrines, and he accepted them both. Oh he knew there were South Sea Islanders and people with sticks through their noses, every kind of ritual and ceremony all over the world, and there were Mohammedans, Hindus, Buddhists, Sikhs, Jains, all respectable religions. But he was not faced with the problem of coming to terms with all of these, since they did not flourish in Scotland. What was God doing allowing so many perversions of his truth? Did he prefer it that way? Or was there no truth apprehensible by men, only aspects and facets of an incomprehensible totality? That was the view that made most sense. But you couldn't really say that all beliefs and practices represented partial glimpses of a mysterious whole. Some beliefs were patently absurd, some practices were cruel and beastly. Polytheism and idol worshipping were clearly wrong, and so were horrid things like human sacrifices. A witch doctor was not an acceptable variation of a rabbi. The rabbi subscribed to a fortnightly illustrated publication called *Peoples of All Nations*, which he later had bound, and our hero would gaze fascinated at pictures of outlandish rites performed by exotic tribes. So various a world, such a varied humanity, made universalism very difficult. Yet was the little segment of history that had carried the Jewish people forward in time from Abraham the only true bit, the only bit in which God was really involved, with all other people and events just goyim and their misguided ways? Or should everyone believe that his bit was the only true bit for him and be happy to let others think the same about their bits? That seemed to him to be his father's position. The rabbi did not want the leopard to change his spots, the Christians to cease being Christians or the Moslems to cease being Moslems. As long as they were nice to the Jews, the Jews would prefer them to be as they were. There were, the rabbi explained on one of the few occasions when our hero took this tricky question up with him, what the Talmud called the seven laws of Noah, laws which were kept by the righteous Noah long before the Law was promulgated on Sinai, and good people of all proper religions adhered to these basic ethical principles. Whatever unacceptable theological ideas they employed to justify those principles, if they adhered to the principles they could be recognized as good people and lived with as neighbours. Nevertheless, they looked forward to a universal theism of the purest kind prevailing some day among all men, and towards the end of the sabbath morning service the congregation sang the concluding sentence of a central Jewish prayer: *bayom hahu yiheyeh adonai echad u-sh'mo echad*, In that day shall the Lord be one and his name one. That was the one far-off divine event towards which all history was moving, the last step in progress. But he himself found the present quite satisfactory and was happy to be growing up in Edinburgh in the first part of the twentieth century.

It wasn't really the twentieth century, of course, but the fifty-sixth, the Jewish year, *annus mundi*, dating from what was once thought to be the year of creation, but though on formal ceremonial occasions the Jewish dating was used the rabbi and his family used the Christian dating as the normal secular way of doing things. True, they used BCE (before the common era) and CE (common era) instead of BC and AD in Jewish publications, because BC and AD had unacceptable theological connotations, but at school for example he would never have dreamed of deviating from the usual practice. These were not important matters. He could have wished that the early Christians had not perversely changed their day of rest from Saturday to Sunday, in order to differentiate it from the Jewish sabbath, for it would have been a great convenience if Jewish and Christian sabbath had coincided, but the shape and flavour of the weekend with religious shabbos followed by quiet and undemanding

Sunday was so well established that he found it hard to imagine a world arranged otherwise. He liked the sound of Edinburgh church bells, though they did not summon him anywhere, and he liked Cowper's lines about the origin of Robinson Crusoe:

> But the sound of the church-going bell
> These valleys and rocks never heard,
> Ne'er sighed at the sound of a knell,
> Or smiled when a Sabbath appeared.

Wordsworth objected to the adjective church-going as applied to a bell, describing it as an instance of the strange abuses which poets have introduced into their language, but while it is true that a church-going bell does not go to church, neither does a dining-room dine or a wishing-well wish or a visiting-card visit. A dining-room is for dining IN, a wishing-well is for wishing AT, a visiting-card is for visiting WITH, and a church-going bell is for going to church BY or at the sound of. He did not use the Edinburgh church-going bells for this purpose; for him as they sounded just before eleven they proclaimed the genteel permanence of the city's habits and institutions, and he used them self-indulgently to please his mood. What went on inside the churches was a mystery to him. Occasionally he heard the sound of hymns or metrical psalms wafting out, and some of these were familiar, but the service itself, its ritual and order, remained unknown. He knew they didn't kneel in the Church of Scotland as they did in the Church of England, and that provided a certain fellow feeling, but when they stood and when they sat, what prayers they said, what kind of sermons were preached, belonged to the area of blank and alien subjects. He was happy to accept this ignorance. He did not want to pry into the habits of other religions. When his schoolfellows disappeared into the interior of churches on Sundays and when he disappeared into the interior of the synagogue on Saturdays they were each retreating into the special mysteries of their own tradition, determined by their separate pasts. He would see groups standing in their Sunday best outside the church after the service, clutching their prayer books. *Extra ecclesiam. Extra ecclesiam nulla salus*, no salvation outside the church. When he first heard this disturbing phrase he imagined to himself a minister briskly coming up to a group gossiping outside his church and saying reprovingly, *outside* the church there is no salvation. This would be to chide them for standing outside. But it could also be taken to mean the forbidding of offering salvation outside the church. Suppose the minister saw an itinerant preacher from another denomination offering salvation to members of his own (the minister's) flock outside his own church, he might say: No salvation outside the church, as one who says, No spitting outside the church. But spitting inside the church would be a graver offence. Some of the very old Yiddish-speaking immigrants in his father's congregation were accustomed to seeing spittoons in the synagogue which they could use when they felt inclined, and had to be restrained from spitting on the floor in their absence. In Edinburgh tramcars and at tram stops there was displayed the sign: M.O.H. SAYS SPITTING SPREADS DISEASE. It struck him as odd that this was recorded as an observation by M.O.H. rather than stated as a fact. Ah, it's only what M.O.H. says, so we needn't bother. If the notice had read simply SPITTING SPREADS DISEASE it would have sounded more absolute and authoritative. In theatres and concert halls there was the simple command REFRAIN FROM SPITTING, and it was said that two elderly ladies at a concert in the Usher Hall were heard conferring in puzzlement as to what the item about to be played really was when one of them said happily, pointing to the notice, Ah, it's the refrain from Spitting. That sounded less attractive than the refrain from Walking on the Grass. Where e'er you walk cool gales shall fan the glade, Trees where you sit shall crowd into a shade. Prohibitory announcements abounded. NO SMOKING. NO ADMITTANCE EXCEPT ON BUSINESS. NO DOGS EXCEPT ON LEASH. NO HAWKERS. NO STANDING ON THE UPPER DECK. No standing on the burning deck, but the boy stood, whence all but he had fled. Mrs Hemans wrote such he-man poetry it was hard to believe that she was a she-woman. Nobody took her seriously at school. The boy stood on the burning deck with ripe bananas round his neck, they would recite. It was little boys' poetry, all that rhythmic ranting. Felicia her first name was. *Felicia quae potuit poemata fingere multa.* There was an extra syllable at the beginning, but only experts would be bothered. You used to be very pert, didn't you? Yes, I was, but not any more: I'm an ex-pert. In Latin it meant having no part in. *Expers spectaculi sum*, I have no part in the play. But we all have parts in the play, all the world's a stage, at each stage one acts a part, at each act one parts the curtain, in each part one treads the stage. And who coaches you in the great drama of life? The schoolmaster is the stage coach. Open your teeth boy. *A absque coram de.* Two of a tri, three of a di. And what, boys, said the modern language master who started them on German in the VIth, as an experiment, what do you think of that delightful list of prepositions which take either the accusative or the dative AS THE CASE MAY BE? An auf hinter in neben vor über unter zwischen. List, list, O list. Haste me to know't. Duller shouldst thou be than the fat weed that rots itself in ease on Leith Docks. Adieu, adieu. Remember an auf hinter etc. Gunpowder treason and plot. A good plot as ever was laid, our friends true and constant: a good plot, good friends, and full of expectation. Great expectations. Now that did have a good plot. How everything tied together in the end, when Magwitch and Estella and Miss Haversham and Compeyson were revealed as all enmeshed. England expects. Gentlemen who expectorate ought not to expect to rate as gentlemen. Now wasn't that better than M.O.H. SAYS?

It would have been better to put his statement first and then add, sez M.O.H. You could of course put it into oratio obliqua, M.O.H. said that spitting spread disease – or would spread? It depends what you imagine his actual words were. Those words having been said, it remained for the town council to make use of them. That ablative. How absolute the knave is. These things having been accomplished. Such being the case, *quae cum ita sint*. Such being the nominative case in fact. It was a good idea to have a vocative case, but hardly necessary to have it for inanimate objects. Yet poets could use it. O field, I praise thy fresh green grass. O evening star. O little house where once I lived. Wee, modest crimson-tippèd flower. He supposed that if you talked to yourself you would have to use the vocative. O me! I hear you ca-a-a-a-alling me, in the vocative. Ca' the yowes to the knowes. A wild call and a clear call that will not be denied. Ca' canny! The calling coal men called COAL – COAL – COAL all over the city. Call-men. Sometimes in duplicate, COAL – COAL, more often in triplicate, COAL – COAL – COAL, never lingering over the vowel but uttering it briefly and sharply. Sometimes they called BRIQUETTES, but he was not sure what they were. Newsboys shouted SPATCH, NEWS. Cries of Edinburgh. They had Cries of London on a set of cigarette cards. What d'ye lack? Ah, what a question. What did he lack? I want, I want, I want. What d'ye lack? Fancy an itinerant street-vendor (who was not a vendor *of* streets as a money-lender was a lender of money but a vendor *on* streets), fancy an itinerant street-vendor forcing one to search one's inner desires. Well what *do* you lack? What, what, what? Everything or nothing. All lives, all experiences, all roads. On holiday, exploring a new countryside, he had to choose one of two beckoning paths, only one could be trodden at a time. (Later, when he read Robert Frost's poem about the road not taken, he found the shock of recognition overpowering.) It was not that he wanted to be everybody, but he wanted to know from the inside what it was like to be everybody. Someone glimpsed from the train walking in a field, a face at a window: who were they *really*? And in that special sense he wanted to be a sea-captain, a kilted highland soldier, an explorer, a trawler fisherman, a landowner on a beautiful country estate, a rustic innkeeper, a tramp, a concert violinist, as well of course (but this was a more direct and simple ambition) as a great poet. What d'ye lack? The whole world. He wanted to know it all, embrace it all, be it all. He had moods of enormous charity, believing that he and only he was capable of fully understanding everybody's desires and feelings and inner states. And yet, sitting alone by his open bedroom window on a summer evening looking out on the back greens of Livingstone Place he was content, content, content, knowing that he could both concentrate and dissolve in his own imagination, his own mood and feeling, anything and everything that mattered in the whole wide world. Lost in himself, wondrously, happily lost in a trance of acceptance and receptivity, all was within him, in stillness and tensely balanced inner passion he was transformed into a burning-glass that focused the rays of all human light into a cold fire. It was a miracle of rare device, a stately pleasure dome with caves of ice. Hot ice and wondrous flaming snow. And he knew that Kubla Khan was a poem about making poetry, a poem about the poet's necessary state of mind. Of imagination all compact. And there the record was, black marks on a page, they spoke, the dead poet spoke, he was in the poet's presence. It was frightening when he really thought about it. You read a book, a poem, a novel, and took for granted your absorption in the world created by the writer and coded in black marks for you to decode it may be centuries later. This was much more marvellous than the gramophone. There were the books standing on the shelf, waiting for their authors' imagination to be summoned back into vivid present life by a reader. What was the status of books when they were not being read? Like the score of music not played. And many people could read the same work or play the same piece of music at exactly the same time in widely separated places. A British exile in India reading Keats while he read the same poem on Blackford Hill, an American reading Dickens in California at the precise moment when he was reading the same chapter of the same novel in a corner of his Edinburgh dining-room. So God could speak simultaneously to different people in different places. He had some glimpse of how like the lastingness and ubiquity of literature was to a concept of the divine voice. Do they know when you read them after their death? If he wrote something and some boy centuries later were to read it and say, Yes, yes, I know what he means, he is speaking to me, what then? He would never be aware of that recognition, never hear the greeting, and he grieved for his future ignorance.

Time was what it all came back to. Time said the invigilator at the end of the period allotted for the exam, time said the maid knocking on the bedroom door at half-past seven, time said his mother when she came to clear away the school-books from the dining-room table, time said his father when they ought to set out for the synagogue, what's the time, there's no time left, have a nice time, all in good time, once upon a time. Time in history and English exams was terrible, for he was prone to write long long answers to the first question and then have to finish the others in panic, racing against the clock. And time was irreversible. One couldn't say, let's take this day again and do it differently, let's see what happens if we try it another way. Sometimes it went so slowly, sometimes it went so fast. What was it like not to exist, to have no awareness of the present? He cast his mind back, back, he saw himself as a little boy playing with a wooden engine, writing his first letters in a copy book, and before that? Disappointingly, it slipped away into darkness. What was it like not to have existed all those thousands of years before he was born? He didn't know. And yet he had been in that state of non-existence. He wrestled with this. Here he was, everything in the universe, so far as he was concerned, coming through his consciousness. Everything had meaning only in so far as it struck his own self. Of course it was the same with everybody else and their own selves. But he wasn't everybody else. His centre of consciousness was his only guarantee that anything was real. Across this sense of isolation came the light of dead minds shining through their books. He was told that every seven years every atom of your body changed and you were therefore a different self. He could believe it. Was he the same now as he was when a helpless and inarticulate baby? Yet surely he would be the same when he was older, and never forget as a man the self he had had as a boy. The child is father of the man, and I could wish my days to be bound each to each by natural piety. I could wish, yes, anybody could wish, but was it really so? What would he be like as a responsible adult man, earning money, bringing up his own family, making solemn decisions with other grown-ups? Wouldn't that involve a clamping down on the wild inner freedom to think and feel and indulge different kinds of mood? Yet poets who were adult men had written poems that showed him clearly that they had not given up these inner freedoms. He did not believe that poets and novelists were permanent children, irresponsible and feckless, unable to cope with the adult world; he did not believe this at all. Shakespeare managed his affairs very well and retired to Stratford. Shelley it is true behaved irresponsibly, but Keats didn't – it wasn't his fault that he was consumptive and died young as a result. No, he clung to the fact that many poets and novelists had inhabited the adult world perfectly easily, and at the same time preserved – indeed, enlarged – that capability of inducing and exploring inward states that for him was so much a part of his being a youngster. Well, there was no point in arguing with himself about it: time would tell. Time always told. You told the time and time told you. Curiously enough, he had had difficulty in learning to tell the time as a small boy, perhaps because nobody bothered to teach him. In Class H – was it? – Miss Smith had sent him to look at the clock in the school hall and come back with the right time, and he had most shamefacedly to tell her that he could only tell o'clock and half past. So she sent another boy. When that boy came back he said it was half-past eleven, and he realized with a pang that he could have got away with it without the shameful admission, for it was one of the times he could tell. How had he been left deficient, when other boys of his age had mastered the art of time-telling? He told the story to his mother when he got home from school and she briskly set about remedying the deficiency. It turned out to be quite easy really. He encountered a sundial once in a friend's garden, and saw with astonishment how the sun got it right. A simple and ingenious idea. He thought that a sundial could more properly be called a time-table and was surprised that no one had thought of that before the schools and railways took the word over. There were these two kinds of time-tables: the school one, which you were given at the beginning of each session and carefully copied out in neat little boxes and pasted into the inside of key school books, and railway time-tables, which were much more exciting, and which enabled you to go imaginary journeys all over the place. The little blue Murray's diaries – the rabbi always carried one in his waistcoat pocket, for he travelled a lot, giving lectures in other cities – showed all the trains that went from either Waverley Station or Princes Street to all over Scotland and England. London had a long narrow column, and you could go three ways, two from Waverley and one from Princes Street. He could sit for hours with a Murray's diary deciding where to go and when, but better still were those larger and more complete time-tables which enabled you to plan connections and go from place to place. Railway time-tables were really place-tables, showing the places where trains went to. But of course they showed the times when trains left and arrived: place was defined by time or was it time that was defined by place? Oh that was the year we went to Romanno Bridge for our holidays, that was when we were at Crail, that was when was where . . . *Et ego in Arcadia vixi. Veni vidi vixi*, I came, I saw, I LIVED. That's how it was. Each summer he possessed another seaside village, another country place, and lingered over it in memory during the following winter months. Past time was measured by places. Even the hours of a day. In bed, in the dining-room, crossing the Meadows on the way to school, and then the different periods, Maths, Latin, History, English, Greek, Physics, Geography – seven periods during a school day, each in a different classroom, each with its own flavour and feeling, and the inties in between. Like that song about the roast beef of Old England. Hot on Sunday, cold on Monday, Wednesday and Thursday too they make it into Irish stew.

> What gives the p'liceman
> The strength to blow his whistle?
> It's the little bit of fat
> And the little bit of gristle
> In the roast beef of Old England
> That makes us what we are today.

But who ate fat and gristle? It was put in for the sake of the rhyme. Oh rhymes, what crimes are committed in thy name. I like a sandwich of salmon and shrimps, you never find imps in salmon and shrimps. Was it at Port Seton that the pierrots sang that ridiculous song, with those desperate imps introduced as a last resort rhyme, a last seaside-resort rhyme? But a good and fitting rhyme was a great satisfaction. It was a matching, a chiming, a manifestation of order, a reflection through man's use of language of God's producing order out of chaos and so creating the world. The procession and recurrence of the seasons, the breaking of waves on the shore, the structure of flowers and sea-shells, were in a way great natural rhymes. Yes, nature had both rhyme and rhythm, and that was why one felt at home in it. For men's minds responded to rhyme and rhythm (and to rhyme and reason, lack of which was proverbially senseless), the universe was God's epic poem and every person and creature and thing and force in it rhymed with SOMETHING. The most diverse things were linked. Did he who made the lamb make ME?

Me? I wake in the morning and resume myself from the shadows and figments of the night, bit by bit memory reasserts my identity as consciousness strengthens and I become progressively aware that I am me, here, now. I am what I was. God said I am that I am, because he was outside time, but my self is a constantly expanding bundle of memories. Trivial fond records. Remember, recollect, recall, bear in mind, be mindful of. There were active and passive kinds of remembering. If we were enjoined to remember actively the fifth of November, the rhyme should be

> Be mindful of
> The 5th of Nov.

rather than

> Remember remember
> The 5th of November.

Not that the fifth of November means anything special to me, whose ancestors were not in the country at the time of that Catholic plot to blow up a Protestant Parliament. Engrafted memories of others' pasts have doubtless helped and enriched me, but the me that is helped and enriched emerged from a more private history. I am a first person singular, a singular first person, and I have to remind myself that all those whom I see as third persons and talk to as second persons are first persons to themselves. This is the great mystery. It's amazing how we all get along, not wasting our time brooding over firsts, seconds and thirds but taking up the telephone, hello, is that you, are you there, this is me, I'm telling you, you surprise me, I say I say I say. You know what I mean? Do you don't you do you don't you know what I mean because what I mean is what I mean and not what you may turn it into when you hear it. Do you read me? Me to you. Over. Message received. Me to you. Over. You mean you to me. Over. Yes, me to you. Over. Are we overheard? Are we understood? Take me with you. Com-prenez? I am apprehensive that you may not have apprehended. Or I may not. Do I recognize myself in your response to me? O wad some power the giftie gie us to see oorselves as ithers see us. Do I really want that? We would then no longer be ourselves. You are not yourself today. Well, I'm not absolutely myself, just selfish. Closed up in one's own identity, a selfish shell-fish. Clam, secretly. The secret bivalve, clamping its halves together, symbol of isolation or of union? A clam destined to a clandestine existence? No, there are clans of clams, societies, relationships, even among molluscs. Hello, are you the Clam Macdonald? No clam, I'm a Mussulman. Of the two, which is the oyster? Which is the carpenter of the two? I weep for you the walrus said, I deeply sympathize. But to weep FOR is not to sympathize, that is to weep WITH. And that is hard. Who truly suffers or rejoices with me, sym-pathizes or co-gauds when I suffer or rejoice? Yet how we welcome gestures of sym and co. I ran home across the Meadows to tell my parents that I had won the Sir Robert Cranston Memorial Prize for essay writing. With no one to tell, where would the joy have been? The solitary golfer who got a hole in one was driven to despair when he realized that there was nobody with him to witness or attest his triumph. Narcissus was your only true communicator, yet how barren, how bitterly barren, never to see yourself reflected in others' eyes, always and only in your own.

I wasn't always brooding like this you know, mostly I took life as it came, affected by the weather, welcoming Friday, relishing fresh scones and jam, losing myself in books. I communicated with objects. My father gave me a little wrist-watch when I was twelve and at night I would put it under the pillow beside the flashlight and I would talk to them both. We formed a nocturnal society. Who would be so silly and sentimental as to talk to a watch in the daytime? But at night Ticky was a real character and the sound of his voice coming through the pillow on to my ear was part of a real dialogue. The flashlight had a bulbous magnifying-glass on the top of the hinged case, but you could fold back the top and expose the ordinary little bulb shining without magnification. The light was so white and clean after I had put in a new battery, then as time went on slowly became yellow and feebler. The progressive decline of Flashy was sad to observe, but a new battery eventually resurrected him, symbol of immortality. Feeling better now? Yes thank you. I would shine the light under the bedclothes, a white palace lit up. So I shine a light now, illuminating what I was. And was the child father of the man? Shall I tell how the story ends? It does not end, it slips and slides onwards, the 'already' merges continually into the 'not yet', and the child mutates and disappears yet remains, colouring the adult mind with more than memories, furnishing, yes that's the word, furnishing the conscious and the subconscious, a mind bien meublé. Do I mind being meublé? It is the condition of existence, to be démeublé is to be dead. I sometimes used to think, What if I lost my memory completely and had no awareness at all from moment to moment of who

I was, lost all continuity of personality? Would I be a person at all? Suppose someone said: Tomorrow you will lose all memory of what you have been, so that the person you will be tomorrow will have no contact in his mind or feeling with the person you are today. If after this happened somebody inflicted grievous pain on you, who would be feeling that pain? Would you be right (supposing I told you now, before you lost your memory) to dread that pain, or could you say, That person will not be bound to me by any continuity of memory, so to all intents and purposes he will not be me, so it won't be me who will be hurt, so I don't need to dread the coming pain? I could never make up my mind how to answer that question. As well as the problem of continuity of personality there was the question of uniqueness of personality. Once – playing the violin in public immediately after it had been completely re-strung so that the unstretched strings kept slipping and I got more and more wildly out of tune so that I had to stop in the middle of a sonata and retire in total shame – I tried hard to comfort myself in my humiliation by thinking that I was the only person in the whole universe who responded to the situation in that way, so why bother to carry my wholly personal burden, why not escape from my self and think and feel about the matter as someone else (and EVERYone else was someone else)? It wouldn't work, though. Yet it wasn't difficult to identify myself with somebody I was reading about. Indeed, there the opposite situation prevailed, for I had to keep telling myself that it was only an invented story when something painful was happening to a character with whom I had become emotionally involved, and assert my own identity in contrast. Yet I was tempted, in inventing stories and situations, to go to the extreme edge before bringing the characters involved back to safety and happiness. I used to imagine cases of misunderstanding and growing coldness between two people who really deeply loved each other and keep on postponing the moment of clarification and reconciliation, so as to make it all the more moving and profound when it did come. And in real life too I sometimes did this, exacerbating a quarrel with masochistic anguish wanting to say but putting off saying, No no, I didn't mean that, let's start again and be as we were. At the back of my mind there was an archetypal tragic situation when that moment was postponed, postponed, postponed, always with the intention of relishing it the more when it did come, but something happened and it never did come, it was too late. Why did I indulge in such fancies? Was it in order to add to the emotional quality of living, to the resistance of experience which required to be overcome and in overcoming which one put vividness and colour into what might otherwise have been a pallid existence? Has that anything to do with the *oikeia hedone*, the peculiar pleasure, of tragedy?

But I was not a tragic boy; far from it. I had frequent impulses to clown, to make a nonsense out of what other people were taking seriously. Sometimes I had a sudden urge to contribute something totally absurd to a serious discussion, to say when listening to the geography master talking about rock formations, And that is why mince-pies always move sideways, or Steam-rollers are cheaper with strawberry jam. Nonsense verses would muster themselves in my head. The pigs from Piccadilly are performing in the park, The dirty dogs from Darlington are dancing in the dark, Baboons from Bessarabia are buttering their buns, And grenadiers from Glasgow are a-greasing of their guns. When Herbert Hoover became president of the United States I associated his name with the Hoover vacuum cleaner, which advertised that it beats as it sweeps as it cleans, and one night in bed there came vividly into my head, to the tune of Solomon Levi, a ridiculous verse which I kept singing for years:

My name is President Hoover and I keep a grocer's shop,
There are biscuits at the bottom and tomatoes at the top.
So if you want your groceries, come form a single file
And wait for President Hoover who will serve you with a smile.

(CHORUS)

O President Hoover
It beats as it sweeps as it cleans.
O President Hoover
Fetch me that tin of sardines.   &c.

Why? O reason not the need, these frothy irresponsibilities on the surface of daily living were I suppose a testimony to an excess verbal vitality; they welled up unbidden and caused me unreflective happiness. Do I recall them? Very well then I recall them. As I do not recall the broody poems, the imitative sonnets, the Spenserian stanzas, the sunsets and moonrises and other literary-picturesque performances with which I filled notebooks. Those were consigned to the flames with my belated discovery of post-Georgian poetry which brought with it an appalled conviction that my poems were all second-hand and derivative and showed no truly original poetic force. But the silly verses and the nonsense poems were never written down, and so were never burned. They were invulnerable to criticism and to time. And oft when on my couch I lie in vacant or in pensive mood.

These are the words, *eileh ha-d'varim*, these are the words which Moses spoke unto all Israel beyond the Jordan. The opening of Deuteronomy, which in Hebrew is simply called *d'varim*, words. Or it might equally mean things. Or affairs. That always seemed to me perfectly logical. When Adam named the creatures in Eden he was saying what they were. And when Moses spoke unto all Israel beyond the Jordan we are told that it was in the wilderness, in the Arabah, over against Suph, between Paran and Tophel, and Laban, and Hazerot, and Di-zahab. This was a local habitation and a name with a vengeance. The place names give authenticity to his speech. He spoke then and there. He had a *locus loquendi*. The place names were for named places. Words spoken in places for which the words were Arabah, Suph, Paran and Tophel, would obviously be quite different from words spoken in places for which the words were Edinburgh, Perth, Aberdeen and Inverness. Scottish songs were always naming places, ye banks and braes o' bonnie Doon, the birks o' Aberfeldy, there was a lad was born in Kyle. And Wordsworth tended to be locally specific. Lines written a few miles above Tintern Abbey. Lines written near Richmond, upon the Thames, at evening, composed upon Westminster Bridge, and a little-quoted poem that leapt out of the page at me when I first leafed through his collected poems, A Jewish family in a small valley opposite St Goar upon the Rhine. Hamelin Town's in Brunswick, by famous Hanover city. The lake isle of Innisfree. Adlestrop. These are the words, place names, thing names, person names, and reality is mediated through them. In playing fancifully with words we can create alternative realities in our mind. That's what it is. Real literature uses language to interpret reality, word literature constructs out of words an alternative reality that does not obey the laws of the one we know from experience. A red and yellow somersault, inquisitive and vain, Trundles a pair of brackets down the causeway in the rain. Tell me, weird sisters, do you expect sunshine, rain or hail tomorrow? Hail, Macbeth. Some hail and some rain? All hail, Macbeth. He was foiled in the end by a verbal trick, a trick of names, Birnam Wood and Dunsinane. Ships are solemnly named with champagne. Some orthodox Jews, when their baby is dangerously ill, formally change its name in a synagogue ritual in order to cheat the Angel of Death.

> The merchant to secure his treasure
> Conveys it in a borrowed name:

> Euphelia serves to grace my measure,
> But Chloe is my real flame.

Then why break security in the very measure in which you are supposed to be trying to hide her real name? A rose by any other name will smell as sweet, because it's still a rose. What Juliet actually said was, That which we call a rose, etc. The way her sentence has been abbreviated in popular remembrance is significant, indicating that rose is still its *real* name. Now I always knew that names could be switched, that there were Hebrew equivalents for English words and kinds of naming you used to other Jews which you couldn't employ in talking to the boys at school. Yet this increased rather than diminished my awareness of the importance of naming. An early childhood recollection is of an uncle who said, Avoz a goose, which seemed to expect the reply were you? or even vos you? Avoz was how some Yiddish-speaking Jews would say I was. But *avoz* was also the Hebrew word for goose (in the Ashkenazi pronunciation). So my uncle was informing me that *avoz* meant a goose. It took me some time to discover this, and in the difficulty of my apprehending his purpose lay the joke. I encountered this kind of verbal play almost from infancy, always with reference to more than one language. Since *dog* was the Hebrew for fish, would a little Hebrew fish be a puppy? And – a subtle one this, asked regularly by my father at the Passover Seder – who was Danto? The second verse of a seder song begins, *Danto melech gerar*, Danto king of Gerar. So who was Danto? King of Gerar of course, an unsuspecting guest, showing off his Hebrew, promptly replied. But no. Danto is the second person singular past tense of the verb to judge, and means thou didst judge. So *Danto melech gerar* means, Thou didst judge the king of Gerar. Hebrew lent itself to jokes of this kind. I got wise to them early, and was never caught more than once.

Words were an invitation to use them. There were formulas for beginning stories. It was a dark and stormy winter's night, and the rain came down in torrents. The Duke said to Antonio, Tell us a tale. And the tale began as follows: It was a dark and stormy winter's night, and the rain came down in torrents. The Duke said to Antonio, Tell us a tale. And the tale began as follows: It was a dark . . . A maternal aunt used to recite that to me. The Duke. Antonio. Shakespeare's world. Other names had other suggestions. Brooks of Sheffield is sharp, my mother used to say, indicating that we children were picking up more from a grown-up conversation than we were supposed to. Years later I came across the phrase, Little pitchers have big ears, and recognized Brooks of Sheffield. My father, referring critically to a troublesome female member of his flock, referred to her as Mrs Hotzyplotz, which came to be his name for anybody whose identity he wished to hide. But Brooks of Sheffield was often able to discover the identity of Mrs Hotzyplotz. Hoots, toots, ma heart is in ma boots. That fine comic Dave Willis, playing the part of a pirate condemned to death, was asked by the judge if he had anything to say. Aye, he replied, I feel rotten aboot the whole thing. Litotes. Might be a character in a Greek play or a seventeenth-century play about classical characters. Now say, Theramenes, whence heard you this? Ask not, Litotes, for I may not tell. And does the great Litotes fear to speak, Whose eloquence so oft hath moved us all? Ah jest not dear my Lord. Figures of speech I have put from me, and my words are numbered. Dwarf enters and stabs him from behind, saying: So are thy days, proud man. *Accipe hoc.* It was in *The Talisman* that I met this Latin phrase on the lips of an assassin: Take that. But when I firs.t read it it sounded so like a perfect imitation of a double hiccup, accipe hoc, that I interpreted it as such. There was a story of celebrating students asking the waiter for a bottle of hock and jocularly calling it hic-haec-hoc. When it failed to arrive and one of the students protested the waiter said, But I thought you had declined the wine sir. Ladies in Victorian novels fell into a decline and the Roman Empire declined into a fall. My loot, be still, as the burglar said to his bag of swag. When I first read Fifteen men on the dead man's chest I thought to myself, no wonder he was dead, how could he breathe with fifteen men sitting on his chest? It was some time before it dawned on me that it was the other kind of chest.

But man does not live by words alone, and memory has as much a visual as a verbal texture. Brightly lit interiors, figures in a landscape, rooms, doors, staircases, paths, railings, streets, school desks, corridors – they form an immense pattern, synchronic not diachronic in spite of having been woven in time. So here we are, each carrying his interior pattern. Sometimes in a Dutch painting we look into a room and recognize that it has been lived in, that it has been part of someone's daily experience. And we feel a pang, because it is not our experience, but it might have been, it is not our memory, but it might have been, it is recognizable but strange, familiar but different, not part of our own interior pattern but *almost* a remembrance, as Keats defined the effect of poetry. In this almost lies the poignancy of so much human communication and the appeal of so much in the arts. Almosting. All human society is an almosting of inter-relationships and we must be glad that there remains a gap between the communicants, a slip between the cup and the lip, a limitation to the totality of expressiveness. For if we could communicate absolutely, wholly, and not have to stretch and strain and strive, testing words and trying out gestures and always always aware of the frustrations of approximation – if we had no need to wrestle with the medium and it all came easily, fully, completely, then art would not be possible and human individuality would not be possible and we would be melted in a world of soft comprehension. Can we glimpse here a justification of the existence of evil in the world? It is an analogy, anyway. Art must not be perfect or it would not be perfect art. Something of resistance must remain in the finished work, some indication of the recalcitrance of the chosen medium, some suggestion of the incompatibility between words or musical sound or colour and form on the one hand, the reality of human experience on the other, if the work of art is to make that disturbing appeal combining recognition and strangeness. And in the gap between vision and expression the work of art finds its own autonomy, unexpected meanings come to light, worlds of value are born and reflect back on the world we started from, and we look around us differently. Oh we can be deceived, though. Intimations of immortality may lie cruelly: Heaven lies about us in our infancy, and also lies *to* us. Promises, vistas, intuitions, convictions even, may fade into doubts, disappointments, frustrations, emptinesses. But if we are lucky wonder remains, and doubt mutated into wonder rather than wonder worried into doubt is the richest human state. And uncertainty makes for infinite expectation, disappointment if unaccompanied by certainty can point to renewal:

> All, all of a piece throughout;
> Thy chase had a beast in view;
> Thy wars brought nothing about;
> Thy lovers were all untrue.
> 'Tis well an old age is out,
> And time to begin a new.

Disillusion or optimism? They can be more closely related than most people think.

The world's great age begins anew. The final chorus in Shelley's 'Hellas' echoed often in my young mind. A brighter Hellas, a loftier Argo, another Athens, and I would add a rebuilt Jerusalem. But the line, The world is weary of the past, I could not go along with. Progress, reform, continuing enlightenment, yes, but all judged in the light of memory, given meaning by history. You can't draw a line and start afresh, after 1066, after 1485, after 1789, after 1914. Today is always the end product of all our yesterdays. I used to worry about causation. Was it all the result of climate? You could argue that very plausibly. Or consider the point the history master once made: In the Middle Ages there was no artificial cattle feed, so most livestock were slaughtered before winter set in and salted down or spiced for the winter, only a few beasts surviving weakly to be carried out into the newly growing pasture in the spring. Salt and spices were thus a necessary condition of survival in the winter. When the land route to the Far East, source of spices, was blocked by the fall of Constantinople in 1453, alternative routes had to be found. Hence the voyagers, the discoverers, the opening up of the New World and passage to India. The voyagers needed better navigational instruments than they possessed, which meant better astronomy, so in response to the needs of exploring seamen the new astronomy arose. And in its wake came modern science. So the modern world arose as a consequence of the need to discover new spice routes after 1453. True or false? Neither, surely; you could take any cause in a long chain and single it out as the original one. But causes marched back infinitely and where you began the chain was purely arbitrary, and causes also marched together, innumerable factors operating at the same time. So the truth about causation could never be known. So all explanatory history consisted at best of half-truths. Was history decisively influenced by the character of individual great men? Yes and no. My father would cite the proposition that if Cleopatra's nose had been a fraction of an inch shorter the history of the world would have changed as an example of the absurd views of historical causation that could be held by those who did not realize that history was guided by God for a purpose. Yet I couldn't help being fascinated by this point about Cleopatra's nose. Some decisive battles of the world were won by accidents of weather or of misunderstanding or of some other kind. The chain of events that led to my father's meeting my mother might have led in any one of hundreds of other directions if certain accidental occurrences had not taken place at different times, and if the meeting had not taken place the I that is now writing would not be in existence, I would not be here recalling my reflections on causation, yet the world would be going on carrying its past with it just as it is going on now. Or would it? I sometimes had a sneaking fear that everything was a product of my own consciousness. I did not want to think this, the thought really frightened me, the idea that the whole of history was a construct of my own mind and that there was no guarantee that anything ever occurred except my own sense of awareness opened vistas of appalling loneliness and responsibility. Fortunately such thoughts occurred rarely, for they were kept at bay by opposite feelings of intense human curiosity, a genial inquisitiveness about what it was like to be other people and what it must have been like to live at different periods in the past.

At school the classics master quoted the lines of Agathon: *monou gar autou kai theos sterisketai, ageneta poiein hass' an e pepragmena.* This alone is denied even to God, to make what has happened into what has not happened. I found this a fascinating thought. One might never know everything that happened in the past, but it remained there, unchanging and unchangeable, and each moment as we moved forward in time more events were rendered unchangeable by passing through the irrevocable time process. It occurred to me that we faced the future backwards, as we faced the unfolding view from the back of a moving train, able to see the ground we had traversed but wholly ignorant of what the future would bring. And with every is being constantly processed into was, was remained the triumphant part of the verb. King Was ruled the world. All story was history, even invented story, for that was the history of someone's imagination. And my story like his story is history. And history is mystery. For the only question that seemed to me truly philosophical was the mysterious one to which there was no possible answer: Why should anything ever have occurred? Why should there be events at all? Why should there be ANYTHING? One could not conceive of there being simply no existence of any kind, what would that total nothingness *be*? But it wouldn't be at all. These speculations made my mind reel, and I could never sustain them for very long. It was a relief to get back to the simple practicalities of the history books. Robert the Bruce, well aware of the mighty force advancing against him, posted his men . . . Oh well aware, Robert the Bruce, well done sir, Scots wha ha'e, up guards and at 'em, ae toot an' y'er oot, as the beadle said to the man in church with the ear trumpet. There's decisiveness for you, no messing about, pithy phrase promising firm action. Ae fond kiss and then we sever. Sever, Robert? Surely a blot on a fine song. Poor old Burns needed a rhyme for ever, that old tyranny of rhyme again. Well my dear, it's getting on for six, we'd better sever. Severance is such sweet sorrow. When we two severed in silence and tears. Am I being too severe? Procul este, severae! The

Emperor Severus built a wall between the Tyne and the Solway Firth and died at York. Plain Mr York of York, Yorks. That was Rowntree's, whose different varieties of chocolate played a significant part in my awareness of advertising in the middle (was it?) 1920's. Motoring chocolate, containing nuts and raisins, seemed a highly imaginative innovation: we used to eat it after bathing in the cold North Sea or Firth of Forth. That was when the fourpenny and six-penny slabs came in, too large and expensive for individual buying, but bought by the paterfamilias for family use. The old penny bars were more familiar; twopenny bars, thicker and wider, were normally beyond my means. There were Fry's and Bournville as well as Rowntree's. Another commodity whose advertising caught my attention about the same time was Colman's mustard. They mounted a fierce campaign in the newspapers to persuade people to take freshly made mustard with every meal and invented an institution known as the Mustard Club which gave rise to a number of popular jokes. Has father joined the Mustard Club? Has auntie joined the Mustard Club? Why should such things have coloured my childhood imagination? Like the man in the monocle advertising Sharp's super-cream toffee. A toff he was. A knut. Those monosyllabic dandies figured prominently in jests made by my elders about young people. They seemed to bring somehow a whiff of the London music hall, of which I only knew through the transfiguring mediation of Scotch comics.

> While strolling one day, to a music hall I went,
> I put my hand in my pocket and I hadn't got a cent.
> I just turned my trousers round about:
> Instead of going in they thought that I was going out.
> So that's how you do it, that's how it's done,
> That's how you diddle-iddle-iddle-iddle-um.

That was Bob Merry at Leven. The last verse of this haunting song took us to York:

> I once took on a bet with a friend of mind at York
> To drink a bottle of whisky without pulling out the cork.
> He was a mug: soon I had his tin:
> Instead of pulling out the cork I simply pushed it in.
> So that's how you do it, that's how it's done, etc.

At first I couldn't make out what the tin was, associating it with mug as a tin mug. It was a slang word for money that I had never before heard, though I finally tumbled to it. It was interesting, I used to reflect, that we called tin cans tins and Americans called tin cans cans. Americans canned things while we tinned things. This made possible one of my father's favourite jokes, about salmon being so abundant off the north-west coast of North America that they eat what they can and they can what they can't. Come fill up my cup, come fill up my can, come saddle your horses and call up your men. We used to sing 'Bonny Dundee' at school, and Mr De la Haye explained the historical background. I used to imagine Viscount Dundee seated on his horse holding out something that looked like an empty salmon tin, to be filled with ale. And let me the canakin clink: a soldier's a man, a life's but a span, why then let a soldier drink. Blessed art thou O Lord who createst the fruit of the vine. Iago uttered no such blessing, but Shylock must have, though Shakespeare didn't know it. Divided and distinguished worlds, but my darting consciousness joined them.

So back to the self we come. There needs no ghost, my lord, come from the grave to toll me back from thee to my sole self. No escape. And no way out or way back, you had to make your exit by the far door, which was death. It was extraordinary when you came to think of it, this relentless one-track movement, one-trap life. It was not that I feared death for myself, because I had Hazlitt's feeling of immortality in youth, but I did for others, and I was conscious of us all being at different stages of a line that stretched in one direction only. Would transmigration of souls be of any help? I read about this and it interested me as a possible way out of irreversible time and the limitations of identity, but again I stuck at the problem of memory. What did it matter if I had led an alternative life some time in the past if I was never to be aware of it in the present? And if any possible future existence I might lead as another person altogether carried with it no memory of the self I was now, how could it in any sense be me that would be leading that existence? Orthodox religious ideas about immortality in heaven concerned me very little. I found it hard to imagine convincingly the nature of a disembodied soul, and though Judaism did officially believe in the soul surviving after death the belief was never as central to it as it appeared to be to Christianity. My father never discussed the matter. On only one occasion do I remember the question of life after death coming up; it was after dinner on a Friday evening and we had a visitor, who somehow turned the conversation in this direction. My father said, in answer to a direct question, that it was hard to believe that God had created man with all those faculties only to allow him to be snuffed out for ever at the end of his short life. But in any case, he said, our real immortality is that we live in the hearts of those we have loved and taught. Loved and taught! I found this an intriguing combination, and when I heard the two words come together on my father's lips I had that sudden frisson that I got in moments of deep feeling, as though I sensed a revelation. My father then swiftly changed the subject, embarrassed at having been drawn to say what he did say.

The emphasis in Judaism is on leading the good life in this world, not so much for any specific reward (though the Hebrew Bible is full of promises of rich happiness if all God's commands are obeyed) as because this was God's intention for man and because this is the only way in which a healthy society can be maintained. I was brought up to believe this. And why not? If everyone behaved with decency, kindness, charity, and order, wouldn't society be better off? The end, as I understood it, was a social one. Good behaviour did not guarantee health and wealth to the individual (the Book of Job had knocked that belief on the head), but it guaranteed health and prosperity to society. So underlying the observances and the ritual and the daily prayers and the synagogue chanting lay this reasonable, almost utilitarian view of life. No wonder my father was so much at home in the Scottish Enlightenment! There were of course other Jewish traditions, mystical traditions, the legends of the chassidim. But these were not for my father. I never learned of the existence of Jewish mysticism, never a word about the kabbala or about the Ba'al Shem Tov, from my father. The rabbi who regularly quoted *mens sana in corpore sano* was no believer in divine madness, in *furor religiosus* or any other kind of furor. *Meden agan*, nothing in excess, may have been written above the Delphic oracle, but it was rabbinical wisdom too. The Yiddish word for the ultra-orthodox who practised a passionate scrupulousness in observance was *meshuggah-frum*, crazy-pious, and when I first learned about the eighteenth-century disapproval of religious enthusiasm I thought of my father's disapproval of the *meshuggah-frum*. He was in everything Apollonian rather than Dionysiac. The eldest is fairest but all are divine. Ah, Antiochus Epiphanes, if you had spoken words of hellenic moderation rather than hellenistic superstition to my ancestors during that fateful confrontation with the Hasmoneans there might have been no Maccabean revolt, and instead a combination of Platonic idealism and Jewish ethical monotheism that might have spread over the world and saved two thousand years of suffering. True, that would have meant no festival of Chanukah, and no Christmas either for that matter, but instead there could have been a great festival of light at the time of the winter solstice participated in by all good men. *Bayom hahu*, in that day shall the Lord be one and his name one. But of course alternative histories are impossibilities. What didn't happen is forever impossible as a past. We are back in history's single track again, and how can I complain of that, because I am I because of it. I am because I was, I was because history was, and history was because because because.

There are tricks we play to shake meanings out of all that muddled mass of memories, perceptions, insights, forebodings, knowings and not-knowings. To put words together this way, that way, the other way, is to interrogate experience, perhaps find a whisper of an answer. Mirror mirror on the wall. In the end it is all that there is to believe, it reflects great credit, that mirror, as we stare back at ourselves. Ourselves? Yes, plural indeed, a long long line of was making up that present is. Abraham our father, canst work i' th' earth so fast? A worthy pioneer! Jacob, dreaming dreams no mortal ever dared to dream before. Moses our teacher, how art thou translated! David, sweet singer in Israel, so excellent a king! I see you all. When we were very young we played the singing game:

> Here's a poor widow, she's left alone,
> She has no one to marry upon.
> Come choose the east, come choose the west,
> Come choose the one that you love best.

As a child playing that game I could not choose. I had no special affection for any of the party girls, I wanted everyone to be in it and to be in it with everyone, choosing both east *and* west. There is another version of the song, which goes:

> Here's a poor widow from Babylon,
> With six poor children all alone.
> One can bake and one can brew,
> One can shape and one can sew,
> One can sit at the fire and spin,
> One can bake a cake for the king.
> Come choose you east, come choose you west,
> Come choose the one that you love best.

Babylon, in an Edinburgh children's game! The impossible choice between east and west! I choose both, I choose all, *nihil humani a me alienum puto*. Everyman, I will go with thee, and be thy guide, in thy

222

most need to go by thy side. Judah Halevi, thou shouldst be living at this hour! Walter Scott, I greet you from your own romantic town. David Kimchi, I think of your grammarian's funeral. Ah, Robert Louis Stevenson, you were right: The level of the parlour floor was honest, homely Scottish shore, but when we climbed upon a chair, behold the gorgeous East was there! Nathan ben Jehiel of Rome, Jehiel of Paris, Maimonides, Moses ben Nahman, amoraim, geonim, composers of piyyutim, talmudists, commentators, expositors, *beannachd libh! Shalom aleichem!* And shalom to you, P. B. Shelley, Alexander the great Pope, Wordsworth who had the cheerful faith that all that you beheld was full of blessings, and Tennyson – do not forget Alfred, Lord! I who speak the tongue that Shakespeare spake pronounce a *b'rocho* on you, a benison, as a thank-offering, a *todah*. Be near me when my light is low all of you, all of you, poets, prophets, Jews, gentiles, whom I see behind me and at my side, my wasness of is. What a lot of you it took. Though I am only one of millions whom you unwittingly worked for, I claim you, I adopt you all equally as ancestors, Scot and Lot, Celt and Semite, mystic, wonderful. I came to pass, here I am, *hineni*. From a multiple past I came to pass, creating a new past as I pass, so many onces upon a time and each time upon a place. One, two, three O'Leary. Are you there, King Leary, ruler of the passing moments? But who's counting? No matter: causes keep moving into consequences thus creating their own destiny. I face the future perfect when all that I know shall have been. Then I too shall be an ancestor, my was moving into others' is. But as I write this all history has narrowed itself down to me, here now. I am not history, history is A. N. Other, always there, weaving patterns in time. He makes history, I receive it, wondering.

> His story
> History.
> My story
> Mystery.